WHEN DIVORCE CONSUMES THE MATERNAL INSTINCT

WHEN DIVORCE CONSUMES THE MATERNAL INSTINCT

How to Promote and Protect A Special Parent - Child Relationship When an Ex-Spouse is Difficult

Robin R. Allen

NIPOMO PUBLISHING COMPANY

BELVEDERE

www.nipomopublishing.com

For Information:

Nipomo Publishing Company
Post Office Box 407
Belvedere, CA 94920

(415) 435-9200
(866) 897-9200 (toll free)
(415) 435-1887 (facsimile)

e-mail: *nipomopublishing@earthlink.net*
Web site: www.nipomopublishing.com
Ordering information page 305

Printed in the United States of America
Cover Design by Tania Alexander of Corporate Design Systems

When divorce consumes the maternal instinct:
how to promote and protect a special parent-child relationship when an ex-spouse is difficult/
Allen, Robin.

ISBN 0-9718058-0-6   LCCN: 2002091058

1. Divorced parents -- Psychology. 2. Parenting, Part-time.
3. Children of divorced parents -- Family relationships. 4. Custody of children.
5. Divorce -- Psychological aspects.

This book is dedicated to all families of divorce.

Now is the time to make positive and effective changes for a new family structure.
Learn how to promote and protect a special parent/child relationship after divorce.
Ask questions, search for alternatives and take control of your new destiny
with confidence and fairness!

✴ ✴ ✴ ✴ ✴

OTHER BOOKS BY ROBIN R. ALLEN

THE COMPLETE GUIDE TO PARALLEL PARENTING

CONTENTS

PART ONE

PARALLEL PARENTING: ESTABLISHING A SEPARATE BUT EQUAL POLICY

Parallel parenting is introduced, discussing the positive aspects of the parallel structure for the parents and children of divorce.

A key principle to implementing a successful parallel parenting model is *non-interference*. • Why is non-interference so important? How can divorced parents learn to acknowledge, accept and support the principle of non-interference?

PART TWO

WHEN CONFLICT IS ONE~SIDED
HOW TO RECOGNIZE THE MOTIVATION
WHEN A PARENT BEGINS TO INTERFERE WITH THE CHILD~PARENT BOND

It takes only one parent to create conflict, yet promote the image that both parents are involved in the struggle. Conflict is defined, illustrating how a motivated individual can use the legal system to keep the other parent engaged in the discord. One-sided conflict may become a life sentence for millions of unassuming divorced parents.

This chapter investigates some of the emotional and psychological issues that compel parents to misbehave in the aftermath of divorce. Staying enmeshed with an ex-partner's problematic thinking may ultimately undermine a parent's good intentions to maintain a healthy parent/child relationship. • Before establishing a parallel parenting plan it is important to understand *why* such a plan is needed and to explore some of the psychological dynamics that can be created during the divorce process.

This chapter introduces and summarizes some of the motivational factors that may be involved when a parent tries to interfere with a parent/child relationship. This chapter is based on the research presented by Stanley Clawar and Brynne Rivlin (published by the American Bar Association) and provides the reader with an overview of some of the basic elements of destructive post-marital behavior.

This chapter introduces the *female factor*, with further explanations of why mothers may brainwash and alienate their children against the father. Recognizing that both men and women are capable of alienation, this chapter discusses the woman's ability, motivation and participation in exhibiting the characteristics and behaviors described throughout this book.

Is it simply curiosity, overly concerned about the children or should it be considered stalking? Some parents will use the children as the conduit for information after divorce. Stalking an ex-partner *through the children* presents an entirely new perspective on divorce and can be an integral component when an embittered ex-partner seeks revenge. • Current literature does not expand on the correlation between stalking, divorce and the *use of children* to perpetrate the stalking behavior. This situation may be far more prevalent than researched, and this chapter exposes some very disturbing insights.

PART THREE

GETTING OFF THE DANCE FLOOR ~ GRACEFULLY

This chapter highlights how to establish a stable foundation for the child using a new premise, the *essential elements*. Each *essential element* creates a specific blueprint for the child's future, separate from the other divorce issues. • Special emphasis is placed on learning how to differentiate and negotiate an agreement of the *child related issues*, including discussion and explanations of the legal doctrine, the *best interest of the child*.

9. Mediation

Mediation and alternative dispute resolution have proven to be a satisfactory and less expensive way to resolve disputes. In the highly or even moderately conflicted situation, mediation can be very difficult. This chapter discusses how to find a mediator that will support and facilitate the parallel parenting model and how to succeed with the mediation process.

10. In the Same Place at the Same Time

When sharing children there are always situations when ex-partners will be in *the same place at the same time*. In the beginning stages of separation and divorce parents are often unsure of how to interact in such close proximity. This natural confusion creates many '*opportunities*' for parents to misbehave. Guidelines and boundaries are presented to make even the most uncomfortable situations tolerable.

PART FOUR

CREATING SUCCESSFUL BOUNDARIES
HOW TO PROMOTE AND PROTECT AN SPECIAL PARENT~CHILD RELATIONSHIP WITHOUT UNNECESSARY INTERFERENCE FROM THE OTHER PARENT

11. Access, Schedules and Parenting Time

This chapter defines child custody, visitation and parenting time. Examples of comprehensive, structured visitation and custody agreements are included with guidelines on how to establish boundaries and ground rules for the visitation schedule. The parallel parenting custody arrangement promotes autonomy and helps promote and protect a special parent-child relationship.

12. The Calendar, Conflict and Special Events

Special events pose a unique situation for all families of divorce. Special events are the significant highlights and celebrations in the child's life, and may become emotionally charged events for the parents. • This chapter defines special events, and presents solutions to help minimize the confusion and loyalty issues that often accompany the emotional and developmental milestones of a child's life. Sample agreements are presented to help families of divorce enjoy and celebrate these special events.

Obstruction of Visitation: One of the most abused and unmanageable situations of divorce. When the dynamics of divorce are complicated, the visitation schedule may become *the perfect tool* for a parent possessing alienating qualities. Without specific guidelines and schedules, an alienating parent may succeed in obstructing and/or denying access of the child to the other parent. • Examples, definitions, risk factors, warning signs, sample agreements and realistic enforceable sanctions are presented in this chapter.

Neutral exchange is a near perfect solution to help minimize separation anxiety for the child and parental conflict at exchanges. Separation anxiety, emotional outbursts and reactions at the time of transitions between homes are common in divorce. The parents and the children may contribute to the chaos, and some parents may use the transition to manipulate and disrupt the exchange process. Neutral exchange is the answer to end the commotion that is often encountered during exchanges of the child. This chapter describes why, when and how to facilitate a neutral exchange.

This chapter describes some of the emotional games parents may play to involve their children in the divorce process. Termed by some professionals as *psychological warfare* these games should be redefined as *emotional abuse of the child*. This chapter explores the nature of these common psychological games and how the young and naïve mind of a child can be manipulated. Brainwashing games can be fun, and children are unaware of the destructive outcome. Realistic scenarios, definitions, problems encountered, detection and prevention techniques uncover the unthinkable.

The telephone and other communication devices may become the basic tools that are used to obstruct or interfere with visitation when there is an unhealthy parent-child post divorce alliance. In these situations, communication devices may be used as an intrusive and manipulative way to disrupt the other parent's time with the child, and may significantly interfere with the parent-child relationship. This chapter investigates the different levels of problematic communication, with corresponding solutions and guidelines to help overcome this common scenario.

Illness of a child may present a broad spectrum of different scenarios for families of divorce. For some parents, an illness may create an opportunity to interfere with a child's access to the other parent, resulting in obstruction of visitation. For other parents, losing custody or sharing the child with the other parent (even a couple of evenings a week) may trigger a strong emotional sense of loss. These parents may actually *need* the child to be sick to foster their own parental instincts. • This chapter investigates illness (real or imagined) including definitions, behavioral manifestations, solutions and how to involve the school and health care providers for immediate and logical remedies.

Health care is one of the *essential elements* in a child's upbringing, and involvement in the child's health care should be a primary goal for all parents. This chapter provides examples and guidelines for communicating with the child's health care professionals and offers solutions for some common issues that occur after divorce. Forms and letters are included for ease of use.

Some parents may have difficulty disconnecting emotionally from the other parent after divorce. These parents can easily create a new emotional arena by declaring a false 'emergency situation' for a child. In other situations, the emergency may be very real, even life-threatening. • This chapter defines urgent and emergent care and presents solutions with clear guidelines on how to deal with boundaries when a child is sick, hospitalized or dying.

All parents should be encouraged to participate in their child's educational experience. The academic experience spans the majority of a child's minor life which means their friends and families, teachers, administrators and coaches are all involved in a child's growth and development for more than a decade! • Forms, letters and special guidelines are introduced in this chapter to help a parent maintain a neutral and helpful alliance within the school community.

Extracurricular activities pose some of the most challenging aspects of post divorce life. Extracurricular activities include all the activities in which a child participates outside of school and family life. Extracurricular activities comprise a large percentage of a child's time, and incorporate vital social and developmental stages of a child's life. There are many complexities to the *extracurricular factor*, and this chapter is designed to help parents choose and support activities for their child after divorce, including guidelines for parental attendance and boundaries at the events.

Kidnapping is a growing concern with approximately 350,000 parental abductions per year. This chapter includes researched risk factors for parental abductions, official forms, national and international contacts and resources for any member of the legal team. For the concerned parent, this chapter will be an invaluable source of information.

PART FIVE
THE RESOURCES

A comprehensive glossary of terms including psychological and legal terminology with easy to understand definitions.

APPENDIX

ACKNOWLEDGEMENTS

*Grateful acknowledgment is made for permission to reprint excerpts
from the following books. These books have all been excellent and valuable resources.*

CAUGHT IN THE MIDDLE: PROTECTING THE CHILDREN OF HIGH-CONFLICT DIVORCE
Written by Carla B. Garrity and Mitchell A. Baris
Copyright © 1994 by Lexington Books, An Imprint of Macmillan, Inc.
Reprinted by permission of John Wiley & Sons, Inc.

CHILDREN HELD HOSTAGE: DEALING WITH PROGRAMMED AND BRAINWASHED CHILDREN
Written by Stanley S. Clawar and Brynne V. Rivlin
© 1991 American Bar Association
Reprinted by Permission of the American Bar Association

IMPASSES OF DIVORCE: THE DYNAMICS AND RESOLUTION OF FAMILY CONFLICT
Written by Janet R. Johnston and Linda E.G. Campbell
Copyright © 1988 by Janet R. Johnston and Linda E.G. Campbell
Reprinted with the permission of The Free Press,
an imprint of Simon & Schuster Adult Publishing Group

IN THE NAME OF THE CHILD: A DEVELOPMENTAL APPROACH TO UNDERSTANDING
AND HELPING CHILDREN OF CONFLICTED AND VIOLENT DIVORCE
Written by Janet R. Johnston and Vivienne Roseby
Copyright © 1997 by Janet R. Johnston and Vivienne Roseby
Reprinted with permission of The Free Press,
an imprint of Simon & Schuster Adult Publishing Group

MUNCHAUSEN BY PROXY SYNDROME: MISUNDERSTOOD CHILD ABUSE
Written by Teresa F. Parnell and Deborah O. Day
Copyright © 1998 by Sage Publications, Inc.
Reprinted by Permission of Sage Publications, Inc.

SURVIVING A STALKER: EVERYTHING YOU NEED TO KNOW TO KEEP YOURSELF SAFE
Written by Linden Gross
Copyright © 1994, 1998, 2000 by Linden Gross
Appears by permission of the publisher, Marlowe & Company

THE BEST PARENT IS BOTH PARENTS: A GUIDE TO SHARED PARENTING IN THE 21ST CENTURY
Edited by David L. Levy J.D., President, The Children's Rights Council
Copyright © 1993 by Children's Rights Council
Reprinted by Permission (1-800-787-KIDS)

PUBLISHER'S NOTES

This book was written to provide readers with general information about the divorce process, some issues encountered by families of divorce, and for reading entertainment purposes only. It is not intended to replace an attorney or to provide psychological, financial, legal or any other type of advice. The law and methods for dealing with this book's subject matter frequently change and are fact specific.

If expert assistance or counseling is needed, the services of a competent professional should be sought and the reader should not act upon information contained in this book. The author, publisher and distributors of this book shall not be liable or responsible to any person or entity with respect to loss or damage actually or allegedly resulting, directly or indirectly, from information, ideas or suggestions contained in this book.

This work is based on the author's observations and interviews with parents, children, lawyers and other professionals dealing with families of divorce. The author has changed the names and identifying characteristics of subjects included in the work to protect their privacy. The people, events, and circumstances depicted in this book are fictitious and represent an amalgamation of common reported circumstances. Any resemblance of any illustration to any actual event, or of any character to any actual person - whether living or dead - is purely coincidental.

The author of this work has added value to the material herein through one or more of the following: unique and original selection, coordination, expression, arrangement, and classification of information.

Any case involving psychological, physical or emotional abuse, including the brainwashing, alienation or programming of a child, should be treated carefully on an individual basis by professionally qualified individuals.

WELCOME!

Welcome to a new outlook and perspective for families of divorce. When divorced parents read this book there is often an overwhelming response of excitement and hope. "You mean there really is a life with autonomy when sharing children after divorce?" And, I cannot count the number of times I have heard, "I wish I had read this book when *I* was getting a divorce." And then the stories begin. Stories often consisting of a common theme of discouragement and sadness about sharing children in two homes and the resulting chaos and confusion regarding *"family boundaries."*

Often there is dismay. "Why didn't my attorney tell me I had these options? These incredibly simple ideas would have made all the difference in the world for me!" Or, "Why didn't my attorney discuss with me the possibility that some parents will try to ruin a parent-child relationship? And why didn't they offer solutions for me when they knew it was beginning to happen?"

Well, now is the time to take a proactive role for all individuals involved in the process of divorce.

FOR THE DIVORCE PROFESSIONAL
HELP YOUR CLIENTS REDUCE THE OPPORTUNITIES FOR CONFLICT AFTER DIVORCE AND GIVE THEM AN ADVANTAGE FOR CREATING A NEW FAMILY STRUCTURE SUCCESSFULLY!

The ideas and solutions in this book will help attorneys, judges, mental health professionals, parenting coordinators and special masters guide their clients toward a less chaotic and disruptive life after divorce. With thoughtful preparation, you will be able to explore *new alternatives* and offer *unique options* to these families. These innovative alternatives will help these families succeed in their transition to their new family structure and the new family relationship. In turn, this will reduce the over utilization of precious court resources, and will promote alternative conflict resolution strategies.

FOR THE PARENTS OF DIVORCE
TAKE A PROACTIVE ROLE IN YOUR NEW DESTINY!

All parents involved in divorce - whether newly separated or years later - should unite in their quest for peace and autonomy for their new family structure. Parents of divorce should ask more questions and search for alternatives to the traditional boilerplate divorce. Ask your attorney, judge and other divorce professionals to help you find alternatives and options that will promote and protect your relationship with your children after divorce. Ask questions, present ideas and discuss alternatives that will help you succeed in your new life with your family. Read this book, and promote the ideas presented to secure a unique and special relationship with your children for years to come!

How to Use this Book

This book was designed specifically for ease of use, with each chapter dedicated to a special area of concern. If you are a parent, or divorce professional, the ideas and suggestions presented in this book can be tailored to each specific situation without confusion or the bundling of other issues.

For example, if a divorcing family is fortunate enough to experience only mild conflict (about one or two child related issues) then those issues can be explored quickly, with solutions and ideas presented clearly for easy implementation. As an illustration, if parents are experiencing difficulty about the choice and participation of their child's extracurricular activities, the reader can simply turn to Chapter 21 to review alternatives and ideas for successfully promoting and participating in the child's extracurricular activities after divorce.

On the other hand, it may be necessary to explore this book thoroughly for alternatives and options to help both parents participate equally and fairly in the growth and development of their child for many years to come. For example, a parent may begin to misbehave, and demonstrate parental qualities that would indicate an intention to interfere with a child's relationship with the other parent.

In these situations, this book can be used to explore the various motivational and underlying factors that may precipitate a parents efforts to meddle and interfere with a parent-child bond. With these insights, parenting plans can be coordinated and tailored to support and preserve the child's relationship with the other parent.

To that end, this book includes chapters dealing with some of the more complex issues involving more complicated divorce dynamics, such as Parental Kidnapping and Child Abductions (Chapter 22) Obstruction of Visitation (Chapter 13) or Psychological Warfare and Games of the Child's Mind (Chapter 15).

In any case, "*let your fingers do the walking*" and explore all the alternatives and ideas presented in this book. Families of divorce deserve the best possible chance to pursue healthy parent-child relationships after divorce, and I encourage all readers to take advantage of the ideas and insights offered throughout this book.

PREFACE

There are many interpersonal dynamics entering the equation when parents misbehave during and after the divorce process. When I started to research parental misconduct following divorce, there was considerable attention focused on the concept of *parental alienation*. As I watched in dismay, the debate over the definition and criteria of *'alienation'* took precedence over the real issue, becoming as political in the world of divorce professionals as the debate between international politicians about the war in Iraq- 2003!

It has been over a decade, and many professionals are still at odds regarding the correct labeling, diagnosis and treatment of a very common post divorce scenario: one parent attempting to alienate or brainwash a child against the other parent after divorce. Fortunately, as the debate continues, there is one commonality in the wide spectrum of professional opinion and that is *'alienation'* does, in fact, exist.

And yes, like every political hot topic of this generation, there is also a strong debate about gender. Are both men and women capable of alienation or trying to interfere with a parent-child bond? The answer is unequivocally, yes. Do men and women alienate for the same reasons and in the same manner? No, they do not.

While the title of this book may raise an eyebrow to current political correctness, it is important to understand it has been written to help both men *and* women, the fathers *and* mothers (and the professionals who work with them) who may spiral into the trap of behaving badly and contributing to the interpersonal conflict after divorce.

When used as a positive divorce tool, this book offers hundreds of ideas and creative insights to help parents disengage from the their own emotional pain and the polarized positions that often create a post divorce standoff. This book emphasizes the realities of post divorce impasse, and endorses why establishing appropriate boundaries should be paramount in the presentation of options to families of divorce.

This book is written to help parents, and divorce professionals establish *healthy boundaries* during the divorce process. These boundaries are intended to help create healthy post divorce relationships that will facilitate more options for a much needed and refreshing autonomy for the new family structure.

Destructive post divorce behavior has been occurring unbridled after divorce for generations. And for generations, the legal system has held a steady unhelpful line, expecting parents and children to function after divorce without providing them guidance for success or offering them solutions to a future without conflict.

Now is the time to make positive and effective changes for these families of divorce. Read on, and learn how to promote and protect a special parent/child relationship after divorce. Be a part of the solution and the bright new future this book proposes for all children and families of divorce.

PART ONE

PARALLEL PARENTING

ESTABLISHING A SEPARATE BUT EQUAL POLICY

1.

Introduction to Parallel Parenting

Most books on the market regarding divorce, separation and custody emphasize co-parenting, open and frequent communication and 'getting along' with the other parent. While the models presented in these books sound logically based and convincing, many parents have a difficult time cooperating and managing custody of their children without some level of conflict.

Making matters worse, the legal system in the United States imposes rigid ideas and beliefs on families of divorce. These legal standards often force parents to interact and make important decisions about their children prematurely and without careful consideration. Usually, the timing of these premature and often *binding decisions* about the children coincides with the complex technical process of the divorce. These important decisions about the children and the 'future family' are often made impulsively, under tremendous stress, and without considering the long-term ramifications to each member of the family.

The initial phases of separation and divorce are psychologically exhausting, and many parents cannot separate the *'child related issues'* from the emotional, financial and material aspects of the divorce. At this sensitive and traumatic time parents often feel they are being financially compromised. They are inundated and overwhelmed by legal maneuvers such as demands for discovery of finances, dividing precious assets, selling the family home, establishing custody, negotiating child and spousal support. Understandably, it is very difficult for these parents to cope with the new situation of divorce. Being in court, interacting with an angry spouse, sharing the children, dealing with attorneys and all the other issues often create high-conflict and high-drama during the divorce process.

This book is designed to help parents make informed decisions about their children. It approaches the subject of *sharing the children* by establishing 'boundaries' to protect the children (and the parents) from parental conflict. These boundaries are created to shield the children from the gruesome process of divorce and the outcomes of conflict that can last for years. This book is designed to benefit parents who are in the beginning stages of separation and divorce as well as for parents who are struggling with post-divorce conflict long after the divorce has been finalized. For judges, attorneys and mental health professionals this book offers full-proof solutions to protect the children, narrowing the opportunities for post-divorce conflict. This book also offers suggestions to manage almost every scenario imaginable for families sentenced to a 'life of conflict after divorce.'

The vital statistics of divorce are clearly illustrated by Gary Neuman, the creator of the nationally recognized *Sandcastles Program* for children of divorce.

> "*The Hard Facts About Divorce*: In the United States, one in every two marriages ends in divorce, and two-thirds of these families include minor children. As a result, every year approximately one million new kids become "children of divorce.' More prevalent than drug abuse, teenage pregnancy, or the death of a parent, divorce is the most common problem facing kids today. Only about 40 percent of those born in the mid-1980's can expect to grow up in a home with both biological parents present, a trend the U.S. Census Bureau predicts will continue into the next century. Currently, approximately 37 percent of all American children live with a divorced parent. Experts project that before reaching eighteen, approximately one quarter to 35 percent of American children will spend some time in a step family; two-thirds of these children will have step- or half siblings." [1]

In their outstanding book, *The Name of the Child*, Janet Johnston and Vivienne Roseby further define the statistics of divorce,

> "… approximately one million children each year experience their parents' divorce in the United States, over a span of two decades more than five million children will be affected by ongoing parental conflict; for two million children, this condition will be permanent. (Glick, 1988; Maccoby & Mnookin, 1992)." [2]

In another excellent book, *Impasses of Divorce,* Janet Johnston and Linda Campbell state,

"This book [*Impasses of Divorce*] has addressed the plight of an increasingly large population of families for whom divorce is not a relief from an unhappy marriage because it does not signal the end of parental disputes. Instead it may signal the beginning of chronic struggles over the children between distressed parents, or disturbed patterns of parent-child relationships where the children bear the long-term burden of preventing their parents from destroying themselves and each other. The outlook for these children is ominous, even grim, with disturbing implications for the next generation unless we can find better ways of helping them." [3]

It is my opinion there is a way to help these children and their parents both during and after divorce. I strongly believe that children and parents can benefit from a *parallel parenting model.* A parallel parenting structure maximizes both parents access to their children, while minimizing the likelihood and opportunity for parental interference and conflict.

Parallel parenting is a structured and well-defined parenting model. Parallel parenting may also be defined as 'similar parenting,' 'equivalent parenting' or 'matching parenting.' If introduced and initiated properly, parallel parenting can promote autonomy for the new family structure and immensely enhance the child's new life in two homes. Parallel parenting gives the child the opportunity to love and experience each parent separately, while minimizing the opportunities for loyalty issues so often encountered in divorce situations.

Unfortunately, the parallel parenting model is not readily available, per se. You cannot walk into your attorney's office tomorrow and say, "I want parallel parenting." However, it does exist and is touted by many experts under different guises and definitions. Interestingly, many experts state they do not like parallel parenting yet when given a different definition it is *often* the model they choose when all else fails.

In my search for parallel parenting examples and models, I did find a parallel parenting order from the Judicial District of Edmonton, in Canada. I have included this information in Appendix A, as an example of a forward thinking court; a court that recognizes the potential benefits of a parallel parenting structure.

This book proposes (whenever possible) that separated and divorced families should begin with the parallel parenting model. When handled appropriately, children in *parallel parenting families* will be protected from parental disputes, essentially *buffered* from the conflict that may exist. Because of the *parallel structure* these children will not experience the day-to-day conflict, therefore enabling them to experience 'each family' as their own and separate family. The *parallel time* spent with each parent maintains the feeling of cohesiveness of the family unit. Specifically, it allows the child special access and guarantees autonomy so that the child can experience and love *each parent*. In essence, the parallel parenting model provides continuity, stability, access and attachment for children of divorce.

While many people may be critical that you cannot get along with your ex-spouse (or do not want ongoing contact with them) there are also many experts who support the '*separate but equal policy.*' Being married to someone you are not compatible with or no longer in love with is difficult enough. Trying to raise children with someone you do not like, do not respect or cannot trust is often more difficult than actually living with them.

A very successful attorney and good friend of mine said it perfectly. "I simply do not understand how the (legal) system thinks people can get along about their children after divorce when they were so unsuccessful getting along between themselves when they were married." So simply stated, this may well be *your life* after divorce.

During their extensive research of divorce, Janet Johnston and Linda Campbell followed up on the outcomes of divorced families two and three years later. They made the following observations and conclusions in their book *Impasses of Divorce*:

> "More commonly, the decreased intensity of the dispute was achieved by parents avoiding each other assiduously. They never met or talked with one another, did not interfere in each other's lives, and pursued their own style of parenting. Rather than joint decision making around the needs of the child, each followed a policy of noninterference with the other. This 'parallel parenting' worked partly because they had a very structured time-sharing agreement and partly because, as noted above, the children did not protest or make other demands. These parents accepted the inevitability and routine of the children's visiting arrangement, while voicing to the counselor when they felt it was futile trying to change the situation, ('She'll never change! It's not worth it!'), because they did not want to fight anymore or because they were invested in a new relationship elsewhere. The fact that their children lived in two separate worlds did not seem problematic providing that those two worlds never crossed and the children were not caught in contradictory expectations. However, in these cases, visiting schedules are often extremely rigid and unresponsive to the child's changing needs. Where a fixed visiting schedule was not in place, the child often found it difficult to summon up the courage to initiate contact with the other side. Hence visiting became less frequent or gradually ceased entirely over time.
>
> Several parents, all but one of whom were fathers, withdrew their demands to see the child. They withdrew in frustration with their ex-spouse, because they were driven away by the parent-child alliance, or because they felt depreciated and angry at a court order...." [4]

When interpreting this and other similar readings, it is often revealed that parallel parenting truly can work for all parties involved. Parallel parenting supports the non-interference policy. When the parallel parenting model is designed with careful thought and foresight (for example, a well defined calendar arrangement, efficient decision making remedies and guaranteed access) it allows the parents to live their lives free from conflict, enabling them to concentrate on the important interpersonal relationship with their children.

Most experts agree that the parenting plan should meet the child's changing developmental needs, and this *can be accomplished* with the parallel parenting model. It is important to take the time and make the effort to negotiate a parenting plan that incorporates a child's changing developmental needs and supports the parallel parenting model. The energy engaged in this effort will create the foundation for your *new life* with *your child*.

Therefore, it may be one of the most important decision making processes you will encounter in your life.

Creating a well-defined parenting plan and agreeing on a separate but equal policy eliminates many of the 'control games' often surrounding even protected and predetermined situations. Ideally, the opportunities for conflict and unnecessary negotiations regarding parenting and the children will be kept to a minimum with an effective parallel parenting plan.

In this book we will illustrate many cases where one parent has moved on emotionally, and the other parent uses every opportunity of contact to create problems or pry further into the privacy and life of the other. Families caught in this type of situation (described appropriately by Johnston and Campbell as *impasse*) need precise parenting guidelines and boundaries, narrowing the opportunities for conflict.

Some families cannot make even minor changes to their parenting agreements without experiencing an abuse of the process or increased conflict. Consequently, the children may be constantly caught in the middle of the parents negotiations and disputes. Although most experts try to encourage cooperative parenting, studies and research indicate that many families of divorce engage in a parallel parenting scenario on their own.

"In an ongoing study of custody arrangements in California, the Stanford Child Custody Project found that most parents with joint custody functioned like parents with sole custody, despite the divorce decree. One parent, usually the mother, performed most parental tasks, and the children spent most of their time with that parent.

However, researchers have found that even in joint custody arrangements parallel parenting develops (i.e. each parent operates as an independent unit, rather than sharing parenting or co-parenting)." [5]

Studies such as this reinforce the idea that a parallel parenting model may be the most comfortable and natural evolving solution for divorced families. Perhaps the legal system is expecting too much of parents insisting they should be joined forever through their children. Therefore, establishing useful parallel parenting guidelines and boundaries may be the most logical and efficient way for these families to succeed. These boundaries will protect the parent/child relationship, protect the child's wellbeing and will promote autonomy in the new family structure. These boundaries will also create helpful guidelines for a clear and beneficial separation for divorcing parents.

In the final pages of their excellent book about divorce, *Joint Custody With A Jerk: Raising a Child with an Uncooperative Ex*, Julie A. Ross and Judy Corcoran state:

"When You Really Can't Stand Your Ex: If you and your ex are at extreme odds, prevent as many meetings, confrontations, and problems as possible. Instead of picking up your child from your ex's house, try to agree that whoever has the child must drop him off at the other's house. It's less territorial, and it tells the child that you approve of the visit and that he's not being taken away but given over. Also, consider a neutral exchange place, like school or a restaurant between both houses.

If you can't stand to be together, even for school and sporting events, arrange to sit on opposite sides of the place. One mother and father agreed that she would get the right side and he would get the left, just like guests at a wedding, when it came to school auditoriums, ballet recitals, and Little League games. Other parents split up the games and recitals, with one going to dress rehearsal or alternating sporting events.

If you can arrange it, don't share clothes, toys, and other possessions. Give your child his or her own set of things, including pajamas and toothbrush, at your house (or pack a permanent set for the other parent's house, if necessary) so there is less to carry back and forth, less for you to account for and to argue over.

When your child is visiting the other parent, don't call. It can disrupt their time together...." [6]

Ross and Corcoran wrote a very meaningful and wonderful book offering ideas and suggestions for getting along with the ex-spouse and putting animosities aside. Again, without a label, they defer to the 'parallel parenting model' when all else has failed and ex-partners cannot get along.

Initiating a parallel parenting plan at the onset of the divorce process will help the children by diminishing the amount of contact and the opportunities for conflict between newly divorcing couples. Establishing a parallel-parenting model creates an early and basic guideline for these families. As time goes on, the post-marital conflict may subside. Then again, it may not. If there is even *moderate conflict* after a reasonable length of time, then the parallel parenting model should remain in place.

Protecting the *children and the parents* from any potential conflict should be paramount in the minds of attorneys, mediators, mental health professionals and judges. Great emphasis should be placed on supporting the parallel parenting model, as it protects the children and the parents from ongoing opportunities for disputes and conflict.

(Endnotes)

[1] Neuman, G. M. with Romanowski, P. (1998). *Helping Your Kids Cope With Divorce the Sandcastles Way.* 1st Ed. New York: Random House. p. 15.

[2] Johnston, J. R., Ph.D., & Roseby, V. Ph.D. (1997). *In the Name of the Child: A Developmental Approach to Understanding and Helping Children of Conflicted and Violent Divorce.* New York: The Free Press, A Division of Simon & Schuster, Inc. p. 4.

[3] Johnston, J. R. & Campbell, L.E.G. (1998). *Impasses of Divorce: The Dynamics and Resolution of Family Conflict.* New York: Free Press, a Division of Macmillan. p. 255.

[4] id., p. 253-254.

[5] Neuman, G. M. with Romanowski, P. (1998). *Helping Your Kids Cope With Divorce the Sandcastles Way.* New York: Random House. p. 15.

[6] Johnston, J. R. & Campbell, L.E.G. (1998). *Impasses of Divorce: The Dynamics and Resolution of Family Conflict.* New York: Free Press, a Division of Macmillan. p. 255.

[7] Bray, J. H. (1998). The Family Schedule, Crafting Custody and Visitation Arrangements that Work. Chicago, Illinois: *American Bar Association, Family Advocate*, Volume 21, Number 1, p. 32.

[8] Corcoran, J. & Ross, J. (1996). *Joint Custody With a Jerk: Raising a Child with an Uncooperative Ex.* 1st Ed. New York: St. Martin's Press. p. 227.

2.

Non-Interference
The Key to Success of Parallel Parenting

"The noninterference principle can strengthen the parent-child relationship and enhance the emotional climate of family life. It lessens nasty side effects like competition, nosiness, and manipulation. Noninterference gives the children a sense of security and continuity. Children know what to expect and eventually see how two homes with no fighting can work." [1]

Isolina Ricci, Ph.D.,

"In essence, good fences make good neighbors and even better fences make joint custody and shared parenting easier with an ex-spouse."

Anonymous

In order for parallel parenting to succeed both parents need to acknowledge the fundamental principle and the basic concept of 'non-interference.'

If the divorce situation began smoothly with your ex-partner, do not underestimate how quickly your *'friendly'* relationship can deteriorate. Many factors can contribute to the deterioration of the previous working relationship. Therefore, all parents should be prepared to secure useful boundaries for the new family structure in an effort to avoid unnecessary interference from an ex-partner. In her wonderful book, *Mom's House, Dad's House*, Isolina Ricci defines the non-interference principle and boundary issue with great clarity.

> "When parents adhere to the noninterference principle, parent coopera-
> tion is strengthened, and the children see a new, different, but still united front
> from their parents. Non interference is the workable way to respect your part-
> ner in parenting and to share authority and responsibility. Children need not
> play one parent against the other to feel power. Child power through manipula-
> tion is a frightening substitute for parental strength and responsibility." [2]

> "The most important ground rule for your new working relationship is
> also crucial for your move away from your marriage and your shared intimacy.
> This important rule is that you each delineate and maintain your separate terri-
> tories. Put simply, Mom's house is her bailiwick and Dad's house is his. What
> you do in your own home, and how you parent the children there, is your busi-
> ness. What the other parent does, likewise, is her or his business. When the
> children are living with you, you have authority and responsibility. To preserve
> autonomy, you must maintain your own territory courteously and firmly and
> you must keep your nose out of the other parent's territory as well." [3]

What about the parent who refuses to accept your right to autonomy and non-interference?

Unfortunately, not all individuals will acknowledge or respect logical boundaries, and this may inevitably lead to increased conflict and frustration between ex-partners. As a proactive measure, it is important to be prepared for potential '*boundary breaks.*' It is equally important to be aware of the myriad of '*emotional games*' that may accompany efforts made by an ex-partner to interfere with your life and your life with your children.

> ***Take for example,*** the mother in Connecticut who refused to allow the father
> visitation time with their child without some type of interference. She even pro-
> jected her intentions to interfere with visitation when she wrote to the child's psy-
> chologist, "I have every intention of interacting with my child regardless of who
> has custody at the time." This mother employed endless manipulative and emo-
> tional games to control the father's time with the child, and she actively involved
> the child in the process.

This mother could not tolerate being separated emotionally from the father. Essentially, she was '*stuck in time*' and suffered from what some experts label, a '*divorce hangover.*' Every visit or interaction with the child by the father resulted in the mother interfering, manipulating or becoming emotionally involved.

The pattern of interference spanned over a decade, and even after hundreds of hours of intervention the mother continued with efforts to interfere with the father's parenting time. There was no relief for this father. He could not maintain a relationship with his child without the mother's intentional interference. As one mental health professional stated to the father, "Just face it, this truly is a life sentence."

Anne Walthers coined the perfect term in her excellent book, *Divorce Hangover*. Walthers states, "[The] Divorce hangover is the *unfinished* emotional experience of the divorce." [4] Walthers also makes the excellent observation that "the divorce hangover does not discriminate. It can affect anyone, regardless of sex, social or financial status, or even who initiated the divorce." [5]

Many parents are affected by a *divorce hangover*, struggling with the emotional separation necessary after divorce. Some examples of post-divorce behaviors that may indicate a divorce hangover include:

➢ Unnecessary interaction or communication with an ex-partner.

➢ Fabricating issues to guarantee interaction with an ex-spouse.

➢ Creating an argument about very minor issues, just to stay connected.

➢ Arranging to *coincidentally* be in the same place at the same time as the other parent after divorce.

➢ Arranging to *coincidentally* meet with the children during the other parent's custodial time.

➢ Staying '*emotionally engaged*' with the ex-partner, whether they are communicating with you or not.

➢ Dwelling on the details of the separation and divorce.

➢ Obsessing over the ex-partner's new life, new mate or spouse, and how they spend time with the children.

Danger Zones - Divorce Hangovers and Non-Interference

Despite how well your post-divorce relationship with your ex-partner seems to be working, make sure that you discuss boundary issues with your attorney. Throughout this book, there are many provisions addressing appropriate boundaries that can be used in a legal agreement. These provisions can be used in the marital settlement contract or parenting agreement. Ideally, the presentation and concern for boundaries should also be included in the legal judgment.

If you have already signed an agreement that does not include clear language defining appropriate boundaries (and you are experiencing problems with your ex-partner), you will need to modify your existing agreement or create another agreement. In addition, the fact that you are experiencing difficulty with your ex-partner may justify the inclusion of '*consequences*' or '*disincentives*' in the agreement to deter the other parent from intrusive, unnecessary or destructive conduct.

Disincentives should be designed to discourage certain behaviors that are affecting your relationship with your children and your ability to parent them autonomously in your own home.

Sharing children is not always easy. If the conflict between the parents escalates (instead of diminishes) the remedies to correct the problems become more difficult to establish as time progresses. Establishing appropriate boundaries and guidelines early in the separation process should make the transition into the new *working parental relationship* with an ex-partner easier.

One of the keys to a successful relationship with your children is to loosen the ties with your ex-partner: physically, legally, materialistically and emotionally. A priority and goal for a divorcing parent should be to concentrate on building a strong and meaningful relationship with the children, and to release oneself from the binds of the previous marital bond.

This goal may be very difficult to achieve when there is constant or destructive interference from an ex-partner. When one parent has physical custody or visitation time with the child, the ex-partner does not need to be there as well. If you need to discuss issues about the child with the ex-partner, then communicate those issues when you are not spending time with the child, for example, when the child is at school or involved in other activities.

This book illustrates various methods and ideas of how to implement the non-interference principle in your every day lifestyle. Remember, the basic idea is to cherish time with your children. Time with your children should not be diluted with unnecessary interaction or interference from the other parent.

In the next few chapters, we will explore some of the reactions and motivational factors that can occur during the separation and divorce process. When reviewing the various motivational factors researched and presented, it is important to realize how much influence and power an ex-partner may truly have in your life after a divorce. Specifically, an ex-partner has the unique ability to occupy your personal space and the special time you have with your child.

For example, an ex-partner knows intimate facts and details about the other parent and their lifestyle. If so inclined, an ex-partner also has the ability to create many different scenarios to maintain a relationship (no matter how unhealthy) with the other parent. As a result, this unhealthy contact with the other parent provides the devious or malicious ex-spouse the means and motivation to maintain control of the other parent's time with the children.

It is very important to be consciously aware of the 'evolving relationship' with an ex-partner. It is also crucial to manage that relationship with some clarity, emotional distance and objectivity.

(Endnotes)

[1] Ricci, I. (1980). *Mom's House, Dad's House: Making Shared Custody Work.* 1st Ed. New York: Collier Books, Macmillan Publishing Company. p. 98-99.

[2] id., p. 98-99.

[3] id., p. 98-99.

[4] Walther, A. N. (1991). *Divorce Hangover: A Step by Step Prescription for Creating a Bright Future After Your Marriage Ends.* New York: Pocket Books, a Division of Simon & Schuster. p. 6.

[5] id., p. 7.

PART TWO

WHEN CONFLICT IS
ONE ~ SIDED

HOW TO RECOGNIZE THE
MOTIVATION WHEN A PARENT
BEGINS TO INTERFERE WITH
THE PARENT ~ CHILD BOND

3.

It Only Takes One
Understanding One~Sided Conflict

_____

_____

It may take two to dance, but it takes only one to miss a step and cause havoc on the dance floor. As we will explore throughout this book, it takes only one parent to create conflict, thereby creating a high conflict situation. One parent may be happy, trying to maintain the status quo with their children and the new situation. The other parent may be unhappy, have severe feelings of loss of the divorce and needs continued contact with the other parent to maintain the lost or threatened relationship.

When a parent is *conflict-oriented*, they do not want to agree or cooperate with the other parent, yet, they will insist on having contact. The contact initiated by the conflict-oriented parent will usually lead to disagreements, arguments and discord. This type of interaction presents the parent trying to avoid controversy with a very difficult situation. The parent who does not want conflict, may not have an effective way to cope or protect themselves from the never ending issues that can arise about the children and the divorce. After all, there are countless day-to-day decisions that need to be made about children.

To make matters worse, it is easy for the conflict-oriented parent to make the situation appear as if both parents are enmeshed in the post divorce conflict. The conflict-oriented parent *needs to present the image of 'both parents fighting'* to maintain the lost relationship, protect their threatened position and to keep others interested and engaged.

Conflict oriented individuals will create disagreements about very minor issues and at whatever cost to themselves and the children in the process. Unfortunately, when one parent cannot disengage and chooses to maintain the relationship through conflict, it is the child who often becomes the true victim of the divorce.

In their excellent book, *Caught In the Middle,* Carla Garrity and Mitchell Baris discuss *moderate conflict*:

> "Parents in moderate conflict who choose or are awarded joint legal cus-
> tody have many opportunities for disagreement. After the first painful year or
> two, some parents settle into milder patterns of conflict. Others, however, con-
> tinue to argue over the numerous joint decisions that must be made under this
> custody arrangement-- decisions about the children's education, health care,
> religious training, and extracurricular activities." [1]

Janet Johnston and Vivienne Roseby make the following observations in their book, *In the Name of the Child:*

> *"The Chronicity of the Parental Conflict:* "In general, the more intense and
> prolonged the divorce conflict and the more exposed children are to parental
> disputes, the more likely the children will be drawn into an alignment with one
> parent and become alienated from the other. This is an expectable outcome, and
> parents should be warned of this possibility early on in counseling. Of course,
> the optimal goal is to have them cease fighting and cooperate in their parenting,
> but this is not always possible. Instead, the counselor can help parents to con-
> struct protocols for communication, barriers to constrain their interaction (e.g.,
> no in-person contact), and buffer zones for the child (e.g., exchanges at a neu-
> tral, safe place). Antagonistic parents are encouraged to develop separate, par-
> allel parenting relationships with their children, governed by an explicit court
> order that documents their access schedule, times, dates, and place of exchange
> for all occasions. The need for collaborative decision making should be kept to
> a minimum, with mediators or arbitrators used when necessary." [2]

Johnston and Roseby elaborate further stating:

"The Parents' Contribution to Alienation: THE ROLE OF THE ALIGNED PARENT. It is important to consider the psychological dynamics of each parent in creating and maintaining the aligned/alienation syndrome within the highly conflictual divorcing family. Both the covert and the overt tactics of the alienating parent have long been recognized and are well described elsewhere (Clawar & Rivlin, 1991; Gardner, 1987). In general, the alienating parent has been portrayed more or less unsympathetically, as one who is primarily vengeful and malicious. From our perspective, separation and divorce for these parents is typically experienced as loss (with accompanying feelings of anxiety, sadness, and fear of being alone). It is also experienced as rejection (together with feelings of shame and failure). Consequently, these vulnerable people can become acutely or chronically distressed. For relief, some turn to their children for nurturance and companionship, as allies against the world and as the salve for their wounded self-esteem. Others, in an effort to defend themselves from the humiliation of rejection and failure, project all the blame onto their divorcing spouse, whom they now view as the bad parent: endangering, neglectful, and irresponsible. As a result, they feel self-righteously compelled to fight to protect their children from the other parent.

To have their own needs met, the children must reflect whatever the wounded parent needs and wants. Consequently, these children can become vigilant and highly attuned to the parent. The child fears that disappointing or abandoning the depressed or emotionally volatile parent (often the mother) may result in being ignored, rejected, punished, or even destroyed by that parent. Alternately, sensing an apparent omnipotence in caring for a distressed parent, the child acts as though the parent's survival depends on his or her constant vigilance and caretaking. For these reasons, the child may find it extremely difficult if not impossible to leave willingly for visits to the nonresidential parent, fearing what might happen to the left-behind parent during his or her absence, or out of anxiety at disappointing and betraying that parent by 'going over to the other side.'" [3]

Staying Off the Dance Floor

Again, parallel parenting is mentioned as a *possible cure* for situations when the potential for ongoing and unhealthy conflict exists. It is imperative to identify and assess each parent's ability to be separate from the other parent as early in the divorce process as possible. Specifically, it is essential to determine one's own motivations for contact with the other parent.

Maintaining written documentation (a journal of communications) can help a parent differentiate between necessary and unnecessary communication with the other parent. Was the visit by the other parent necessary? Was the telephone call timely in relation to the child's visit? Was something 'fabricated' for a reason to call and have contact?

All these questions will be explored further throughout this book. Conflict of any nature should be taken seriously, and the origins and motives of the conflict should be assessed. For example, if one parent is creating situations to initiate unnecessary contact with the other parent, then special boundaries and '*buffer zones*' should be created as soon as possible.

When one parent is creating and promoting the conflict, the other parent needs to take swift action. The more enmeshed one becomes with a conflict-oriented parent the harder it is to separate the fact from the fiction. As stated previously, it may appear that *both parents* are equally responsible for the conflict.

Take for example, the mother in Illinois who filed continual legal motions against the father to maintain contact with him. In this case, the mother would not agree to simple parenting requests made by the father and would create conflict at every opportunity, every exchange of their child and for *any reason*. In her legal motions, the mother accused the father of many atrocities and begged relief from the court to chastise the father with sanctions and punishments. As an additional insult, the mother would request of the court that the father pays all her attorney fees and costs, based on the father's superior ability to pay.

In essence, this mother had nothing to lose. She was able to create unrelenting conflict, receive the ongoing contact and attention she so desperately needed and the father was ordered by the court to accept financial responsibility for all the drama and legal costs. As one attorney stated, "This is mere entertainment for her and the court is giving her exactly what she wants."

In situations like this, the allegations made and filed by one parent may be false, yet the accused parent has to defend themselves and will, therefore, be drawn into the conflict. These victimized parents are often forced to respond to false allegations and participate in the one-sided conflict or risk losing custody and visitation rights with their children.

These revolving court appearances are extremely costly and can be emotionally exhausting. Many victimized parents find themselves at the mercy of the court, and have to sort through a maze of perverse issues created by an angry, conflict oriented ex-spouse. Often, the one-sided conflict becomes so camouflaged within the court battle it is never revealed, and *both parents* are viewed as participants in the post divorce discord.

One strategy for these victimized parents is to keep accurate and detailed records of their interactions with the ex-spouse. The documentation should not become an obsession, but rather an avenue to promote clarity and rationality to an unfavorable situation. While keeping accurate and detailed records may help a victimized parent demonstrate that the other parent is '*conflict oriented*,' the documentation may also help a victimized parent achieve some emotional distance, allowing them to assess the situation with more objectivity.

For many victimized parents, one-sided conflict often feels like an attack or an ambush on their parenting time and their parental rights. Unfortunately, it often takes many years and thousands of dollars before these victimized parents can minimize the confusion created by the one-sided conflict.

Conflict is never in the child's best interest and parents need to learn how to minimize the impact of one-sided conflict. It is not an easy task, and all professionals involved in the divorce process should make the *diffusion of conflict* a priority. Unfortunately, the process of divorce remains highly adversarial, contributing to the power of a parent who needs conflict.

Position yourself as early as possible to decrease your contribution to the conflict.
Get off the dance floor with the other parent.
Let them dance the ugly dance of conflict alone.
Over time, this strategy will benefit you and your children immensely.

(Endnotes)

[1] Garrity, C. B. & Baris, M. A. (1994). *Caught in the Middle: Protecting the Children of High-Conflict Divorce*. New York: Lexington Books, An Imprint of Macmillan, Inc. p. 58.

[2] Johnston, J. R. & Roseby, V. (1997). *In the Name of the Child*. New York: The Free Press, A Division of Simon & Schuster, Inc. p 197.

[2] id., p. 197.

4.

Why is She Doing This to My Children and Me?

Before establishing a parallel parenting plan it is important to understand why such a plan is needed and to explore some of the psychological dynamics that can be launched during the divorce process.

You may think if you could figure out why your ex-spouse is exposing your children and you to emotional trauma, you may be able to change their behavior. "If only I knew what was bothering her, I could make things better." It is astounding how many parents (particularly fathers) continue to try to please the ex-spouse even though they are experiencing extreme difficulty trying to co-parent with them after divorce.

Richard Mikesell, Ph.D., who is also a strong advocate for parallel parenting, was explaining about relationships and the influence of moods in interactions. He explained that people who are "mood driven" often act on their mood which will turn into their reality. When emphasizing the importance of differentiating between moods and reality he cleverly stated, "Remember...(for men who were attracted to mood driven women), back then you were the *solution* to all of her problems, now you are the *cause* of all of her problems (at the time of divorce.)"[1] His advice for *all parents*, "Don't make their mood your reality."[1]

So What is the Bewildered Parent to do?

One healthy recommendation is to stop asking yourself *why!* Stop wondering if you can do something to change the ex-spouses destructive behavior. To do so puts you squarely in the middle of the ex-partners manipulative and controlling behavior. It is unfortunate that an ex-partner is responding to the divorce in a negative manner, but it is *their problem* and they are responsible for *their own reactions* to the divorce process. *One parent is not responsible for how the other parent feels or reacts to the divorce!* To enmesh oneself emotionally with an ex-partner after divorce to 'save, help or assist' them will not change the underlying emotions or motivational factors that drive the malicious or vindictive ex-partner to behave destructively.

Understanding *some of the possibilities* motivating your ex-spouse to behave badly may make life a little easier for you, but constantly asking yourself why will only hinder your own personal growth. Staying enmeshed with an ex-spouse and their problematic thinking will ultimately undermine your good intentions to establish and maintain a healthy relationship with your child.

One can spend an inordinate amount of time wondering why. This time is much better utilized enjoying and loving your children. In essence, spend your time wisely with your children: learn to love and care for them free from the potential negative *emotional baggage* so commonly present during and after the divorce process.

Many factors may play a part in contributing to destructive behavior displayed by an ex-partner. The list below outlines some of the motivational factors that may be contributing to your situation. These motivational factors have been thoroughly researched and are extremely valid. All parents should carefully explore these factors if they are concerned about the welfare of their children. Every divorce has unique dynamics. Some divorce situations may involve only one or two of the factors listed below, other divorce situations may involve more or all.

It is important to assess each category carefully to identify if it pertains to your particular situation. Hopefully, by comparing your personal circumstance with these categories, it will help whenever you are confronted with an adverse situation involving the ex-spouse.

Educating oneself about the various '*divorce dynamics*' that can emerge during separation may also help diffuse some of the negative emotional reactions that often accompany adverse situations. If parents are educated and made aware of the motivational factors leading to adverse behavior, it may help them remain more objective, thereby toning down the emotional charge. Making a connection between a specific divorce situation and each category listed below may also help eliminate the natural urge of asking, *"Why is this happening to me?"*

Understanding some of the underlying motivational factors may also help a parent learn how to *maintain some control of their emotions and reactions* to the numerous adverse situations that can arise after divorce. Parents should be encouraged to assess a situation and identify which motivational categories they are dealing with. This knowledge may help these parents remain more objective, actually becoming a building block for new coping skills. Being able to identify and *'label'* destructive behavior may help a parent learn how to react with less negativity, thereby protecting the children from further harmful parental behavior.

In their excellent book, *Impasses of Divorce*, Janet Johnston and Linda Campbell explain some of the psychological reasons that parents remain enmeshed in an unhealthy relationship. They state,

> "Common to both types .... is the defensive use of disputes over custody and visitation to ward off the painful sense of loss, sadness and loneliness experienced in the divorce. To varying extents, these parents are unable to tolerate and accept the pain of the loss of separation from the spouse or child. Hence they are unable to mourn, grieve, and let go of the child, spouse, or the marriage itself. This is manifested in different kinds of disputes. [2]

> "Some try to prevent the actual loss for occurring by prolonging or clinging to the marriage. They do anything to set up roadblocks to the end of the marriage, refusing to settle anything, including plans for their children." [2]

> "Others, feeling hopeless, try to control the speed of the divorce and use mediation and counseling to put off the impending inevitable loss." [2]

> "Some try to deny the loss by refusing to acknowledge the full reality of the separation." [2]

> "Rather than deny the reality of the loss or resist its occurrence, other parents try to ward off and defend against the feelings of loss by denigrating the spouse and rationalizing that the marriage was not worth it." [2]

> "Simultaneously, many cover their sadness over the loss with anger." [2]

> "Fighting is also a means of maintaining contact and fending off loneliness." [2]

> "The custody dispute allows parents to live out the fantasy that they are still together in some way." [2]

"In an attempt to ward off loss, parents often turn to their children as replacements for the spouse. They become emotionally dependent and lean on their children to soften the loss, using the children as companions or confidantes. The intensity of their need for the child as surrogate parent or spouse increases with the stress of the divorce and with the severity of parent's own vulnerabilities." [2]

"Some parents used their children as a bridge to the ex-spouse, for example, by insisting on increased visits or being present at the child's exchange to ensure their own (not the child's) contact with their ex-mate." [2]

"Other parents, over-identify to varying degrees with their children and project their intolerance of sadness and fears of being alone onto the children. Then they seek to protect their children from these distressful emotions and consciously view the custody suit as a means of doing so. In the end, the child's distress and their own loneliness is ameliorated in this flurry of protective activity." [2]

What happens when parents fall into these psychological stalemates?
How does their destructive behavior manifest itself?
What potential outcomes does the destructive behavior lead to?

Stanley Clawar and Brynne Rivlin wrote an excellent book (published by the American Bar Association) based on their extensive research on the programming and brainwashing of children. Covering a 12-year study period, they reviewed approximately 1000 cases. Clawar and Rivlin selected seven hundred of those cases because "they were complete enough for a full data analysis."

Clawar and Rivlin identified what they believe to be the most common motivational factors for parents who program, brainwash or alienate their children from the other parent. Clawar and Rivlin state, "One, many or all (motivational factors) may be operational at any given time." [3]

★ ★ ★ ★ ★

The Most Common Motivational Factors for Parents Who Programme/Brainwash Their Children

1. Revenge
2. Self Righteousness
3. Fear of losing the child
4. Sense of past history
5. Proprietary perspective
6. Jealousy
7. Child support
8. Loss of identity
9. Out of sight; Out of mind
10. Self Protection
    a. Alcoholism or drug addition
    b. Incest or child abuse
    c. Abductors
    d. Criminal Involvement
    e. Mental health
    f. Problematic social relationships or life-styles
    g. Re-existing or new physical health problem
11. Maintaining the marital/adult relationship through conflict
12. Power, influence, control and domination [4]

✱ ✱ ✱ ✱ ✱

*Understanding the basic motivational factors
that may drive parents to interfere with a parent-child relationship
is a crucial step to help maintain, promote and protect
a special and autonomous parent-child relationship after divorce.*

(Endnotes)

[1] Mikesell, R. H. (2001). 13th National Conference of the Children's Rights Council, Bethesda, Maryland, Lecture: *Parallel Parenting Strategies: Keys for Success in High Conflict.*

[2] Johnston, J. R. & Campbell, L. E. G. (1988). *Impasse of Divorce: The Dynamics and Resolution of Family Conflict.* New York: The Free Press, A Division of Macmillan. pp. 102-104.

[3] Clawar, S. S., & Rivlin, B.V. (1991). *Children Held Hostage: Dealing with Programmed and Brainwashed Children,* Chicago, Illinois: American Bar Association, p. 37.

[4] id., p. 38.

5.

Who Would Do Such a Thing?

Is There Really a Motivation to Interfere With a Parent~Child Bond?

As discussed in the previous chapter there are many potential motivational factors that influence the beliefs and behavior of an unhealthy, vindictive or brainwashing parent. We examine some of these factors below. At best, each category is a brief overview. For information on any category, I encourage the reader to review the excellent book by Stanley Clawar and Brynne Rivlin, *Children Held Hostage, Dealing with Programmed and Brainwashed Children.* This book was published by the American Bar Association and is an excellent resource for <u>anyone</u> (parent, attorney, judge, mental health professional, special master or parenting coordinator) involved in the process or business of divorce.

I am very grateful to the American Bar Association for granting permission for this material to be reprinted. Clawar and Rivlin are two of the few researchers who have openly acknowledged that women may possess the intent, desire and ability to program and brainwash their children against the father. Without the inclusion of this notable research, it would leave the reader wondering if women would really use their children to satisfy their own needs or possess the means to retaliate against the ex-partner.

Listed below are some of the more common motivational factors Clawar and Rivlin identified in their research. Of the numerous motivational factors Clawar and Rivlin state, "It is important to remember that one, many, or all of these motivational factors may be operational at any given time." The following brief excerpts for each category are provided to give the reader a very *basic understanding* of the motivations that may be involved when a parent attempts to interfere with the parent/child bond.

1. *Revenge*

"Often, the underlying motivation for programming/brainwashing is revenge against the other parent. Revenge is one of the most common and powerful reasons for these behaviors, and it often emanates from a sense of rejection. The reasons for revengeful behavior may be subtle or obvious. Feelings of revenge may be derived from perceived emotional injuries of the past and a deep need to retaliate.

Additionally, unresolved feelings of rejection, wrongdoing, injustice, helplessness, jealousy, or possessiveness that the revengeful parent experienced in his or her own childhood can rise again to influence present perceptions and behavior." [1]

"Our findings show that former spouses will experience and exhibit more difficulty in minimizing powerful feelings of rejection and the urge to retaliate when

1. they were given no choice or opportunity to try to reconcile their marriage when informed of an impending separation or divorce
2. infidelity was discovered
3. they were immediately replaced as a love object
4. a spouse rushes into a relationship with the person who 'broke up' the marriage
5. a spouse remarries
6. the parent has had a life-style of clear-cut role definitions that revolved only around family, house, spouse, and children
7. the other parent develops a life-style of greater happiness, affluence, ease and comfort.

These parents are often unable to separate their own retaliatory needs from the child's needs and rights to be with the other parent. Avenging their anguish through punishment, they may attempt to exclude the parent from the child's life.

Blind to the child's need to ensure continuity and closeness with the other parent, they can only irritate, aggravate, and litigate, sometimes successfully incorporating the child into their world of hostility. Finally, the revengeful parent feels that he or she has assumed some power over the target parent." [1]

Clawar and Rivlin go on to describe, "Programming/brainwashing as a method of revenge may also be utilized by parents who perceive themselves as having 'lost' by being forced into the divorce, an unacceptable custody decision, and/or a poor property settlement. The attempt is to re-equilibrate the loss and avenge what was lost in the divorce outcome." [2]

2. *Self Righteousness*

"Attitudes of self-righteousness stem from a genuine belief in being the better parent. Some of these attitudes concern who was more involved historically in the child's life—who was there for the birth process, evening feedings (some fathers state that they have done everything but breast-feed their infants), doctor's appointments, shopping, birthday parties, school conferences, and so on.

'The Battle of the Mores' is fought with weight scales that measure who is more involved, more moral, more religious, more financially solvent (and thus able to provide more), more intelligent, more educated, more cultured, more musical and artistic, more fun, more responsible, has more time, or knows more about the child. Of course, parents involved in such battles are never going to convince each other of their respective supremacy. With this implicit understanding, these types often desire litigation, where a judge must ascertain whose case is more convincing when parents are hell-bent upon gaining primary custody and/or excising a parent-child bond.

Such parents may deeply believe that they are more appropriate in their view of life, goals for the child, and their superior ability to parent. In this self-righteous parental game of competition, the court becomes the arena in which the final judgment will prove who is the better parent." [3]

3. *Fear of Losing the Child*

"Some parents fear losing their child emotionally if not physically. Even in shared physical custody situations, fear may exist concerning the possible loss of a child.

A parent may perceive many threats to a relationship with his or her child. These threats are especially magnified when conditions of distrust exist between the birth parents. Frequently, one feels that the other parent does not value the continuity of the parent/child bond. In fact, parents may explicitly state this to each other, as in the following examples:

It's not important for 'my' son to spend any time with you.
My new wife can be a better mother to our daughter than you can.
You have nothing good to offer the child.
It would be best if you never saw the kids again-they wouldn't even miss you.
You've got rotten values-the kids shouldn't be exposed to that life style.

Statements like these and others are certainly incendiary and create a sense of paranoia in parents, which compels them to reactively hold on more strongly." [4]

"Unwillingness or inability to share children can occur after a period of cooperation between parents. The unwillingness may be triggered or initiated by the acquisition of a 'new family' through remarriage or by a surrogate stepparent arriving on the scene. These kinds of changes often become a real threat because the parent may fear loss through a usurpation of his or her role in the child's life. Programming, in some cases, may even be a result of pressure from the stepparent upon the biological parent to gain sole custody of the children. Often, stepparents can become the programmers and destroy cooperative custodial arrangements that have existed over time between the birth parents." [4]

4. *Sense of Past History*

Clawar and Rivlin define this phenomenon as, "One parent perceives herself or himself historically to have had more, or major, involvement in the child's life and should, therefore, continue to be the main caretaker. This point of view is usually associated with traditional mothers who feel that they have contributed more than the father in terms of daily contact and child rearing and should continue to be the main parental contributor to the child's life. These mothers tenaciously hold to the philosophy that they are more knowledgeable about the child's needs—be they nutritional, medical, dental, religious, educational, attire- or hygiene related, social or emotional." [5]

"They (the mothers) do not adhere to the concept of parental sharing. These women subscribe to the 'most competent' parent theory; other input, observations, participation, and resources are rejected because they are not up to the birth mother's standards of excellence in child rearing." [5]

"Whatever the reason for one parent being involved in the greater portion of parenting, a past history of (or a belief that one has had) significantly more involvement often plays a motivational role in programming/brainwashing." [5]

5. *Proprietary Perspective*

Regarding a "proprietary perspective" Clawar and Rivlin state, "Many mothers feel that they have a greater right to possession and ownership of children as a result of pregnancy and childbirth—'He's not getting her; I carried that child in my womb, and she's mine' will often be emphatically stated. Many women maintain proprietary views of their children and steadfastly believe that a special bond exists between mother and child through the process of conception and birth that fathers cannot share.

Women who adhere to this philosophy of motherhood do not believe that fathers, comparatively, are as capable of providing nurturing and care, attentiveness and understanding, love, time, communication, or emotional investment. In fact, to many, a father who fights for custody is an enigma, not only to the mother of his children, but to many members of his own family, to male counterparts, and to female acquaintances." [6]

"To these women, fathers are just not viewed as being significant and necessary to a child's healthy present and future development. It is most difficult to convince them otherwise; research to the contrary, discussions, counseling, mediation/conciliation, or even court orders may prove ineffective." [6]

6. *Jealousy*

"Some parents may have had an amicable relationship post divorce and a successful, cooperative custody arrangement until the introduction of a new partner in one parent's life. This shift in cooperative parenting is especially difficult when the other parent has not become romantically involved. Underlying reasons or problems related to custody revolve around unresolved reconciliation fantasies; jealousy over the child having a good relationship with the new partner; feelings of loss, abandonment, displacement and replacement in the child's life.

Many single parents fear that when the other parent remarries, that parent may show the court a change of circumstances and request modification of a custody order. Often, these parents express to their children that they have chosen not to date or remarry and will remain devoted, unlike the other parent, who has chosen to love someone else. This message is unhealthy as a type of emotional blackmail and places a heavy burden on a child

(1) to view one parent as a devoted martyr;

(2) to believe that he or she owes that parent reciprocity in terms of singularity of the relationship;

(3) that the remarried parent chose another partner over the child; and

(4) that people have to ration love." [7]

7. *Child Support*

"Unfortunately, for some families, financial gain is an impetus behind child custody goals. Parents embroiled in custody conflicts frequently make allegations of this nature to the court and to children. Children may be drawn into the custody conflict through protectiveness of a parent's financial security." [8]

8. *Loss of Identity*

"In cases where a woman has been in the role of traditional housewife and mother, to lose custody, share custody, or be forced to have a diminished amount of time is to suffer a loss of identity. On the social-emotional level, no substitute function can replace her only meaningful role, that of mother.

Mental imagery even before custody problems appear can be powerful. Thoughts of not being needed by one's child on an hourly or daily basis can create a panic reaction. What to do with the time and energy becomes problematic. Rather than utilize the freedom to pursue personal interests, take a course, start a career, spend some solitary time, or see friends, many of these women instead strategize to maintain or reinstate their role.

A frequent stratagem of such women is to continuously remind the children about how lonely it is at home without them. Before the other parent arrives for pickup, the mother will tell the child, 'Don't worry, we will be together again. Two days will be over soon. I'll be here waiting for you, and then we'll have fun.' Children who exquisitely feel a parent's loneliness and desperation each time they leave may carry with them a heavy burden of guilt that they cannot easily forget, despite being engaged in enjoyable activities and family life within the other home.

Unless such women can modify or diversify their role structure, they may firmly establish themselves in evanescent roles that can become bases for depression, constant feelings of loss, and a strong motivation to unconsciously or consciously program a child in order to regain the original maternal role. A great amount, if not the totality, of anger is directed toward the father, whom she believes to be punitive toward her rather than just exercising his parental rights to participate in raising his children. As children are being pulled away, the parents' reaction is to hold on more tightly. These parents are unable to share, primarily because they cannot enter into or develop other roles when the children are not present.

There *are* cases in which fathers who have been the primary caretakers or coequal caretakers experience the same sense of loss and subsequent need to hold onto or regain the lost role. The desire by a father or a mother to be deeply affiliated is not a problem. Programming and brainwashing a child to obtain the goal is." [9]

9. *Out of Sight, Out of Mind*

"For many, out of the vortex of emotions one experiences during separation and divorce, is the persistent need to distance oneself physically and emotionally from the source of pain. This is especially true for those who remain in love with the estranged spouse and desirous of the marriage while the ink is still wet on their divorce papers. Creating distance is also a motivating fact in programming and brainwashing for those who are consumed with hatred and rage. As long as the emotions persist unresolved, the brainwashing parent will attempt to relegate the target parent to nonentity status. A more pernicious situation cannot be found than the admixture of *two* parents who seek to accomplish the same goal: that of removing a child from the target parent's world—only to solve their own need for distance from each other. One child involved in this cross-fire said, 'I want to live with my grandparents -- my mom and dad are crazy.'" [10]

10. *Self Protection*

"Motivational factors in brainwashing are operative when parents behave in self-protective ways that serve as a shield from scrutiny or detection. These parents may fearfully anticipate that if certain discoveries about them were made, they could conceivably lose contact with a child through a custody battle, imprisonment, or institutionalization. Parents who fall into this category are those who are involved in

(a) alcoholism or drug addiction,

(b) incestuous or abusive practices with their children,

(c) plans to leave the residential area, state, or country, abducting the child,

(d) crime,

(e) institutionalization or mental tenuousness whereby custodial contact and ongoing parenting privileges could be curtailed,

(f) problematic social relationships or life-styles to which a child should not be exposed, or

(g) treatment for a threatening health condition (AIDS, multiple sclerosis, cancer, and so forth) and fears losing contact with the child." [11]

11. *Maintaining the Marital/Adult Relationship Through Conflict*

"Severance of marital ties in some cases can be accomplished with surgical precision, reducing trauma so that both parties can proceed into life in a healthy manner. Or it can be experienced as an amputation performed by an unskilled charlatan, leaving the individuals depleted emotionally and financially, hostile and damaged when one or both persons choose to maintain the relationship through conflict. There are innumerable battlefronts available to the conflict oriented, most of which are abusive to one or both parties." [12]

"The continuation of the relationship in its new form as a denouement of the marriage is often more lethal to children than actual separation and divorce because no child is completely insulated or immune from ongoing conflict. Therefore, acceptance, adjustment, and healing remain beyond reach for many children, especially those who are incorporated into angry conflicts." [12]

12. *Power, Influence, Control and Domination*

"The children who are most severely damaged socially and emotionally from divorce are those whose parents are driven to entirely exclude the other parent from the child's life through power, influence, control, and domination. In most cases, anger and hatred are the forces behind a consuming need to prevent the other parent from having any positive input into the child's life. Despite warnings from family members, friends, professionals, judges, or even their own attorneys regarding potential catastrophes to their children, they remain insensitive. They are convinced that they are operating in the child's best interest.

Wallerstein and Kelly coined the term 'embittered-chaotic' to describe parents whose 'intense anger was associated with a disorganizing disequilibrium... The embittered-chaotic parent never shielded his or her child from divorce bitterness and chaos.' [13] It has become our experience that virtually no intervention defuses the blind rage that these fathers and mothers adopt as a code to live by that can overshadow children's lives for years. Anyone not in agreement with their perception becomes identified as the enemy or outgroup.

Unwilling to admit to the target parent's value in the child's life, they systematically attempt to dominate all parental spheres." [14]

✸ ✸ ✸ ✸ ✸

I believe the work by Clawar and Rivlin is invaluable. The brief summaries above (from Clawar and Rivlin's book) are added here to give the reader an overview of the basic elements of potentially destructive post-marital behavior. All these adverse parental actions affect children of divorce.

For parents, you may find it helpful to return to this chapter periodically. When you have the irresistible urge to ask yourself why certain events are happening, refer to the sections above. Do your best to place your current situation into one or more of the categories.

Hopefully (with practice) the next time you are confronted with an unpleasant experience or situation with the ex-partner, you will be able to recognize the behavior and label the motivational factor. Learn to maintain emotional distance, control and objectivity. Most importantly, move swiftly to get your children *and you* out of the middle of the conflict and confusion as soon as possible.

Celebrate your knowledge (to yourself).
Then enjoy your children and the special time you have with them!

For the divorce professional: You see some (or perhaps all) of these behaviors every day. A key to helping these families disengage from the conflict and the dismal future of discord, is to help them learn to recognize the motivation that often drives the anger. With professional insight and guidance you can educate your clients, offer them alternatives to succeed in their new family structure and help facilitate their ability to deal with the undesirable side effects of divorce.

(Endnotes)

[1] Clawar, S. S., & Rivlin, B.V. (1991). *Children Held Hostage: Dealing with Programmed and Brainwashed Children*. Chicago, Illinois: American Bar Association. pp. 37-38.

[2] id., pp. 37-39.

[3] id., pp. 39-40.

[4] id., pp. 40-41.

[5] id., pp. 42-43.

[6] id., p. 43.

[7] id., pp. 44-45.

[8] id., p. 45.

[9] id., pp. 45-46.

[10] id., p. 46.

[11] id., pp. 47-64.

[12] id., pp. 64-65.

[13] J. Wallerstein and J. Kelly, *Surviving the Breakup* (New York: Basic Books, 1980), 28.

[14] Clawar, S. S., & Rivlin, B.V. (1991). *Children Held Hostage: Dealing with Programmed and Brainwashed Children*. Chicago, Illinois: American Bar Association, p. 66.

6.

Would a Mother Really Program Her Child?

If so, Why?

———————————

————————

This chapter expands on the previous discussion of motivational factors and will explore further why some mothers may tend to display alienating characteristics. In this era of 'political correctness,' the argument and implication that women would do such atrocities to their children (more than men) have been met with strong resistance. After all, as a sophisticated society, *we have been programmed* to believe that all mothers are good, and will always have good intentions toward the love and nurturing of their child. Yet, everyday the media informs us otherwise, as we see an increasing number of cases of mothers who inflict emotional or physical abuse, neglect and even the murdering of their own children.

Again, it is important to emphasize there is still a strong political debate that continues to brew regarding gender and the motivation, opportunity and actual alienation of a child from the other parent. In the past two decades there have been many professional pioneers including Richard Gardner, Ira Turkat, Stanley Clawar and Brynne Rivlin, who advocated strongly (in the beginning) that women alienate and brainwash children more than men. Then there was a change in the tide, and the political and feminist influence poured in, to moderate the bad news. As a result, and the undeniable reality that men are also capable of alienation, many of the pioneers reversed their public opinion regarding gender and the brainwashing of children.

For example, Richard Gardner spent years trying to reverse his initial observations that women alienated children more than men. It is believed by some that his change in opinion was influenced partly by a feminist political agendum that included tactics as far reaching as harassment. Nonetheless, he diligently worked to clarify his professional position and opinion that now includes a strong balance between *men and women* alienators. Ira Turkat blended his labeling from *Divorce Related Malicious Mother Syndrome* to *Divorce Related Malicious Parent Syndrome.* And as one can imagine, the debate and relabeling continues as you read this chapter!

I can only emphasize again, that *both* men and women are capable of alienation, and this book is not written to rekindle the argument. I chose to include the work by Clawar and Rivlin because I truly believe that the content of their research is justifiable and presents the motivational factors *of mothers* very clearly and concisely. Despite the debate of which gender alienates more, Clawar and Rivlin present some very compelling factors that all parents and divorce professionals should review and absorb as possibilities in the aftermath of divorce.

Yes, men may brainwash and alienate their children, but I believe their motivation and opportunity varies strongly from those of women. So, I encourage all readers to drop their defenses about 'gender graphics,' and learn more about why a mother may attempt to alienate a child from the father. Only with these insights can we help those children unfortunate enough to be caught in the middle of the ugly divorce fallout of brainwashing and alienation.

Why Would a Mother Program Her Child?

In their book, *Children Held Hostage: Dealing with Programmed and Brainwashed Children*, Stanley Clawar and Brynne Rivlin discovered (through their clinical and research findings) that both men and women could be involved in the programming and brainwashing of a child after divorce. They also discovered (depending on their technique) there were "striking" differences between the sexes, concluding that, "...females were more likely to fit at the extreme end of the continuum in degree and type of programming/brainwashing. Using Wallerstein and Kelley's term, women were more likely to be 'embittered/chaotic spouses.'" [1]

The following brief excerpts selected from the categories created by Clawar and Rivlin are provided as "possible explanations" of why women may program their children against the father. These "explanations" are a result of Clawar and Rivlin's interviews with men, women, attorney's, judges, children, and their own ideas.

1. *Birthright* [2]

"Many women have felt justified in their desired and actual programming and brainwashing because of their views of the pregnancy and birth processes...."

"These statements and others indicate the view that because women have a biological linkage, they have a special social and emotional linkage to the child that men cannot understand. Furthermore, the women often argued that the linkage is two ways – meaning that the child has a special feel and connection to the mother that is impossible to develop with the father. In the more hostile cases, women have referred to men as 'sperm donors,' 'just supplying some genetic material,' 'having no involvement after we had sex,' and other statements of separateness and disassociation of the male to the pregnancy, birthing, and postbirth process."

"Of course, one cannot deny that there may be a special relationship between mothers and children because of these biological processes. This however, is not the issue. The issue is that this fact of life is used as a rationale for keeping distance in, if not severing, the father-child relationship. Also, it is, at times, employed as a basis for denying any specialness in the relationship between father and child."

2. *Proprietary-Exclusionary Perspective* [3]

"Women, inordinately, held to a proprietary view of children. They indicated that the children were theirs, and they were more likely to speak in possessive terms. They would talk about 'us,' 'our home,' 'our life,' 'my children' or 'my family' and use other indicators of ownership."

"The proprietary view often extends to a sense of complete control and direction. Parents who hold to a proprietary view often develop exclusionary philosophies. The idea that the children are the property of the mother may extend into her assertion that she should also make all decisions concerning their education, medical care, social life, travel, holiday celebrations, religion, and other core aspects of their lives."

3. *The Family and Women are Synonymous* [4]

"Many women adhere to the idea that family life is really intimately connected to them, more so than with a male."

4. *Female Identity and Parenting* [5]

"Because of the above factors and other considerations, the social-psychological identity of women is often more bound up in their linkage to children than is that of men. Therefore, a woman may view a loss of a child, even sharing the child, consciously or unconsciously as a loss of part of her status in life. If being female is intimately bound up with the status of mother, and there is a diminution of mothering that can be performed, then by definition a woman could experience a feeling of status displacement or status loss."

5. *Financial-Support Needs* [6]

"At times, women need to maintain the children, or longer periods of contact with the children, in order not to lose support for the children and themselves. Obviously, if a more egalitarian situation develops in the future, this reason for employing programming/brainwashing may diminish. It should be noted that there are some cases where men also programme and brainwash the children in order to reduce their need to directly support the mother and children. However, our research indicates that this group is statistically smaller than the group of women who engage in such activities."

6. *Lack of Other Resources* [7]

"In addition to having less economic power, women may also have a lower social status in the community, less access to legal and professional resources, and fewer opportunities in the job and career marketplace. Because of these and other resource problems, women may resort to forms of postmarital combat that employ their verbal skills. Because of women's economic, social, legal, political, and career differentials, they sometimes need to employ whatever power is at hand for them."

"It appears, too, that men may be able to, because of their superior economic, social, and career positions, employ other mechanisms of seduction in regard to the child. For example, the development of a more interesting and exciting life-style is possible with greater economic resources. Women often feel in competition with this life-style presentation (new household pets, horses, houses, cars, entertainment, and the like) but may not have the economic resources to equalize the situation. Therefore, relying on programming/brainwashing may be seen as a 'court of last resort' in this conflict."

7. *Continuity and Family History* [8]

"An argument women often make is that because they had the majority of contact and upbringing experience with the children prior to the divorce, they should continue in this role during and after the divorce. In fact, at times, the women seem perplexed as to why there should be *any* changes. Arguments that times are changing, that men can become better fathers after a divorce, that children need both parents after a divorce and should have contact with them, and related arguments often fail to make any headway in the face of this idea of continuity and family history."

8. *Negative Opinions of Men's Capacity to Parent* [9]

"Many women adhere to a view that men are not as capable of parenting as women."

"If the mother is not there, she may believe that the child is more endangered in terms of health, welfare and safety (even though there may be no evidence that such dangers exist). She projects that, 'Something could happen, I might be needed, and I won't be there for them.'"

9. *Peer Group Expectations* [10]

"Women, more so that men, may be under social expectations from friends, siblings, parents, and others to maintain the full parenting role. This 'other' orientation means that the women are under scrutiny and in some ways have to meet expectations that exist in the community around them."

10. *Fear of Another Loss* [11]

"The most severe case of programming/brainwashing of children by mothers occurred when they were left for another women, believed there was another woman, or discovered a new woman in the life of the father."

"The presence of another woman/man created the most contamination compared to any other single factor. We call this the 'paramour factor.'"

"Losing the children to any degree, for some of the women, meant loss of respect from others, loss of income, loss of another battle ('He's gotten everything, he's not getting them'), and other associated ideas of loss. Sometimes children are used as a stopgap measure for the feelings of loss."

11. *Desire to Move or Leave a Geographical Area* [12]

"In many of the cases, women were forced to relocate their residence because of money, a new relationship, career, or the selling of the home. In some cases, it was not a forced move but a desire to 'create a new life and get out of here.' Sharing the children can be very problematic in these circumstances and can work against the freedom of the mother to leave the area. Therefore, mothers often relied on programming and brainwashing as a tool in helping the children become part of the total move. Men employed this technique at times, too, but much less frequently."

12. *Desire to Create the New Family* [13]

"Women, whom we have already noted as more sociohistorically connected to the image of family than men, were more likely to make arguments that the new family (mother, stepfather/paramour, and children) was important and, at times, better for the children than the 'old family.' Men had a desire to create new families, too, but were less likely to use programming/brainwashing to facilitate the children's involvement in the new family image. Mothers applied a great deal of pressure to children to 'call him Daddy' (the stepfather). Many conflicts revolved around attempts to get children to call the biological father by his first name after the mother remarried."

13. *Opportunity* [14]

"Because they often have more time with the children, women have the sheer opportunity to programme/brainwash them more. This includes, of course, unintentional as well as intentional dimensions. As we noted, most mothers ended up with the majority of physical and decision-making aspects of custody after divorce."

In their summary of the sex differences in programming and brainwashing, Clawar and Rivlin state,

"... women often indicate to us that they feel justified in giving negative messages to the children. In other words, the end result justifies the means. The overriding feeling present by the majority of women in our study is that something is being taken away from them, rather than being added to the life of the children, if the children are more involved with their fathers during the separation and after divorce." [15]

Obviously, more research needs to be conducted in all these areas. Clawar and Rivlin conclude in their findings the importance that additional studies are needed relating to the sex differences regarding the programming and brainwashing of children. They also felt that it would be crucial to study men and women who *do not* brainwash their children so that profiling and opinions can be more conclusive.

The research, study and subsequent findings done by Clawar and Rivlin are included to help validate the observations made in this book, and to provide a more solid foundation to identify the need for a different parenting model when such circumstances arise. In cases where any of these motivational factors, or elements of destructive parenting exist, a parallel-parenting model may well be the best model for these families of divorce.

Divorce professionals and parents need to take a more proactive role in protecting the parent/child bond when any of these motivational factors exist. To that end, divorce professionals (including judges) need to embrace and endorse "well-defined, enforceable custody and parenting orders" that will protect and promote a parent/child relationship after divorce.

(Endnotes)

[1] Clawar, S. S., & Rivlin, B. V. (1991). *Children Held Hostage: Dealing With Programmed and Brainwashed Children*. Chicago, Illinois: American Bar Association. p. 155.

[2] id., pp. 155-156.

[3] id., p. 156.

[4] id., p. 156.

[5] id., p. 157.

[6] id., pp. 157-158.

[7] id., p. 158.

[8] id., pp. 158-159.

[9] id., p. 159.

[10] id., p. 160.

[11] id., p. 160.

[12] id., p. 161.

[13] id., p. 161.

[14] id., p. 161.

[15] id., pp. 161-162.

7.

Licensed to Stalk!

Is it Simply Curiosity, Overly Concerned About the Children or Should it be Considered Stalking?
Using the Children as the Conduit for Stalking After Divorce

"The only thing my ex-wife really wants is a reaction from me,
an emotion she can hold on to. The strange thing is she will accept *any* emotion
or reaction .... love, hate, a smile, anger, even rage or the complete denial of her
existence ... as an indiction that I still love her and care about her. And if I do not
give her a reaction or an emotion, she will provoke me into doing so. It is very
similar to stalking behavior. A stalker will stalk you until you react, so they can
feel reassured that you are emotionally connected and care."

A father stalked

Only time will tell whether your ex-partner will resort to some of the destructive
behaviors and tactics described in this book. It is important to remember that in the throws
of separation and divorce, many things can go awry. Therefore, precautions should be taken

to protect your environment and your relationship with *your* children. While you may not think of your ex-partner as a stalker, you may benefit from the insights and advice of stalking survivors.

Most of the components in this book are examples of how an ex-partner can, if so inclined, try to damage your life and your relationship with your children. Throughout this book, we discuss how some parents are seriously affected by divorce and the detrimental effect their behavior and actions can have on an ex-partner and their own children. I believe that stalking an ex-partner, *through the children*, is very possible when an embittered ex-partner seeks revenge against the other parent. Simply playing "*I Spy*" (discussed in Chapter 15) is a serious form of stalking, and while the children may be young and unaware, they are learning to play a very dangerous emotional game.

The idea that a parent may resort to using a child to support their stalking behavior has created a significant amount of interest with friends and professionals alike. I believe there is a strong correlation between the standard definition of stalking and the potential for a parent to *use a child to stalk an ex-partner after divorce*. After all, the current research on stalking clearly delineates that the relationship between intimate partners poses a unique situation for stalking behaviors.

There are many different definitions of stalking, and each state has a particular variation of the legal definition. In general, stalking may be defined as:

> ➤ *"The willful, malicious, and repeated following or harassment of another person."*

> ➤ *To harass may be defined as engaging in a "knowing and willful course of conduct directed at a specific person that seriously alarms, annoys, torments or terrorizes the person and that serves no legitimate purpose. The course of conduct must be such as would cause a reasonable person to suffer substantial emotional distress."*

> ➤ *"Course of conduct is defined as "a pattern of conduct composed of a series of acts over a period of time, however short, evidencing a continuity of purpose."* [1]

What the literature and the law fail to examine is the *use of children* by a stalking parent to gather information about their victim, the ex-spouse. This single element, *the children*, creates an entirely different category of stalking. It is my personal belief that the use of children to stalk an ex-partner is far more prevalent than researched or discussed and is often overlooked as emotional abuse by the courts and psychological community.

Take for example the mother in Wisconsin who stalked her ex-husband persistently through her child. During the initial stages of the separation and divorce this mother would telephone her ex-husband repeatedly just to talk to him, often fabricating issues to discuss about their child. As with many stalkers, the telephone became a source of connection with the father and a convenient tool of harassment. The telephone at the father's house could ring up to 15 times in one day, sometimes resulting in trivial conversations about the child, other calls resulting in a disconnection and a dial tone. The telephone calls became regular and harassing.

The mother would also park her car down the street from the father's home, watching his daily activities and monitoring his schedule. Sometimes she would sit in her car with her child, other times she would sit alone. The father did not always lock his doors at home and the mother would often come into his home when she knew he was away.

When the father met someone new, the mother increased her efforts to stalk the father and his 'new friend.' The mother justified her actions stating *"I have every intention to make it my business to know <u>exactly</u> what is going on in his home, especially if this new person will be spending time with <u>my child!</u>"*

In another example, an obsessed mother in South Carolina would question and interview her three young children when they would return from a visit with the father. She would then buy the exact same movies, video games, bikes and other toys the children had at the father's home. The mother would then tell the children that *"her toys"* were *"better and fancier"* than the father's, though they were exactly the same.

Through her children's observations and dutiful reporting of information, this mother created a 'mirror' of the father's home. By mirroring the father, the mother was able to systematically diffuse special aspects of the children's life with their father. The contribution of this systematic diffusion ultimately undermined the unique and special relationship this father *could have had* with his children.

In these two examples, the mothers demonstrated stalking tendencies at the onset of the separation process. Because of the previous marital relationship, and the joint custody arrangement of the children, these mothers could pursue their victim (the ex-husband) without ramifications. One father was unsuccessful in his effort to obtain a restraining order to secure his privacy. The judge in the case stated, "Well, she is the mother, and you just need to let her do what she needs to do. After all, you have a child together!" When the father pleaded that the mother was stalking him, the judge ruled it as a "ridiculous allegation."

Unfortunately, for the parent being stalked, the belief that a child is being used in the stalking process may be very true but will not be easy to overcome in daily life, and may be very difficult to present to the court. The family law courts in the United States are not designed to spend the time or do the necessary investigative research regarding such allegations.

More likely, the court may consider allegations of this nature as unbelievable or unsubstantiated. Divorce brings out the worst in many people, and the courts are accustomed to the many tricks of deceit and dishonesty presented in the courtroom during a divorce or child custody case. Alleging to the judge that your ex-partner is involving your child to stalk you, may not only sound paranoid and narcissistic, but may be viewed as just another element of malice in the divorce court arena.

Malicious or vindictive parents can be extremely deceitful, and they often have no remorse or conscience about lying to the court or others. Unfortunately, in the family law courts, lying is commonplace, and sanctions are scarce for lying and perjury. Malicious and vindictive parents seem to sense the unwillingness of the courts to penalize them for lying, so once they start lying and are not held accountable, they continue with even more brazenness.

Divorce courts are geared for conflict including all the theatrics (based on reality or not) that parents will employ to present and win their divorce and custody cases. Just consider the number of false sexual abuse allegations filed each year during custody proceedings. Therefore, specific steps need to be taken to identify the risk of being stalked by an ex-partner and the potential for the involvement of a child in the process. Every parent should make a careful assessment to protect the child and the parent's right to have a private child/parent relationship.

Throughout this book, we offer ideas and suggestions to help diffuse some of the opportunities that can arise when abnormal parenting behaviors become a part of the divorce equation. We have also emphasized the importance of establishing useful boundaries for families of divorce. If your partner has *ever* shown even mild signs of stalking (in the past or present) then the correlation between separation, divorce, stalking and the use of your child to do so, should be carefully considered.

No one should be obligated to continue an unhealthy relationship, regardless if there has been a marriage, with children or not. Unfortunately, a stalking ex-partner can keep the other parent in a vice, demanding a relationship because of a child. A stalking ex-partner may often try to manipulate the other parent with feelings of guilt or blame, portray the victim (even though they are the aggressor) and try to entwine the other parent in a dependent relationship after separation or divorce.

Setting appropriate boundaries with an irrational, vindictive or malicious ex-partner should be promoted and supported by the legal system, and parents should take a proactive self-protective role when dealing with a stalking ex-partner. It is paramount that this self-protective role is established free from guilt or remorse because of the previous relationship.

This is extremely important advice for parents of divorce. In the beginning stages of separation and divorce, parents are routinely placed in a very grey area regarding boundaries, specifically the amount and frequency of verbal and physical interactions.

Having a child as a product of an intimate relationship creates a unique opportunity for an affected individual to stalk an ex-partner. Individuals with stalking tendencies (or a personality disorder associated with stalking) believe they are *entitled to be a part of the other parent's life*. These affected individuals truly believe they should be included in the other parent's life, even after separation or divorce, and will often extend themselves to great extremes to remain involved with the other parent or try to control the other parent's life with the children.

In her excellent book *Surviving a Stalker*, Linden Gross states:

"The truth is that, for most of us, we're in love not just with the person, but with our projection of what kind of couple we'll make, the needs that he or she will fulfill and the idealized notion of love in general. Before we've even gotten to know whom we're really dealing with, we've fallen in love with what that person could represent to our future.

The individual whose life is a void waiting to be filled, however, takes those feelings and amplifies them. The person with whom he's infatuated becomes his reason to exist. Any contact is better than no contact, any information a way to feel more intimately involved – even if no relationship exists. That emptiness also helps explain the explosion that takes place during the separation or divorces of many couples, when those who have used their relationships to define their identity simply can't afford to let go." [2]

The following excerpts have been chosen to provide a cursory illustration of how different elements of stalking can be present in the post-divorce arena, and *how children* may be involved in the process.

★　★　★　★　★

The interaction between a stalker and a victim may become a game of 'Win-or Lose', almost like a contest or competition of who will outdo or outlast the other.

Parents who are separating should realize that divorce often becomes a high-stake, high-conflict drama that often leads to the legal and emotional battlefield. As one stepfather stated, "We are warring families, and I am but a warrior." Many divorce cases deteriorate into a 'win or lose' mentality, and the individuals involved cannot view the situation objectively. These individuals often become entrenched in the philosophy, "All is fair in love and war and if I can't have it, you can't either. I'll show you."

Our legal system often creates an adversarial environment and often promotes hostility and distrust between separating partners. During the divorce process the hostility and distrust can escalate and any healthy interaction between the individuals may begin to weaken. As the relationship changes between the previously intimate partners, the rapport can easily shift to a contest of who is the better parent, who was the better spouse, who is right and who is wrong, etcetera.

All these elements make fertile ground for warring spouses to become entrenched in the process of humiliating and degrading the other partner. If the chemistry is right and the personality profiles coincide, the possibility of stalking in a post divorce situation should not be overlooked.

"(The stalker) manipulates relationships through intimidation, blames you for not cooperating with him, and minimizes the impact of his own actions. His goal, however inappropriate, justifies all behavior. And his own sense of inadequacy drives it.

Once an individual merges his identity with that of his target, escalation of obsessive activity is almost inevitable. In the face of unrequited love, the stalker raises the stakes for attention and, sometimes for revenge." [3]

As demonstrated throughout this book, individuals unable to handle the stress of rejection or the loss of the relationship may begin to demonstrate significant personality disturbances. If their self-image was poor before the marriage, the loss of the identity of the marriage and family may trigger a strong reaction of blame resulting in efforts to impose guilt upon the other partner.

Manipulation may soon follow. Manipulation allows the hurt individual to feel more in control of the ex-partner and their own emotions. Individuals resorting to manipulation may do *anything* to get the attention essential to their existence. They *need the attention* (positive or negative) to feel complete and to satisfy their own inner insecurities and beliefs that the other partner really does care about and need them.

Individuals in this category could surely use and manipulate a child to create situations in which the other partner *must* interact with them, thereby giving them the attention they so desperately need.

"Deflect weapons of destruction: How your perpetrator chooses to manipulate or harm you is almost beside the point when it comes to stalking, especially since the way a stalker tries to inflict emotional, financial, or physical damage is limited only by his or her imagination. You can limit the impact, however, by how you respond to the situation. When possible, don't play his or her game." [4]

Some individuals will do anything to disrupt or 'ruin' the ex-partner's life. Many divorce cases are riddled with efforts of ex-partners trying to inflict emotional, financial or physical damage to the other parent. One must quickly identify if the ex-partner is demonstrating stalking characteristics, and if they are *involving the children in the process.* If the ex-partner is demonstrating stalking conduct, then their efforts to involve the children in the process may be inevitable. Observe for any signs of stalking behavior and take all the necessary precautions to protect your children and you from the invasive maneuvers that a stalking ex-partner may use.

In general, stalkers often present themselves as reasonable and rationale. In situations such as divorce, a stalking ex-partner can gain control of your emotions through the negotiation process of divorce.

It is important for parents to remember that they may not be dealing with a reasonable or rational individual during the divorce process. In fact, some parents wonder if they ever knew or understood the ex-partner at all. An ex-partner with stalking tendencies will often try to gain control of the other parent through the many negotiations needed to make the divorce final.

Being intimately involved with someone changes your reactions to them. Your reaction may be very different if a stranger walks up to you on the street and begins to bother you, versus an ex-partner approaching you to cause problems. Your reaction will be different because you had an emotional or intimate relationship with the ex-partner. When someone you have cared about in the past begins to act in a strange manner, it is far more difficult to be objective and distance yourself emotionally. Often, there are feelings of guilt during the separation and divorce process. During this fragile time, separating partners are vulnerable and may succumb to the manipulation and 'emotional needs' of an ex-partner, who may use the divorce process as their means to stay connected to the other parent.

Most stalkers are driven to obtain as much information about their victims as possible. Divorcing parents are not excluded from this "search for information." In fact, the divorce process may perpetrate a curious ex-partner into a stalking mania. A mania driven by the need to find answers to questions such as gathering information about the other parent's new lifestyle, professional affiliations, family, home and new relationships.

For the stalking ex-partner, it is easy to jump on the 'information mania highway.' Realistically, an ex-partner has more information to begin with than any ordinary stalker could hope for. As a married or intimately involved couple, confidential information such as social security and drivers license numbers, automobile information (including license plates, registration and loans), bank account information, credit card numbers, loan information, property ownership, mortgage, voting information and professional licensing boards are usually common knowledge between partners. Other vital personal data elements would include your date of birth, mother's maiden name, passwords and pin numbers.

But, the information highway does not stop here. For the stalker, there is also the public record department in each city, county and state in the country. Via this information pathway, a stalking ex-partner can procure the valuable information needed to pry further into the life and privacy of the other parent, long after separation.

In addition, a stalking ex-partner is able to obtain personal information about the other parent through previously established personal relationships such as friends, co-workers and relatives.

An ex-partner has a clear advantage in the information department. Add the normal human element of curiosity and the environment is fertile for stalking behavior! In addition, the design of family law not only allows the stalker to know an ex-partners every move, but actually promotes the flow of information into the stalking ex-partner's (and their attorney's) hands.

Simply calculating child support (which you may be responsible for until your child is 18 or 21 years of age) can lead to the review of every check you have written, and discovery into your most private financial information. Even if you have been separated or divorced for many years, a request for modification of child support can trigger an in-depth review of your current financial situation, including a new spouse's financial resources.

For example, in California, in order to determine child support alone, one must produce the past two years of income tax returns, and through the discovery process, an ex-spouse may have the right to review your detailed financial history. What better mechanism to stalk you with? Imagine all the information that can be gathered by reviewing returned checks and credit card bills during a two-year period!

Even without the family law discovery advantage, a stalking ex-partner has many other alternatives to access personal information. Obviously, a deceitful ex-partner can use this data to obtain confidential information that is supposedly protected by privacy acts and privacy policies touted by most financial institutions. A cunning ex-partner, determined to obtain confidential information, can usually succeed with the combination of the knowledge of private data and crafty lying.

There are many examples of ex-partners who have successfully invaded banking accounts or intercepted valuable financial information about the other partner through financial institutions. Even after years of separation or divorce, financial information can be obtained by using an ex-partner's social security number, bank account number and mother's maiden name.

Some ex-partners have been successful in removing funds from accounts by representing to the bank that they are the 'wife' making financial arrangements for her 'husband.' Customer service representatives rarely know (or care) if couples are separated or divorced.

Another maneuver that has been successful for stalking ex-partners has been the commingling of financial accounts. Linking checking, savings and investment accounts during the marriage can provide a valuable source of information (and potential revenue) for a crafty stalker after divorce.

Other divorced stalking parents may use a child's custodial or trust account to gather financial information. As a parent (whether they established the account or not) they may be able to persuade the financial institution to divulge confidential investment and banking information. Again, these stalking parents have all the necessary identifying information needed to access the accounts. Some parents have been successful in removing funds altogether.

A stalking ex-partner may also pursue gathering information about an ex-partner's business finances or the financial resources of a new partner or significant other. Through a diligent public records search, an ex-partner can discover mortgage and general lending information. This information may include the name of the lending institution, the loan number and the general terms of the loan including specific financial riders.

★ ★ ★ ★ ★

One of the stalkers most successful and telling strategies is to surprise their victims with unwelcomed interactions. The telephone is one of the most notorious instruments a stalker uses to bother or harass their victim. They may telephone their victim repeatedly for conversation, or they may telephone repeatedly simply to hang-up when the victim answers. Any unsolicited interaction between two people, including letters, e-mails, faxes, personal contacts or observation from a distance should be assessed carefully by a potential victim.

The telephone can become one of the most powerful tools a malicious ex-spouse can exploit to hassle and disrupt the other parent's time with the children. Many parents are unsuspecting of an ex-partners malicious use of the telephone or other communication devices. Chapter 16 is dedicated to the destructive use of the telephone by a stalking or intrusive ex-spouse. In general, communication of any nature can easily become disruptive for a child, and parents should be aware of the content and timing of communication with the other parent.

One example of unwanted contact through correspondence involved a mother in Minnesota who continually sent angry and abusive letters to her ex-husband. The letters were insulting and toxic, yet strangely begged the father 'to include her in his new life.' This mother was harassing and stalking the father via her letters.

The father obtained a court order restricting the mother from sending such letters, but the order did not stop the mother from her aggressive campaign. When the letters continued to arrive, the father kept them and cataloged them in chronological order. Within five years, the father had amassed a collection of several hundred handwritten notes and typed letters.

Through this written correspondence, the mother revealed her personality and stalking behavior. In her letters, she would explain in detail how she would gather information from their four children about the father. She would describe her discussion with the children and then format her letter of complaint to the father based on the information she had gathered. The letters would describe in detail how she disapproved of almost everything that occurred during the father's custodial time. In the letters, the mother would complain to the father about his personal and parenting behavior. In closing, she would then beg the father to include her in his activities with the children.

The mother's letters also indicated that she had often observed the father with the children during his custodial time, meaning she had been watching him, *stalking him*, from a distance.

In this example, as experienced by many stalking victims, the court order did not restrain or even deter the mother from sending harassing letters to the father. The mother argued that she had joint custody of the children and that she needed direct communication with the father. She stated that the letters were of "extreme importance in the co-parenting efforts of the children." Often, as so many stalking victims have found, restraining orders mean nothing to a stalker. In fact, many convicted stalkers actually interpreted a restraining order as a positive indication that the victim really cared about them, and wanted the harassing contact.

Stalking and coincidental meetings. Many stalkers will coincidentally appear at events or places they know their victim will be. They do not always interact with the victim, but their presence is obvious. The stalkers main objective is to assure the victim is aware of their presence, yet making it appear as if their simultaneous attendance is entirely coincidental.

Having children with an ex-partner significantly increases the likelihood of this type of 'coincidental stalking.' Some of these obsessed parents will profess adamantly that they need to be at a certain location because of the children, when they are actually at the location to observe the other parent! These stalking parents also know the ex-partner's schedule (because of the daily activities of the children) and they can make these 'coincidental encounters' appear entirely benign.

> *Take for example*, the mother in Colorado who would 'coincidentally' arrange to be wherever she thought the father might be with their child. She would always act so surprised to see them, though she knew exactly what the child's daily schedule was when visiting the father.

The same scenario presents itself for all child related activities. Be very aware of coincidental encounters. Monitoring this type of activity by making brief notes, including dates and times, can help you identify and distinguish between normal and abnormal 'coincidental behavior.'

Most experts on stalking agree that is best not to interact or communicate with a stalker. For families of divorce, this means interacting with the other parent through a third party. Direct interaction with a stalking ex-partner promotes their need for attention and solidifies their belief that the victim parent still wants and needs them. Unfortunately, an ex-partner can create many scenarios to invoke a response from the other parent.

As emphasized throughout this book, be careful how you plan to use *any of this information*, particularly if you intend to present it in legal proceedings. The judicial system is light-years behind dealing with the concept of parental alienation, manipulative and vindictive parents, divorce related malicious behavior and the concept that parents may stalk the other (through their children) for malevolent intent. Presenting any information based on the theory of stalking could backfire on your intentions to protect the best interests of your children. Unfortunately, sharing children with an ex-partner can easily become a license to stalk and interfere in the other parent's life.

Assure that your attorney is well versed in stalking behavior and supports appropriate boundaries for families of divorce. Above all, protect your privacy and your privacy with your children. Remember that pursuing custody or any other litigation involving your ex-partner may open the door to more '*legal stalking.*'

Make your choices carefully and remember:
You cannot change the legal system as unjust as it may sometime seem.
You can however, protect yourself and your relationship with your children,
and that should be your highest priority!

(Endnotes)

[1] Meloy, R. J. (1998). *The Psychology of Stalking, Clinical and Forensic Perspectives.* New York Harcourt, Brace & Company, Academic Press. pp. 31-32.

[2] Gross, L. (2000). *Surviving a Stalker: Everything You Need to Know to Keep Yourself Safe.* New York: Marlowe & Company. p. 7.

[3] id., pp. 47-48.

[4] id., p. 70.

PART THREE

GETTING OFF THE DANCE FLOOR
≈ GRACEFULLY ≈

8.

The Essential Elements:
The Child's Health, Education & Welfare

———————————————

———————————

With the motivational factors defined and explained, it is time to identify some of the important areas that distinguish parallel parenting from other parenting models. First and foremost, the parenting plan needs to establish a foundation of *essential elements* regarding your children.

It is imperative to understand that you may not agree with your ex-partner on many issues going into separation and divorce. You do, however, need to focus and agree to several essential issues regarding your children. These *essential elements* include the basics of parenting and your child's future, including their health, education and general welfare. After an agreement of these *essential elements* is accomplished, you can agree to disagree again.

Many parents begin at an impasse or reach an impasse in the very early stages of the divorce process. Be forewarned, if you cannot (or will not) agree to these essential elements, then rest assured the court will do it for you. *Most importantly, the court has a strict directive to provide for the welfare of the child, and therefore will make decisions for the child when the parents cannot agree.*

The court uses the *best interest of the child doctrine* to make their determinations. It is important to realize that the court does not know you or the details of your situation. The judge relies on the attorneys and how your family and family dynamics are presented to them in court. For example, when a mother claims the father is an alcoholic, the court has to consider this, even if it is untrue. It is imperative to make the best effort possible to *agree on the essential elements* and what is best for your children in these specific areas, instead of having someone else make these important decisions for you.

Remember, this is *not a determination* about custody, child support, spousal support or, sale of the family home. The <u>*sole purpose*</u> to agree on the essential elements is to provide a specific blueprint for your child's *immediate future, separate from all the other divorce issues.*

Make it a priority to define the *essential elements* and agree to coordinate the few major decisions you need to make for your child. These essential elements include your child's legal jurisdiction, which schools your child will attend, what extracurricular activities each parent thinks is important, what medical providers the child will see, what churches the child will attend, and any other issue that may be considered major and *essential* in your child's life. The directive:

The best interests of the child's health, education and general welfare.

Secure a written agreement regarding your child's health, education and welfare as soon as possible. The written agreement should include clauses to make modifications (if necessary) as the child gets older or if there is a significant change of circumstance.

Following the guidelines below for agreeing to the *essential elements* will help clear the 'muddy waters' of the divorce process. Again, this is not about custody, child or spousal support. If you can agree on most of the following elements, you will escape one of the most common pitfalls of divorce.

Often during the divorce process, many of the *child related issues* become distorted and enmeshed with other divorce matters. When this occurs, an agreement regarding the child's *essential elements* cannot be accomplished without making a sacrifice to the many other divorce negotiations. Sometimes this is a deliberate strategy of a divorce attorney, "Wear down the opponent and confuse all the issues." Unfortunately, this strategy plays directly into the hands of a deceitful and destructive ex-spouse.

✸   ✸   ✸   ✸   ✸

Remember:

- ✓ If you cannot agree to the essential elements then someone else will do it for you, e.g., the JUDGE!
- ✓ Remain focused on the essential elements.
- ✓ Make the essential elements a priority for an immediate agreement separate from all the other divorce issues.
- ✓ Do not allow the essential elements to become entwined with the other matters of the divorce process.
- ✓ Do no allow the essential elements to become bargaining chips for other divorce negotiations.
- ✓ Discuss and negotiate or mediate each essential element, one element at a time.
- ✓ Each parent should sign the agreement as *each essential element* is negotiated. (This strategy helps to eliminate the manipulation of the negotiation process and *'parental bartering.'*)
- ✓ Prioritize the essential elements from what you believe will be the easiest to the hardest to achieve resolution.
- ✓ Begin with the easiest element working to the hardest.
- ✓ If possible, sign off (legally) on each element, as it is agreed to. (This eliminates the potential for a 'breakdown' of the process if the more difficult elements cannot be resolved without court intervention.)
- ✓ If negotiations begin to deteriorate regarding the essential elements, reschedule the meeting or negotiations for a specified date in the very near future, for example, no further than 5 days away.

One common strategy of divorce attorneys representing a malicious or vindictive ex-partner is to delay agreements and negotiations, dragging out and entwining all the divorce issues. It is often a successful strategy! The strategy is called *stalling*. *Stalling* benefits the parent trying to manipulate and control *'possession of the child.'*

For example, stalling may benefit the parent who has 'assumed physical custody' of the child during the initial phase of separation. When a parent assumes primary responsibility for a child during separation, it may sway the courts decision regarding custody in the favor of that parent. The tactic of stalling allows the controlling parent to retain 'custody' of the child for an extended period of time, until the legal parameters of custody are decided and clearly defined.

If a parent is actively participating in the stalling tactic, they may be using their forced access to the child to create a stronger parent/child bond, which may also include the brainwashing of a child against the other parent.

THE ESSENTIAL ELEMENTS

I believe the child's *essential elements* should be addressed before any other decisions are made in the divorce process. Judges, lawyers and mediators should strive to settle the *essential elements* before proceeding with any other aspect of the divorce. This would truly be in the best interest of the child. Once these elements are settled, the rest of the divorce can proceed. Deciding on these elements provides the child with some degree of stability when the divorce enters the more complicated phases regarding financial and material issues.

Several elements may be agreed to on a temporary basis, but at least they provide a *beginning for your child's future*. Children are often abandoned during the divorce process, essentially in limbo, until the property and financial settlements are determined. In these situations, the children are often used as pawns for financial retaliation and retribution. Be proactive and make the *essential elements* a priority for your children and you!

Each *essential element* described below has a dedicated chapter in this book to address the issue in detail. This list is presented here as an example to demonstrate the *essential elements of parallel parenting*.

♦ LEGAL JURISDICTION

- ❑ A permanent element – one that should not be changed!

- ❑ Jurisdiction is defined as which state and county will have control of your divorce, custody and other legal decisions regarding your child. It is a legal term, it protects you (and your child) from decisions being made regarding both of you in another jurisdiction.

- ❑ Defining your child's legal jurisdiction should be considered paramount. Legal jurisdiction is discussed in detail in Chapter 22.

♦ HEALTH CARE

- ❑ Portions of this element can be *interim*, until the financial responsibilities for health care costs are legally defined.

❑ Agree on the child's primary health care providers.

❑ If you live in separate towns and cannot have the same providers then list each provider for the mother and the father.

> ❑ The out-of-town parent or the non-custodial parent will designate an alternate health care provider for non-routine or urgent care.

❑ Routine care needs to be established in the child's primary location and legal jurisdiction, if applicable.

❑ In our child's best interest, we agree to the following interim healthcare providers for our child.

❑ We are making this (interim) agreement regarding our child's health care and we both understand that the financial responsibility for the health insurance and health care costs will be determined later.

❑ (If this is an interim agreement) When our financial settlement has been finalized, these providers may change, however, until our agreement is final, we agree to the following providers:

❑ (If this is not an interim agreement) We agree to the following health care insurance and providers for our child(ren):

> ❑ Insurance Company: The following health care insurance will be provided for our child (ren):
>
> Name of Insurance Carrier _____
>
> Address: _____
>
> Telephone #: _____
>
> Policy #: _____

❑ Names of Health Care Providers

> ❑ Pediatrician/Family Practice Provider
>
> ❑ Dentist
>
> ❑ Mental Health Provider
>
> ❑ Urgent Care Facility
>
> ❑ Orthodontist
>
> ❑ Hospital for Emergency and Elective Care

Again, some attorneys will insist on delineating <u>who pays</u> for the health insurance, deductibles, copayments and uninsured costs at this phase in the negotiations. This complicates the negotiation of the health care essential element and can potentially escalate the divorce conflict, starting the financial dispute rolling. The fact of the matter, the court will decide who will be financially responsible for the cost of health insurance and health care if you cannot reach an agreement amicably.

Obviously, the best health care plan is in your child's best interest. If both parents have insurance (through their employers) then choose the best plan for your child's future. Realistically, this could save you thousands of dollars in the future.

The agreement to the immediate health care plan for your children does not need to become a financial issue. Financial responsibility can be decided later, in several different ways. For example:

❑ Each parent contributes to the child's cost of health care insurance and care

_____% Mother

_____% Father, or,

❑ Father pays for health care insurance with a credit to child support payments, or,

❑ Mother pays for health care insurance with a credit to her portion of child support payments.

Chapter 18 is dedicated to Health Care.

♦ EDUCATION

❑ Agree on the schools your child will be attending (especially for the next two years.)

❑ If there is a possibility that your child may attend a private school, then list one school for each public and private category, as responsibility for payment may not have been decided.

❑ *Do not* allow the financial responsibility for education to become a bargaining chip.

❑ Providing the names for both educational systems eliminates the impasse that often surfaces regarding the negotiation of education.

	Private	Public
Pre-School	❑	❑
Primary School	❑	❑
Middle School	❑	❑
High School	❑	❑
College	❑	❑

❑ Obviously, if your child is in preschool at the time of separation, you do not need to designate a college for them now. Try to agree to a 2-3 year educational plan.

❑ Plan for your child's educational choices as far in advance, as possible. This effort will help reduce conflict in the future.

Chapter 20 is dedicated to Education.

◆ EXTRACURRICULAR ACTIVITIES

❑ Each parent will choose one extracurricular activity they feel is important for the child's development. (Each household agrees to support the activity at least two days per week, whether it is practice, lessons, etc.)

 ❑ Activity A (Mother's choice)_____

 ❑ Activity B (Father's choice) _____

❑ This task simply *identifies* what activities each parent believes are important to the child. WHEN the financial piece is settled, these activities can be pursued.

Chapter 21 is dedicated to Extracurricular Activities.

◆ RELIGION

❑ Our child has attended the _____ church of the _____ faith for the past ___ years. We agree that our child will continue attendance at this church and faith to the best of our ability.

❑ We *do not agree* on the religion for our child, and we agree that this matter will have to be addressed later.

◆ PARENTING TIME

❑ Until our custody and visitation schedule is established, we will have the following schedule *(Be as specific as possible)*:

❑ We recognize and agree this may be a temporary or interim schedule:

  ❑ Include the specific days of visitation, the specific time and location of the exchange of the child. For example:

❑ Mother's interim custodial days and times (every other week)
  ❑ Monday after school until Wednesday morning, taking child to school.
  ❑ Friday after school until Monday morning, taking the child to school.
❑ Father's interim custodial days and times (every other week)
  ❑ Wednesday after school, taking the child to school on Friday morning
  ❑ Monday after school, taking the child to school on Wednesday morning.

Example: M = mother, F = father

F/M = father drops off/mother picks up

M/F = mother drops off/father picks up

	S	M	T	W	Th	F	S
	F	F/M	M	M/F	F	F/M	M
	M	M/F	F	F/M	M	M/F	F
	F	F/M	M	M/F	F	F/M	M

Chapter 11 is dedicated to Access, Schedules and Parenting Time.

◆ LOCATION OF NEUTRAL EXCHANGE

❑ Clearly define how, when and where your children will be exchanged.
  ❑ Exchange Location
  ❑ Exchange Day
  ❑ Exchange Time
  ❑ Emergency Exchange Information

❑ Emergency Exchange Information

    ❑   (In the event of an emergency: If the location and time need to be changed, where and how will that be accomplished?)

Chapter 14 is dedicated to Neutral Exchange.

Agreeing on the *essential elements* allows the child their right to continuity of health care, education, extracurricular activities and access to each parent. By agreeing to each of the above, both parents will know where the medical care, school or instruction is to be provided. Again, these are the core elements that need to be solidified before entering into a parallel parenting agreement.

It is very important to realize that the financial responsibility for your child's *essential elements* does not need to be decided at this time. Albeit, many divorcing parents will use the essential elements, and the associated financial responsibility, to promote conflict or 'make deals' during the settlement process. The *essential elements* and the associated finances are fertile issues that often become negotiating chips for the final divorce settlement.

Make every effort to keep the child's essential elements focused on the best interest of the child, and not related to the other aspects of the separation process! Often, it is not clear which parent will be financially responsible for different portions of a child's upbringing. If the parents cannot negotiate the *essential elements* without conflict about financial responsibility, then the initial agreement about the essential elements needs to be made, bypassing the delineation of financial responsibility.

This 'theoretical bypass' needs to be accomplished to promote a temporary settlement regarding the *essential elements*. The temporary settlement is made with a clear understanding that the financial issue will be resolved at a later date. For example:

❑ *Problem:* One parent states they "refuse to contribute or pay for orthodontic care." Essentially, this parent is saying they do not care about the child's teeth. It may be a spiteful position that can lead to significant debate and conflict.

❑ *Solution:* The financial issue needs to be sidestepped. The parents simply need to agree that *IF* the child should ever need orthodontic care, and *WHEN* the financial responsibility is determined or resolved, then *THIS WILL BE* the orthodontic provider of choice.

The same rule applies to education and extracurricular activities. If parents are at an impasse, establish the essential elements first, and then revisit the financial piece later. For example:

❑ *Problem*: One parent wants private schooling but is not willing to help financially.

❑ *Solution*: Until there is a financial settlement, the parents will designate one private school and one public school for the child's educational list. *WHEN* the financial formula for education is resolved, the choice of schools has been narrowed down to two. The child goes to either the private school or the public school.

✶　✶　✶　✶　✶

Sadly, many parents cannot even agree on the choice of health care providers. The divorce is too painful, and conflict may surface regarding every joint decision that needs to be made about the child. This is a common scenario and places parents at an immediate stalemate. If the parents cannot agree on the health care providers, then one parent should choose the dentist and the other parent should choose the pediatrician.

This type of negotiated sharing of parental responsibility can be very successful. Dividing decisions and responsibilities regarding the children (as equally as possible) often helps to diffuse the power struggle, when one parent wants or needs complete parental control of the child. This strategy can also help the parents remain *focused on the needs of the child and the essential elements*.

Once there is an agreement on the *essential elements* (with or without financial responsibility delineated) life in the two homes can begin with less opportunity for conflict, and a more successful transition toward parallel parenting.

Good Luck!

EXAMPLES *of the* 'ESSENTIAL ELEMENTS' AGREEMENT

❑ **Regarding Jurisdiction:** The child will remain in _____ (name of County and State) with _____ (name of the County, State, and Court having jurisdiction of the child. This portion of the agreement is not modifiable. Assure that the correct *LEGALEZE* is added to this portion of the agreement. Assure that your attorney knows what to do!

❑ **Regarding Health Care:** _____(child's name) will see the following providers:

    ❑ **Medical Care:** Pediatrician for medical care:

        _____(Pediatrician's name)
        _____ (address)
        _____ (telephone number)

    ❑_____ (child's name) will see this pediatrician until they reach the age of 14. Then the child will be taken to _____, a family practitioner, for their routine medical care.

    ❑ **Dental Care:** Dentist for routine dental care:

        _____ (Dentist's name)
        _____ (address)
        _____ (telephone number)

    ❑ **Orthodontic Care:** If the child should need orthodontic care, and the issue of financial responsibility is resolved, the child will see:

        _____ (Orthodontist's name)
        _____ (address)
        _____ (telephone number)

    ❑ **Mental Health:** If the child should need mental health treatment, and the issue of financial responsibility is resolved, the child will see:

        _____(Provider name & License)
        _____ (address)
        _____ (telephone number)

❑ **Special Care:** If the child should need special health care and/or treatments, and the issue of financial responsibility is resolved, the child will see:

_____ (Provider name & License)

_____ (address)

_____ (telephone number)

❑ **Regarding Education:**

❑ The child will attend

_____ Pre-school,

(name, address, telephone number)

_____Primary school,

(name, address, telephone)

_____High School.

(name, address, telephone)

❑ Financial responsibility for our child's education _____ has _____ has not been determined at this time.

❑ _____% Mother ❑ _____ % Father

❑ **Regarding Extracurricular Activities:**

❑ The father wants the child to participate in _____.
(The mother will assure that the child attends practice 2 times per week and scheduled games or events during her parenting time.)

❑ The mother wants the child to participate in _____.
(The father will assure that the child attends practice 2 times per week and scheduled games or events during his parenting time.)

❑ Any other extracurricular activity will be considered independent for each household unless decided on and agreed to by both parents.

❑ Choosing an extracurricular activity for the child *does not* define the financial responsibility. It merely helps the parents identify the interests they believe are important for the child. Financial responsibility for extracurricular activities should be considered carefully, as many activities can be very expensive.

❑ Financial responsibility for extracurricular activities has ____ has not____ been determined at this time.

    ❑   _____% Mother ❑   _____ % Father

❑ **Regarding Parenting Time**

    ❑ Until our custody and visitation schedule is established, we will have the following schedule (Be as specific as possible):

    ❑ We recognize and agree this may be a temporary and interim schedule. For example:

        ❑ Mother's interim custodial days and times (every other week)
           ❑ Monday after school until Wednesday morning, taking child to school.
           ❑ Friday after school until Monday morning, taking the child to school.

        ❑ Father's interim custodial days and times (every other week)
           ❑ Wednesday after school, taking the child to school on Friday morning.
           ❑ Monday after school, taking the child to school on Wednesday morning.

❑ **Regarding the Exchange of the Children to the Other Parent**

    ❑ We agree to the following exchange location and procedure. It is recognized this may be an interim exchange location until our custody order is finalized.

        ❑ Exchange Location
        ❑ Exchange Day
        ❑ Exchange Time
        ❑ Emergency Exchange Information
           ❑ (In the event of an emergency, and the location and time of the exchange needs to be changed, how will that be accomplished?)

✶ ✶ ✶ ✶ ✶

As previously emphasized, the earlier the decisions and agreements are made about the *essential elements*, the better it is for the child. With an agreement to the essential elements in place, the child's life will now have *some stability* established before the turmoil of the remainder of the divorce begins.

Once the parents are able to agree on the major decisions about the child (the essential elements), they are free to function more independently of each other, and focus their love and attention on the child during their parenting time. In addition, the agreement to the essential elements provides the child with a reasonably consistent routine in each household, offering considerable continuity for the child.

With these decisions made, the child is buffered from the conflict of the other aspects of the divorce, as the parents will only need to interact *minimally* about the child at this emotionally sensitive time. The supreme advantage to the child is that their basic needs for health, education and welfare are met <u>at the beginning</u> of the divorce process, not at the end! The message from the child:

"Gee, I know my parents are getting a divorce and they do not get along very well.
We don't all live together anymore, but my life is still pretty much the same.
I feel secure, and both of my parents are sharing me and taking part in my life."

"Both of my parents are participating in my special activities,
and they both take me to the same doctor!"

Sounds a little too easy? Probably.
The trick is to agree on the essential elements.
Once that is accomplished, you can disagree again!

9.

Mediation

Mediation has proven to be a satisfactory and less expensive way to resolve disputes. Unfortunately, one of the most difficult things about mediation is that most mediators require both parents to attend the mediation session simultaneously. This can be very difficult in the highly conflicted or even moderately conflicted situation.

I am not sure why mediators insist on seeing both parents simultaneously, especially when there are usually *so many* sensitive issues that cannot be discussed without increasing the level of conflict between the parents. It is my opinion that if a mediator really wants to understand and resolve sensitive issues, they would benefit by meeting with each parent individually. Separate meetings allow the mediator to identify which issues are technically related to the divorce (material, financial or emotional) and which issues are child-related that need to be addressed to improve the family dynamics *for the children*.

Throughout this book, there are ideas and suggestions that require proactive action by the parent searching for autonomy and a future free from unnecessary interference from the other parent. Finding a mediator that will facilitate your needs will require a proactive search. Too often, parents of divorce are '*guided*' by the legal community to mediators that may not support a parent's needs and goals. Diligent research for the best mediator that will accommodate the *parents needs*, will lead to a more meaningful dispute resolution.

In the pursuit of *parallel parenting*, one should carefully research the mediator's philosophy regarding separate meetings. The mediator should not hesitate, and will ideally recommend (without prompting) meeting with each parent individually, especially for the first meeting. If the mediator will not accommodate a parent's request for separate meetings then they *should not* be the mediator of choice. Keep searching until you find a mediator that will provide separate meetings, more commonly known as *shuttle diplomacy* or *shuttle mediation*.

Shuttle mediation provides for confidential information to be shared with a mediator while minimizing the opportunity for conflict. It also eliminates the opportunity for nonproductive communication and enables the parents *and the mediator* to focus on the significant issues.

In her article, *Maybe You Should Mediate*, Althea Lee Jordan states:

> "Some mediators will meet with the parties separately and conduct 'shuttle' negotiations. Others insist that the parties meet together in the same room. The beauty of the mediation process is that the mediator and the parties can customize the mediation environment for their own circumstances and comfort, creating a process and structure sensitive to the needs of the parties and the unique context of the marriage." [1]

Be persistent in your goals for clarity! Do not allow the overwhelming legal process, or individuals who seem to be in control of your destiny, distract you from securing a situation toward less emotional confusion and turmoil. *Mediation should be tailored to your comfort level and understanding!* Do not let others pressure you into an uncomfortable mediation situation. Mediation can be very successful, and eliminating the potential for increased conflict should be paramount!

> *"But I don't want shuttle mediation. I want to hear it directly from you!*
> *I want to know exactly what you are thinking. We need to have direct contact,*
> *for the sake of the children."*

✷ ✷ ✷ ✷ ✷

Mediation, Manipulation and One-Sided Conflict

There are many parents who may use the mediation process as another venue to interact with an ex-partner. As we have discussed throughout this book there are endless opportunities to *'create child-related issues'* necessary in the co-parenting process. Some parents may attempt to schedule mediation unnecessarily. If the other parent does not agree to meet (based on the lack of a perceived need) then the argument could be made that they are uncooperative and unwilling to co-parent.

Take for example, the mother in New York who engaged in the over utilization of the mediation process by scheduling mediation on a very frequent basis. This mother would insist on mediation when she needed an *"ex-spouse fix."* She would often fabricate issues to be discussed about her child, and insisted on joint attendance at the meetings with the father.

The father, however, did not believe there was a need for such frequent mediation. He also believed, when there was a need to mediate, he had very specific and sensitive concerns that he felt should be discussed privately with the mediator. The private mediator supported the separate meetings, but the mother refused to meet separately.

In desperation for a joint meeting the mother filed a motion with the court. This legal motion prompted a mandatory court ordered mediation session. When the father requested separate meetings with the county mediator, the mother refused and convinced the county mediator that it was *imperative* that the parents meet together. She claimed it was *"for the sake of the children."*

To illustrate to the court how "difficult the father was," the mother cited his request for separate meetings as a significant flaw in his ability to co-parent. The mother then proceeded to co-opt the mediator, crying on the telephone and writing letters of appeal. The mother postured herself brilliantly as the victim, stating that she "hoped the mediator (a woman) would understand how difficult it was to co-parent with someone who would not even sit in the same room with her."

Unfortunately, the county mediator *was* co-opted and became sympathetic to the mother's position as *the victim.* As a result, the mediator made a recommendation to the court undermining the father's current custodial arrangement.

Initially (and in her discussion with the judge) the mediator stated she felt the father was being "unrealistic, requesting separate meetings and that he did not appear to be a cooperative co-parent." She later admitted she "did not have the time to meet with the parents separately," even though separate meetings were offered as an option with the county mediation service. "I made the best recommendation I could considering the time constraint and the father's unrealistic demands."

Of special interest is the fact that the children had been doing extremely well with the existing custody arrangement. This was a significant oversight by the county mediator. Once co-opted and sympathetic to the mother's position, the county mediator did not consider or investigate how any change in the parenting model would affect the children. This is an example of how the courts may make a decision based on misinformation. The mediation in this case was conducted in a county that supports non-confidentiality between the mediator and the judge. In other words, as we will discuss in the next section, the confidentiality of the mediation session is not protected, and the mediator is able to divulge confidential information to the judge to be used for settlement or rulings of the case.

The good news is there is hope on the horizon. When looking for a mediator that will provide individual meetings or *shuttle mediation*, keep in mind the following information, recently published by the Children's Rights Council:

> "A Special Masters program to help highly conflicted parents to cooper-
> ate in the raising of their child has been established in several states. One such
> program, in New York State, is a specialized mediation service for parents who
> have a high level of conflict, are chronic litigators and whose children pay the
> price for this conflict...."
> "Because of the high conflict, the parents are usually seen separately, not
> together." "Connecticut and California are among other states offering similar
> programs." [2]

Again, parallel parenting is supported without a label!

✶ ✶ ✶ ✶ ✶

Private versus Court Appointed Mediators

It is important to realize there are different types of mediators available for families of divorce. Mental health professionals often conduct mediation and so do attorneys. There are also excellent trained mediators that are not mental health professionals or attorneys. Mental health professionals usually provide a more emotional and psychological approach to mediation. Attorneys have a more technical and legal approach. There are different styles of mediators and different approaches to the mediation process, all of which can be very effective. The most important variable in mediation is your ability to work with a mediator to achieve your desired goals.

County mediators are either employed by the county or are on retainer to the county for their services. Some states and counties require that couples use the county mediation services before their case can be heard in court. Unfortunately, as with many bureaucratic entities, the county mediators have a very heavy workload and are often not able to dedicate the time needed to mediate complicated and high conflict divorce cases.

A word of caution about the county mediation system: sometimes mediators employed by a specific county are asked to give an opinion to the court. This can work to your advantage or against you. As illustrated in the case above, the county mediator was co-opted by the mother and then made her '*professional recommendation*' to the judge.

Judges are very busy and usually do not have the time to research each individual case. Therefore, they often rely on the opinions and recommendations of a trusted insider, such as a county mediator. The courthouse can be a very political arena, and if a mediator works efficiently with a judge, for example, reducing case load and facilitating settlements out of court, they can hold tremendous weight in how a judge views a particular case.

This does not mean that county mediation services are inferior, ineffective or inadequate. To the contrary, there are many excellent mediators working within the court system. However, higher case loads *can* dilute the effectiveness of a mediator when dealing with high conflict cases. The lack of resources and the available time to work with these cases may also hinder facilitating the *best results* for divorcing families. It is important to understand that many county mediation services are allocated time per case, and high conflict cases usually take more time to mediate than can be allowed.

Private mediators provide mediation services independent of the state or county mandated programs. While they are more expensive, they are able to schedule whatever time is needed to help resolve conflict. Private mediators are also more likely to provide shuttle mediation, as they do not have the same pressure of case load management.

Another advantage to private mediation is that you can personally select the mediator. You can interview them, discuss their philosophies of mediation and investigate for potential bias and personal outlooks. You can also determine their previous experience with cases involving high conflict, parental alienation, borderline and other personality disorders. The interview should also include verifying the mediators experience and attitude toward a parallel parenting model.

During the interview with the private mediator, you can assess if you can have an open and honest dialog with them. You are not given this luxury or flexibility in the county or state system, as the mediator is usually *assigned* to the case.

Make a careful and informed decision about the choice of the mediator. You should be able to trust the mediator on a professional level and work with them in a stressful situation. It is important to acknowledge that a high conflict separation or divorce situation can tax any mediation process.

And remember, the mediator cannot and *should not* take sides. Rather, they should help your resolve disputes and assist your efforts to facilitate the best parenting model you can create!

It is also important to realize that you will pay considerably more for private mediation services, but in the course of your lifetime, the effort to secure a good post-marital and parenting agreement will be well worth the expense.

Research your options regarding mediation
and take your time choosing a competent and educated mediator,
one that will respect your opinions and ideas.

✴   ✴   ✴   ✴   ✴

One Issue at a Time

If you are dealing with an ex-partner who *needs* ongoing contact to '*co-parent*,' (yet any contact results in conflict) you will benefit by addressing only one issue at a time in mediation. There are hundreds if not thousands of examples of parents entering mediation with 'laundry lists' of complaints and issues. Be careful not to be overcome by '*the list.*' A good mediator will help you stay focused on the issues that are important to you, are *truly <u>child related</u> and in your child's best interest.*

Basic Mediation Guidelines

- ❑ Assure that the mediator understands and supports the concepts of 'parallel parenting.'
- ❑ Assure that the mediator will conduct separate mediation sessions with each parent.
- ❑ Discuss with the mediator that you want to focus on one issue at a time.
- ❑ State clearly that you want to resolve each issue before moving to the next.
    - ❑ Resolving each issue before proceeding to the next may actually require signing a contract for each separate issue.

❑ This process is more time consuming and costly, but the result of your efforts will reduce the potential for a breakdown of the mediation process.

❑ Many conflicted parents will not continue the mediation process stating, "Everything is off, my way or else." While time consuming, signing a mediation contract on each individual issue eliminates some of the opportunities for manipulation of the mediation process.

❑ Prioritize the issues, beginning with the most important issues relating to your children and the *essential elements*, their health, education and general wellbeing.

❑ Assure that each issue is singular. Do not 'bundle' issues.

❑ Make sure that the mediator remains "objective (distanced from the conflict) and neutral (not aligned with either party)." [3]

❑ The final parenting agreement should include a clause that states if the parents cannot agree to the elements of the parenting plan (schedules, access, extracurricular activities, etc.), they will first try to resolve their differences with the help of a mediator before going to court.

❑ The final parenting agreement should also include that the mediator of choice, to help resolve ongoing disputes, *will provide shuttle mediation.*

❑ The agreement may include the name of the mediator, but this makes it more difficult to change mediators later in the divorce process, if needed. Proceed with caution on the *absolute designation* of a mediator. The term 'mediator of choice' is less restricting and allows legal latitude and flexibility should things go *awry* with the mediator originally chosen.

❑ Assure that the final agreement is 'fine-tuned' and that your attorney reviews it for legality.

❑ Assure that your attorney reviews any and all agreements for legality and all other issues that will represent your best interests.

★ ★ ★ ★ ★

(Endnotes)

[1] Jordan, Althea Lee. (1999). Maybe You Should Mediate. *Family Advocate: Surviving Your Divorce.* Chicago, Illinois: American Bar Association, , Volume 22, Number 1. pp. 19-20.

[2] Children's Rights Council, Speak Out for the Children, Volume 15-No. 3/4, page 13, Fall 2000/ Winter 2001.

[3] Jordon, Althea Lee. (1999). Maybe You Should Mediate. *Family Advocate: Surviving Your Divorce.* Chicago, Illinois: American Bar Association, , Volume 22, Number 1. pp. 19-20.

10.

In the Same Place at the Same Time

The Ground Rules of Parenting Behavior During Close Contact

There will surely be situations where you and your ex-partner will be in the same place at the same time. This is especially true in the beginning stages of the separation process, before appropriate boundaries have been defined. Newly separated parents are often unsure of how to act when in close proximity. This confusion creates many *opportunities* for parents to be in the same place at the same time and in the danger zone of unhealthy interaction.

When parents are in the process of dissolving the marriage, and have not established suitable boundaries, these *encounters* can be very difficult. It can be very awkward to feel relaxed and comfortable around the children (and society in general) when the ex-partner is present. This is especially true when parents are in the midst of negotiating spousal support, child support, dividing business and other assets acquired during the marriage, protecting separate assets (remember, those you brought to the marriage), selling the family home and engaging in the legal turmoil of child custody.

All these variables contribute to the tension, resentment and anger so often present during the divorce process. It is easy to understand how difficult it is to manage the emotional tribulations associated with divorce. Making matters worse, there are often lies, deceit and malice that cause divorces to become even more bitter and chaotic. So, if you are feeling uncomfortable being around the ex-partner, you are not alone. During this sensitive time, the best system is to avoid direct contact to the best of your ability without missing opportunities to be with your children, their friends and families.

Unfortunately, for some ex-partners, avoiding direct contact may not be that easy. If an ex-partner possesses *even one* of the motivational factors described in the previous chapters, then being in the *same place at the same time* will be more challenging.

Be keenly aware of the ex-partner who is determined to be in the same place at the same time, looking for interaction and the all-important *face-to-face contact*. The beginning stages of separation and divorce provide these affected individuals with the perfect opportunity to be '*innocently omnipresent*' in your life. Remember, they may *need to see you*, not necessarily your children!

★　★　★　★　★

As uncomfortable as these situations can be, there are *ground rules and guidelines* one can follow to make things less stressful. Following these rules can help minimize your vulnerability during a stressful encounter.

➢ Do not be *surprised* or *react negatively* when your ex-partner appears on the scene.

➢ Be cordial, but keep moving. If the children with you, move them along with you gracefully.

➢ If an emotional outburst is possible (by either parent), try to keep a reasonable physical distance between you and your ex-partner. (Public places are not where one wants to demonstrate untoward or angry behavior.)

➢ If the other parent becomes aggressive or insists on interaction that is not productive, then take any immediate *graceful* action to *remove* yourself and your children from the stressful environment.

In addition, it may be helpful to outline parenting behavior in a written agreement. This may help newly divorcing parents establish guidelines in the beginning that will help them behave appropriately in close contact. In addition, there may be some parents who have been separated for some time who may need some guidance when in close proximity. Some ideas may include:

➤ The parents agree to be very careful not make negative comments, innuendoes, facial expressions or disapproving sounds regarding the other parent in front of the children.

➤ The parents agree they should only make positive references about the other parent during their custodial or visitation period.

➤ The parents agree there should be no conflict between the parents in the presence of the children.

➤ The parents agree that if there is a likelihood of an argument or conflict, the parent who does not have custody of the child at that time will leave the premises immediately and make arrangements to discuss the issue with the other parent when the children are not present.

While it may be difficult to monitor this type of agreement, the intent is to establish *ground rules* to protect the children and parents from the unpleasant 'side effects' of parental misconduct. If you cannot say something nice about your ex-partner, do not say anything at all. You do not have to talk about your ex-spouse, so don't!

Save your concerns for a protected environment, with trusted friends and professionals, rather than berate and admonish your ex-partner to your children or to the general public. Being in close proximity to your ex-partner may be very uncomfortable. Maintaining distance and creating appropriate boundaries will help eliminate the opportunity for conflict or unfavorable behavior by either parent.

PART FOUR

CREATING SUCCESSFUL BOUNDARIES

HOW TO PROMOTE AND PROTECT
A SPECIAL PARENT ~ CHILD RELATIONSHIP
WITHOUT UNNECESSARY INTERFERENCE
FROM THE OTHER PARENT

11.

Access, Schedules and Parenting Time

> "It is crucial that we understand not only that parent-child access after
> divorce should be tolerated, but that it should be actively encouraged. Child
> access has too long been treated as an issue of much lesser import to children than
> custodial status or financial care and responsibility after divorce." [1]
>
> *David L. Levy*

After agreeing to your child's *'essential elements,'* the next important step is to establish a comprehensive and structured visitation schedule. This is an important task, and includes establishing *ground rules* for the *visitation schedule*. A structured and comprehensive visitation schedule will help parents succeed in having an autonomous relationship with their child, free from unnecessary interference or obstruction by the other parent.

Most parents rely on their attorney to recommend the best timeshare or custodial arrangement for their children. As much as you may like and respect your attorney, they often do not think about the long-term ramifications of the timeshare agreement. Every family is different, and the pre-packaged visitation schedules often presented to parents may not work for you or be in your child's best interest. There are variations on each visitation theme and one should carefully consider all the issues before signing on the dotted line.

A good attorney will give you several *visitation packages* to consider. When choosing a visitation schedule, carefully assess your personal capabilities and availability for parenting time. Most importantly, assure there is a *modification clause* written into your agreement. Even if the first choice of visitation schedules seems adequate, there are always situations that can arise requiring either a minor or major change to the custody schedule. Without a modification clause, you may have difficulty changing your custody arrangement, even though it may clearly be in the best interest of the child.

The divorce process can be very stressful and confusing! The visitation schedule may seem miniscule compared to dividing assets, divulging finances, moving out of the house, selling the car, liquidating stocks and bank accounts, fighting for custody of your children and negotiating child and spousal support.

With these numerous distasteful issues swirling around in your head, it is important to remain focused on having access to your child, and creating a well-defined calendar!

Without a modification clause, you may have to reenter the courtroom to make even a minor change to your custody arrangement. Reentering the courtroom can be very unpleasant. You may only want to switch one day of visitation, yet find countless issues added to your simple request. Assure there is a modification clause in your agreement protecting your rights to change the visitation schedule with your children, if needed.

In his excellent book, *The Father's Emergency Guide to the Divorce-Custody Battle,* Robert Seidenberg states,

> "Some lawyers are indifferent and will leave a father with an agreement that simply states that the father will have 'liberal' or 'reasonable' visitation. Such an agreement is worthless. If you do not have your visitation schedule spelled out, it cannot be enforced. The more conflictual your case, the more specific you should be in defining visitation. When you have days and times spelled out, it makes a specific commitment. In addition, you should be specific as to where the children will be picked up and dropped off...." [2]

In another excellent book, *The Best Parent is Both Parents,* David Levy states,

> "Even where both parents are universally agreed to be fit and psychologically and socially normal, where their child is agreed to have a loving and emotionally significant bond with both parents, and where both parents provide the child with decent homes and decent family life, it is not uncommon for such parents to experience untold anguish and spend up to $ 10,000 or more in legal fees, simply in order to maintain the right to spend a few weeks a year with their children." [3]

Take for example, the father in Ohio who decided he would like to become more involved with the day-to-day care of his young child. His original custody order already gave him frequent visitation, every Wednesday evening from 6:00 PM until 8:00 AM the next morning. He also had visitation with the child every other weekend from Friday at 6:00 PM until Sunday evening at 6:00 PM. The child was 3-years-old when the original agreement was written. Unfortunately, there was not a modification clause to accommodate for a change of circumstance, or consideration for the developmental growth and needs of the child. The child was now 7-years-old.

Per the written agreement, all exchanges of the child were at the mother's home. The father was obligated to take the child to the mother's house before school. The mother would receive the child in the morning, feed her, dress her and take her to school. The mother also picked the child up from school and had her in her custody for several hours before the father came to pick her up from the mother's home after work.

This time-share arrangement was proposed by the attorney and accepted by the father during the confusing and traumatic pre-settlement divorce process. In hindsight, this custody arrangement created a very disjointed and chaotic situation for the child, especially as she grew older.

Realizing there must be a better way to care for his child the father made a reasonable request to change the existing agreement based on the child's changing developmental needs. He asked the mother if she would be amenable to him taking the child directly to school on the mornings following his overnight visits, and to pick her up from school on the days of his custodial evenings.

The father truly believed these changes were logical and in the child's best interest. He explained to the mother how these changes would provide more continuity for the child, and would also provide a *neutral exchange location.* For the father and the child, neutral exchange would mean no direct contact between the parents at the time of the exchanges.

Unfortunately, these simple and seemingly reasonable requests assumed a life of their own. The father did not realize the hostility and anger consuming his ex-wife. He soon discovered the mother was *relying* on the exchanges of the child to gather information about the father and his plans with the child on each particular day. This information provided the mother with the opportunity to interfere with the father's visits, often resulting in sabotaging his time with their daughter. The mother was also using the exchanges to argue with the father in front of the child, creating conflict over very minor issues.

In this example, the mother was struggling to maintain control of the child and the child's time with the father. The father, on the other hand, was trying to revise the visitation schedule in the best interest of the child.

Life for this father would have been much easier had there been a modification clause in the agreement. Instead, he spent one year and thousands of dollars simply trying to establish *more reasonable and logical access* to his child. The sum of the proposal included a few more hours a week with the child and hassle-free exchanges. These minor changes would have resulted in a more stable environment for the child, providing continuity and a smooth integration into *each* family's normal daily routine and activities.

As David Levy states, "These expensive and conflict ridden scenarios that exist just to modify or adjust existing access orders generally escalate already hostile feelings and will most certainly put your children in the middle of the post divorce conflict." [4]

In another example, when negotiating their annual calendar, a mother in Florida wrote a letter to the father stating she had "deliberately left the summer calendar open so you can choose which three weeks were best for you to spend time with the children."

The father was thrilled with the presumed cooperation and told the children (before the negotiations were finalized) the wonderful summer vacation he was planning. The unassuming father was in for quite a surprise. When the mother received his request for the three-week block of time in August, she became enraged and immediately began to obstruct the vacation.

This seemingly simple request for time during the summer created a new platform for conflict. The mother became indignant, demanding to know why the father wanted "those specific weeks during the month of August," even though she had offered the father "first choice" for the summer months. Apparently, the mother lost sight of her initial generosity and insisted that the father "provide the precise reason he wanted any certain week during the summer, and for that matter, any other special time during the school year."

Needless to say, the father's summer plans were ruined, the negotiation of the calendar deteriorated (dragging on for several months) and the mother insisted on maintaining control of the calendar. She did not have plans for the month of August, yet she had no intention of the father making "good, fun plans" with *her* children.

This is an example of the gaming and control that surrounds even protected and predetermined calendars. These parents had a regular, predetermined calendar during the school year that alternated visitation every other week, major school vacations and holidays. The only opportunity for calendar negotiations was for parenting time during the summer months. The legal agreement stated that the "parenting time during the summer months was to be shared equally between the parents." There were no specific guidelines included for negotiation of the summer calendar.

In this case, one parent had progressed emotionally and the other parent used every opportunity to create conflict and pry further into the privacy and life of the other. This case clearly illustrates the more precise the calendar is designed, the fewer opportunities there will be for conflict. This family could not make even minor changes to the calendar without experiencing an abuse of control and manipulation regarding the time spent with the children.

When custodial and parenting time are not defined clearly, children are often caught in the middle of the parents negotiations. In the example above, the mother had inappropriately questioned the children for information about their upcoming summer vacation with the father. Excitedly and naively, the children told their mother about the vacation plans. One can only imagine what the children were subjected to after eagerly sharing their excitement. And just imagine how the father felt trying to explain to his children why the "great vacation" had to be cancelled.

"When significant conflict prevents parents from working cooperatively, having a clear, predetermined schedule will enable parents and children to know ahead of time when visitation and access will occur and thus may even reduce future conflict over access issues." [5]

Visitation schedules should be created very carefully, with a mechanism in place to modify the agreement when the child's age changes or when there is a significant change of circumstance.

In his insightful book, *The Best Parent is Both Parents,* David Levy lists some very common obstacles that parents must overcome to see their children. Some of the obstacles Levy identifies include:

❑ "The absence of specific, enforceable orders providing for parent-child access after divorce." [6]

❑ "The absence of a means of modifying such orders, even where they exist, to fit new circumstances, without resorting to expensive and adversarial court proceedings." [6]

❑ "The failure of many orders to concretely address the child's needs, desires, and other circumstances in formulating the parent-child access orders." [6]

❑ "The failure of many court orders to recognize or deal with the incidence of one parent deliberately preventing or discouraging access between the child and the other parent, even where it has been ordered." [6]

❑ "The presence of factors which discourage the most beneficial forms of access between parents and children, including the designation of custodial status, the reluctance of the courts to enforce access orders, and the lack of sufficient procedures and mechanisms other than through the court process to enforce or modify access arrangements." [6]

❑ "... the legal system often fails to articulate the specific rights to times when the parent has access to the child or children. Most orders provide for 'reasonable' (or 'liberal') visitation, with the determination of what is reasonable left to the custodial parent, who may be hostile to the non-custodian. Other orders state that rights of parent-child access are to include specific times, but in practice these rights are defined minimally, as those which have been specified." [6]

❑ "... one parent is usually (in approximately 90 percent of court orders) redefined negatively by the law: they become the 'non' -custodial or 'absent' parent, the 'other' parent, the 'contesting' parent. The usual term for access – visitation– underscores the demotion of one parent to the status of a guest in their child's life (and vice versa)." [6]

❑ "... the times usually awarded often do not permit the child and his parent to feel they are integrated into each other's normal, daily lives and activities. They tend to award some part of weekend and holiday periods to one parent and the vast majority of daily routine periods to the other. One parent may be cut out from participation in such things as school activities, helping the child with homework, or other activities which normally take place during the week (Scout meetings, athletic practices, doctor's appointments)." [6]

❑ "... the process of repeatedly confronting one's loss of this contact and relationship with one's children is extremely painful and can cause feelings of sorrow or loss of self-respect as parents; these feelings overwhelm many non-custodial parents, particularly in the context of other personal strains of a divorce." [6]

❑ "... if the custodial parent denies access to the other parent, even where an order for visitation exists, there are, in practice, virtually no usable enforcement mechanisms or remedies available to the non-custodial parent. This is particularly true where access is described only as 'reasonable' in the court order, and wherever that parent's available funds for litigation are limited." [6]

❑ "... as with child-support orders, original access orders are very rarely written in such a way that they provide for any future changes in the divorced family or in the child's age; and the schedule or amount of access ordered for an infant may not be appropriate to the needs of a 10-year-old or 14-year-old child. One, or both parents, may move out of the area. Yet modification through the courts can be prohibitively expensive for many parents, and, if one parent is resistant, the process can be prolonged over several years, producing stress for the child as well as the parents." [6]

✦   ✦   ✦   ✦   ✦

Parenting Plan Considerations and Checklists for the Visitation Schedule
Suggestions for Spending More Meaningful Time with Your Children

Modification Clauses in the Agreement

❑ Establish from the onset that your access, visitation, and/or custody agreement can be modified if there is a change of circumstance.

    ❑ The modification clause should state clearly that the changing ages and developmental needs of the child (ren) qualify for a modification to the agreement.

❑ Most experts agree that the parenting plan must meet the child's changing developmental needs.

❑ *Do not* sign an agreement that does not allow for a modification to the custody arrangement or a modification to have access to the child.

❑ If you have already signed an agreement that does not address a modification for access and visitation, then discuss with your attorney or mediator the best plan of action to prepare for the future should you need to modify your situation.

Decide How Much Time You Want to Spend with Your Children

- ❑ Set aside all other issues regarding your divorce and concentrate specifically on how much time you want to spend with your children.

- ❑ Be realistic and stay focused on this task.

- ❑ Write down your preferences including your rationale.

- ❑ Carefully assess your schedule and what will work for you.

- ❑ *Do not* accept the first calendar presented to you as acceptable without carefully considering other alternatives.

- ❑ Try for larger blocks of time rather than agreeing to fragmented visits.

- ❑ *Do not* accept a custody arrangement just to finalize your divorce. *It is the wrong motivation* and often a tactic used by attorneys to distract you from other important issues. Take your time and stay focused on this issue.

- ❑ Remember during negotiations that what is appropriate for a 2-year-old child in terms of visitation and access is very different than that of a 5, 7 or 12 year old.

- ❑ Make every effort not to become a victim of the outdated custodial theories of '*maternal expertise or the tender years.*' These older concepts of custody and visitation are outdated and insinuate the father may not be able to provide for the infant and toddler as well as the mother.

- ❑ Use the term 'parenting time' (whenever possible) to describe your custody and visitation time with the child.

Creating Your Calendar

- ❑ Purchase a large annual calendar and mark all the important dates you want to spend with your children. Remember that you will most likely be alternating all major holidays and vacations.

- ❑ Get a copy of each child's school calendar. This should include school opening and closing dates, vacations and holidays.

- ❑ Consider the extracurricular activities that your children are engaged in and determine how much you want to be involved in those activities.

❏ Do you want to help coach, manage, teach, etc.? If so, make sure you will have access to your child on those particular days or weeks.

❏ Do not attempt to *hoard* all the special activities and events. *Parallel parenting and two homes means sharing the child's time and events as equally as possible.*

❏ Revisit the proposed calendar over a period of several weeks to make sure you are accomplishing your parenting goals and your rights to spend quality time with your child.

Negotiation Guidelines for Creating an Annual Calendar

❏ Establish in your written agreement that you will be negotiating an *annual custody* calendar for your children. The calendar should run from January 1 through December 31 of each year.

❏ Establish a time line for negotiations for the upcoming year. For example:

  ❏ All calendar requests for the next year need to be submitted to each party in writing by October 1st of the current year.

  ❏ The calendar will be negotiated between October 1st and October 31st for the upcoming year. (This prevents parents from stalling or obstructing the negotiation process. There is a start and an end date to the calendar negotiations.) Rules for negotiation should be clearly defined, if necessary.

❏ All requests and negotiations should be submitted to the other parent in writing.

❏ Consider using a parenting coordinator or mediator to help with the calendar negotiations. It is not uncommon for families to argue about calendar and visitation issues.

❏ If the parties cannot agree, then the calendar issue *must be submitted to mediation within 10 days of the October 31st deadline.*

When the Calendar is Finalized

❏ Once the calendar has been legally decided, create a calendar for your children. Clearly mark the days they will be with you and have the calendar visible for all to see.

❏ Mark 'special occasions' clearly.

❏ Encourage your children to participate in making the calendar. Their input will create a special interest, and they will have a better understanding of how the calendar works, including how the calendar relates to their time spent with you.

   ❏ 2 Exclusive, a company based in Utah has an excellent children's calendar with stickers and a creative flair for children of divorce.

   ❏ This is an excellent calendar tool and is designed to encourage an interactive approach to the child's custodial calendar and parenting time. The calendar can be ordered directly from:

      2 Exclusive   www.whereamitoday.net
      P.O. Box 573690   (801) 966-1018
      Murray, Utah 84157-3690

Exchanges of the Children Should Be Clearly Defined

When negotiating your calendar it is imperative that the agreement addresses where and how the children will be exchanged between the two homes. *Neutral exchange* is discussed in detail in Chapter 14.

❏ Decide where you are going to exchange the children on non-school days.

❏ Do not exchange your children at the other parent's home. Choose a neutral location where the children can be supervised or occupied in a certain activity.

❏ Take your children to school on your scheduled days or have someone associated with *your* family take them to school. (Parents, aunts, uncles, friends of the children, etc.)

❏ Pick up your children from school or have someone associated with *your* family pick them up from school. (Parents, aunts, uncles, friends of the children, etc.)

❏ If possible, avoid exchanging the children on Sunday evening, during your custodial/parenting weekend time. Ideally, the weekend should begin on Friday after school and flow through until Monday morning when the child returns to school.

❏ Always opt for a smooth weekend and deliver the children to school from your home, in good spirits with their homework complete, on Monday morning.

❏ If possible, make Sunday night your traditional night to do something *special* with your children. A barbecue with friends, grandparents, go out to dinner, or something equally special. Your children will look forward to these *Special Sundays* and they will remember them for years to come. (If Sunday is not an option, then designate another day for a *special traditional evening.*

❏ If possible, try to maintain this special family day as a tradition. Maintaining a special traditional evening gives the child a sense of stability regarding *family and lifestyle.* The simple *Sunday tradition* creates something special about *your home and family* and helps to solidify and strengthen the new family structure.

❏ If your custodial arrangement does not include Sunday evenings, then choose a different day to create a consistent family tradition.

✸ ✸ ✸ ✸ ✸

SAMPLE VISITATION SCHEDULES and PARENTING AGREEMENTS

The following examples of verbiage for a parenting plan or custody agreement are included to introduce the basic concepts of a well defined and enforceable calendar. Remember, the more detailed and defined the agreement, the more you will be able to relax and enjoy your children. A well defined calendar assures fewer surprises and less conflict. All the examples below can be modified to accommodate different situations and time frames and can be presented as boilerplates for your calendar negotiations.

As you will discover, there are many examples of visitation schedules. Two excellent books to review regarding visitation schedules are *The Father's Emergency Guide to Divorce-Custody Battle,* by Robert Seidenberg and *Creating a Successful Parenting Plan,* by Jayne Major. Both of these books are exceptional resources for parents, and I encourage further reading of them for other ideas and insights.

In general and unless noted otherwise:

- ❏ *Alternate all annual or major holidays.*
    - ❏ Mother will have the children on even numbered years.
    - ❏ Father will have the children on odd-numbered years.

- ❏ 'Parenting time,' 'Visitation,' 'Custody time,' will begin from the close of school on the designated day until the morning the children are due back at school.

- ❏ Each parent will pick up the children from school and deliver them to school on their days of custody. (Or be responsible for the arrangement of transportation of the child during their custody time.)

- ❏ Summer camp or other extracurricular activities shall be treated as the same definition as 'school' for the purpose of exchanging the children during non-school months.

- ❏ It is best that the child does not go to the other parents home between school and visits.

- ❏ If possible, arrange for after school activities, extracurricular activities or for your child to be with friends or relatives until you can be with them after work. This continuity helps reduce some of the confusing and emotional issues during transitions from one parent's home to the other.

❑ The written agreement should include a clause that states the children will not miss school to accommodate vacation travel. Any exception to the children missing school for travel needs to be agreed to in writing and signed by both parents.

❑ If there is a substantial conflict regarding vacation dates during the summer, the parents will alternate the right for first choice of vacation dates in a given year. For example, the mother will have the first choice of vacation dates in odd numbered years and the father will have first choice of vacation dates in even numbered years.

❑ Some custody agreements include a clause that states each parent has the right of first refusal of the child. This means if one parent is going to be out of town or cannot have the child with them during their regular parenting time, then the other parent is given the first opportunity to have the child.

   ❑ This situation should not require make-up days or exchanges of time when one parent forfeits time to the other parent.

   ❑ Be sure that this type of arrangement does not increase conflict or allow a parent to manipulate custody time.

Parenting Time During the Weekend (Visitation/Custody) Examples:

❑ Each parent will have the children on alternating weekends, from close of school on Friday until opening of school on Monday.

❑ Each parent or their designee will pick the children up from school on Friday and take them to school on Monday.

❑ If either parent cannot pick up the children from school on Friday afternoon, then they will make arrangements for the child to be picked up by a friend, relative, or arrange for transportation to an extracurricular activity.

❑ If the regularly scheduled custody weekend includes a holiday on the Friday before the scheduled weekend or the Monday following the scheduled weekend, then the weekend is automatically extended to those dates.

Parenting Time During the Week (Visitation/Custody)

❏   Try to spend as much time with your children as possible.

❏   If the visitation schedule includes mid-week visits:

    ❏   Clearly define what days of the week the child will be with each parent.

    ❏   Father will have the children every _____and _____night,
                                 (day of the week)   (day of the week)
        from the close of school until the opening of school the following day.

    ❏   Father or his designee will pick the children up from school and take them to school the following morning.

❏   Many fathers are *given* Wednesday as the midweek day for visitation. Evaluate your choices and determine what will work best for your schedule and lifestyle. Any day of the week can be used for midweek visits.

Major School Holidays: *Thanksgiving Holiday*
                                         Christmas = Winter Semester Break
                                       President's Week = Ski Week
                                         Easter = Spring Break

❏   Parents will alternate major school holidays and vacations. Major school holidays are defined as:
    ❏   Thanksgiving Holiday
    ❏   Christmas Holiday *or* Winter Break
    ❏   Ski Week, President's Week *or* Mid-term Break
    ❏   Easter Break *or* Spring Break

❏   For example, the agreement may read:

    ❏   Even Numbered Years:

        ❏   Father will have Thanksgiving and the Ski Week/February Break.
        ❏   Mother will have Christmas/Winter Break and the Spring break.

    ❏   Odd numbered years, the schedule will reverse:

        ❏   Mother will have Thanksgiving and the Ski Week/February Break
        ❏   Father will have Christmas/Semester break and the Spring break.

❑ All vacation and holiday dates begin at the close of school on the day vacation begins and end on the morning when school resumes.

❑ There will be no exceptions to the children missing school to facilitate an extended vacation for either parent, unless agreed to in writing and signed by both parents.

    ❑ For example, there will be no early departure from school for holiday plans or late arrival to school to extend a vacation.

(Some professionals suggest that Christmas/Semester break and Easter/Spring break should be shared between the parents every year. This means exchanging the children in the middle of a vacation. In my opinion, this is not the best arrangement because the continuity of the holiday is interrupted, but sometimes cannot be helped because of work schedules, religious beliefs, etc.)

Summer Visitation/Parenting Time – Examples may include:

❑ At the end of the school year, the parents will alternate the children on a weekly, bi-weekly, tri-weekly or monthly basis until the official summer vacation ends, and school resumes for the children. For example:

❑ The children will be with each parent from Monday to Monday in one, two or three week intervals.
OR

❑ Father will have the children with him for one month (or other designated period of time) during the summer, from July 1 at 9:00 AM until August 1, at 9:00 AM.

❑ Mother will have the children with her for one month (or other designated period of time) during the summer, from August 1 at 9:00 AM until September 1 at 9:00 AM.

❑ The regular school visitation schedule will begin on the first regularly scheduled day that school resumes. For example:

❑ The first *mid-week day of visitation* will begin during the first week that school resumes.

❑ The *first weekend* will begin on the first Friday after school resumes.

❑ Exchanges during the summer months will be at a neutral location, preferably summer-camp, extracurricular activity or a friend's home.

❏ One parent will take the child to the location and leave, making sure the child is safe, comfortable and appropriately supervised. The other parent will pick the child up when the activity is complete, or in the case of a neutral friend, after the other parent has left.

Three Day Weekends: Monday Holidays, Federal or School Holidays

❏ When a federal, school or other holiday occurs on a Monday following a regularly scheduled weekend of parenting time, the children will remain with that parent for the holiday and until the beginning of school on Tuesday.

For example:

    ❏ Memorial Day and Labor Day occur on Monday, making a 3-day holiday weekend. The child will stay with the parent that has regular custody for the weekend, extending the weekend until the beginning of school on Tuesday morning.

The 4th of July, Halloween and Other One Night Holidays or Special Occasions

❏ The parents will alternate the 4th of July Holiday. Each parent will have the child for the 4th of July every other year.

❏ The parents will alternate Halloween annually. Each parent will have the child for Halloween every other year.

    ❏ Halloween may include several definitions for school age children. The parents should recognize all the definitions of Halloween, and alternate the Halloween activities every other year.

    ❏ For example, 'Halloween' includes grades school parades and parties. The parent having custody of Halloween, will have custody of all events pertaining to Halloween every other year.

    ❏ If Halloween occurs during the week, the parenting time for Halloween begins with the school parade and party or immediately after school, until the start of school the following school day.

❏ If either the July 4th or Halloween occurs on a weekend, the parent designated for that holiday will pick up the children from school or activity on Friday afternoon and deliver them to school on Monday (or Tuesday) morning, regardless of whose regular weekend it normally is.

Children's Birthdays

❑ The parents will alternate having custody of the child on their birthday every other year.

❑ For example, the father will have the children for their birthday on odd numbered years and the mother will have the children for their birthday on even numbered years.

❑ Birthdays are a *special occasion* and this may change the regular schedule. Therefore, the designated parent for the birthday will pick the child up from school on that day and deliver them to school the following morning.

❑ If the birthday occurs on a weekend, then the parent designated for that birthday will pick up the children from school on Friday and deliver them to school on Monday morning, regardless of whose regular weekend it normally is.

Parent's Birthdays

❑ If desired, each parent will have the child for their birthday. The father will have the children on his birthday and the mother will have the children on her birthday.

   ❑ Again, if the birthday occurs on a school day, the children will be picked up after school or other activity and will be taken to school or activity the following morning.

❑ Some parents prefer to celebrate their birthday on the nearest custodial day versus disrupting the child's schedule. For example:

   ❑ The father's birthday is on a Wednesday and he does not have custody on that day. He may choose to celebrate his birthday on the next weekend that he has regular custody.

   ❑ This arrangement puts much less pressure on the child, modeling for the child that special events can be celebrated with flexibility. A very important message for children of divorce.

Father's Day and Mother's Day

❑ Father's Day and Mother's Day occur on a weekend. Therefore, each parent will take the weekend that coincides with this designated day. For example:

  ❑ Father's Day will begin on Friday after school or activity and continue until Monday morning for school or other scheduled activity.

❑ Some parents may opt to celebrate Mother's Day or Father's Day on a regularly scheduled weekend, not having the child on the actual Father's or Mother's Day.

  ❑ This strategy allows children to share these special days with step-parents or grandparents of the other family.

    ❑ For example, the father waives Father's Day so that the child can share the special day with the step-father.

    ❑ Sometimes this strategy really helps to alleviate some family tension and loyalty issues. On the flip side, a malicious ex-spouse may twist the meaning, creating more loyalty issues or confusing the child.

Religious Holidays

❑ As outlined above, the parents will alternate Christmas and Easter holiday.

❑ The parent will have the children for Christmas in the years that they have Christmas Break, and Easter in the years they have Spring Break.

❑ Parents should make every effort not to split these vacations and breaks as it provides a special opportunity to spend uninterrupted time with a child.

If One Parent is Jewish and the Other Parent is a Christian

❑ If one parent is Jewish and the other parent is Christian and they do not agree to spend uninterrupted time with the child, alternating the Christmas and Easter breaks every other year, then:

❑ Respect should be given to each parents religious preference. In doing so, the religious holidays will take precedence over the regular custodial calendar or the school vacation calendar. For example:

❑ The *Jewish Parent* will have the children after school until the following morning for each of the following Jewish Holidays. If the holiday occurs during the weekend, the calendar will reflect that the Jewish parent has the child from Friday after school until Monday morning.

  ❑ Rosh Hashanah

  ❑ Yom Kippur

  ❑ Purim

  ❑ The first two nights of Passover

  ❑ The first night of Hanukkah

❑ The *Christian parent* will have the children after school (or other designated time) until the following morning (or other designated time) for:

  ❑ December 24th, [Christmas Evening] and December 25th, [Christmas Day]

  ❑ Good Friday until the morning after Easter Sunday

❑ Some years will have coinciding religious holiday dates. In situations such as this, the parents will need to negotiate a fair and equitable religious calendar, perhaps alternating custody of each coinciding religious date.

Make-Up Time

❑ To reduce confusion, potential for manipulation of the calendar or the opportunity for conflict, it is strongly recommended that 'makeup time' is avoided.

★ ★ ★ ★ ★

Remember, if you are dealing with a manipulative, angry or vindictive ex-partner, the calendar may become fertile ground for disputes. Any opportunity for an *ex-spouse fix* may become the underlying reason to request a calendar change. Requests for changes in the calendar should be kept to minimum, as the increased contact and discussion of plans may create disorganization and conflict.

Keep an accurate log of all requests for changes in the calendar.
Be sure that your calendar is well defined, including the precise dates and times
you will have access to your child.

(Endnotes)

[1] Levy, D. (Ed) (1993). *The Best Parent is Both Parents, A Guide to Shared Parenting in the 21st Century.* Norfolk, Virginia: Hampton Roads Publishing Company, Inc. p. 60.

[2] Seidenberg, R. (1997). *The Father's Emergency Guide to Divorce-Custody Battle.*, Takoma Park, Maryland: JES Books, Inc. p. 133.

[3] Levy, D. (Ed) (1993). *The Best Parent is Both Parents, A Guide to Shared Parenting in the 21st Century.* Norfolk, Virginia: Hampton Roads Publishing Company, Inc. p. 57.

[4] id., p. 59.

[5] Bray, J. H. (1998) The Family Schedule. *Family Advocate: Coparenting After Divorce*, Chicago, Illinois: American Bar Association. Volume 21, no. 1, p. 34.

[6] Levy, D. (Ed) (1993). *The Best Parent is Both Parents, A Guide to Shared Parenting in the 21st Century.* Norfolk, Virginia: Hampton Roads Publishing Company, Inc. pp. 57-60.

12.

The Calendar, Conflict and Special Events

———————————

————————

Some divorce professionals will emphasize flexibility in the custodial calendar, including makeup days, flexibility during the holidays, special events and unexpected opportunities or engagements. Flexibility sounds nice. Unfortunately, when the conflicted family attempts a flexible custodial relationship, it can lead to significant 'gaming of the calendar' and the potential for abuse and manipulation of calendar requests.

The importance of certain events and a parent's desire for custody of the dates can often become a competitive matter. For example, one parent may be competitive about the significance of a particular event, insisting that the child experiences the event from their home only. Consequently, these parents may become argumentative about whether the event occurs in one home versus the other.

Take for example, the mother and father who lived in Arizona and were both members of the local and very active sports club. These parents had many arguments regarding the divorce settlement and had a very difficult time creating a fair parenting plan and custodial arrangement. As a result, clear boundaries were established to keep contact between the parents to a minimum.

The final parenting agreement stated that whoever had 'custody of the children' would have 'custody of the location.' To clarify, whoever had the children on a particular day would be able to use the club, and the other parent was not to interfere with that time.

Unbeknownst to the father, the mother went to the club manager to inquire about the dates for all the 'special events and activities' for the upcoming year. Then, without giving specific reasons to the father, the mother requested all the dates that would give her custody of the children for the 'special events' at the club. The mother succeeded in controlling the sports and social activities at the club with the children and her 'new friend.' As a result, the unsuspecting father was alienated from taking part in events that he would have enjoyed participating in as a family.

The club manager looked at the father in amazement when he casually commented one day that he did not know how all the special activities seemed to end up on his ex-spouses parenting time. The manager stated, "I know exactly what happened. Your ex-wife came in and requested a calendar of all the upcoming events for the next year. She told me she would like two copies so she could give one to you, as the two of you would be discussing the children's activities! You mean she didn't talk to you about sharing the events?"

The club manager became very upset and apologized to the father profusely. She stated people were wondering why the father was never participating with his children in the club activities. As time had progressed, everyone thought he was not interested in being active at the club with his children.

In their excellent book, *Caught in the Middle: Protecting the Children of High-Conflict Divorce*, Carla Garrity and Mitchell Baris discuss special events when considering the parenting plan for moderate and high conflict families of divorce.

> "When parents are unable to celebrate special events peaceably in each other's presence, it is best to hold celebrations in both houses. Children are not at all likely to object, for example, to celebrating their birthdays twice, once in each household. So instead of specifying who gets the child's birthday each year, it can be celebrated according to the calendar, wherever he or she would normally spend that day...." [1]

"Some events, however, cannot be duplicated or divided. In the case of children's recitals or special school programs, parents should agree to keep away from each other if there is a chance they will argue. All too often, we hear children talk about looking forward to performing in the school play but fearing that their parents will spoil the occasion by fighting in front of their friends and teachers. Parents who cannot maintain some physical distance from each other at school events should agree to divide them, even though this means missing some of the milestone events of their children's lives. During the regular season, it will be easy enough to alternate attendance at games or athletic matches; play-off and championship matches, however, pose a harder challenge, especially as the children probably will want both parents to attend. Here again, if they cannot do so without conflict, they will need to divide up these events as well." [2]

Unless you are a long-distance parent, the best policy to use is the parallel parenting model: the parent who has custody of the child has 'custody of the location.'

Considerations for Special Events

❑ It is important to be realistic and realize that children and parents of divorce miss the opportunity to participate in many 'special events' that may have been enjoyed by both parents and the child as an intact family.

❑ As parents, try to be flexible in your attitude about these 'special events.'

❑ Birthdays are special but can certainly be celebrated the day or the week before or after the actual day. For example, a parent's birthday, Father's Day or Mother's Day and other 'special days' can be celebrated with flexibility. In other words:

    ❑ Do not to be drawn into the emotion and drama surrounding these events. Create your own 'special time' with your children without making them feel uncomfortable about missing a special event or special time with you.

❑ If you do not angst over special occasions, neither will your child. Most children can enjoy celebrating special days in both homes separately, on whatever day is deemed the 'special day.'

❑ Parents who overly involve their children or promote guilt about special occasions may be setting their children up for an emotionally abusive experience.

❑ The new family structure should promote parents to create new special days and events with happiness and enthusiasm, *not* with guilt, remorse and control!

Parenting Plan Considerations for 'Special Events'

❑ The parenting plan should clearly define *'Special Occasions,' 'Special Events'* and *'One-Time Only Opportunities'* For example:

❑ A 'Special Occasion' is defined as: _____

❑ *Sports*: Any occasion that occurs only once. For example, a championship or a final play off game at the end of a regular sport season.

   ❑ This *does not* include tournaments played during the regular season, including semi-final or final games played during the tournament.

❑ *Music/Drama*: Any occasion that occurs only once. For example, a one-evening recital or performance.

   ❑ Most plays occur on at least two separate occasions, maybe a Wednesday and Thursday night. Parents will alternate their attendance at these events.

   ❑ Alternatively, if a play or recital is scheduled for only one day, there is often a dress rehearsal or a student-only performance that one of the parents can attend.

❑ *Graduations, weddings and other major one-time milestones:*

   ❑ When both parents are required to attend one-time milestones such as graduations and weddings, the parents agree to sit on opposite sides of the recital hall, church, or place of the ceremony.

      ❑Mother will sit on the _____. (left or right)
      ❑Father will sit on the _____ (left or right)

❑ The parents agree to stay at least 30 feet away from each other.

❑ The child will leave with the parent who has custody at that time, or custody of the event.

❑ Hellos and good-byes will be brief so as not to encumber the child with emotions or guilt.

❑ Each parent will respect the space of the other parent when the brief hello or goodbye occurs.

❑ The parents will not park their vehicles in close proximity so there will not be an opportunity for *'coincidental interaction.'*

    ❑ Mother will park to the ____left ____right side of the parking lot
    ❑ Father will park to the ____left ____right side of the parking lot.

Clearly defined parameters provide the parents with *'boundary controls'* that can be used consistently throughout their lives after divorce. If the child is now two years old, these parameters can be used successfully for the next 50 years. Jane goes automatically to the left, John goes automatically to the right, and the children will not have to endure unexpected conflict or surprise situations.

While it may seem overkill to designate even parking areas, there have been many instances of parents 'coincidentally' parking next to or very near the other parent's car. This coincidental parking is very convenient for the parent who wants contact or wants to interfere with the other parent's custodial time. It can be very difficult to avoid unnecessary contact when the parent with the child is leaving the activity, and the other parent is getting into their car at the same time.

★ ★ ★ ★ ★

(Endnotes)
[1] Garrity, C. B. & Baris M. A. (1994) *Caught in the Middle: Protecting the Children of High Conflict Divorce.* New York: Lexington Books. p. 148.
[2] id., page 148.

13.

Obstruction of Visitation, Parental Alienation and the Visitation Schedule

When the divorce dynamics are complicated, the visitation schedule often becomes an advantageous tool for the parent possessing alienating qualities. Without a clearly defined visitation schedule, the alienating parent may succeed in obstructing and/or denying access of the child to the other parent.

A parent may obstruct visitation in many ways. When a parent obstructs visitation, the underlying message to the child is that the visit with the other parent is not important. Essentially, the child is programmed to think that the other parent is not special and should not be given any consideration.

> The malicious or vindictive parent may obstruct visitation in a variety of ways. The obstructing parent may tell the other parent:
>
> "the child is sick and should not [cannot] go for the visit."
> "the child is late returning from a game or practice and will be too tired to go to 'your' home."
> "the child is not ready and is working on an important homework assignment, 'We really shouldn't disrupt his work.'"
> "the child just does not want to go today."
> "the child changed their plans at the last minute and is staying with a friend, 'You want them to have fun, don't you?'"
> "the child was tired, took a nap, and is still sleeping."
> "the child had a bad day, and should just relax at 'my' home."
> "I completely forgot that I had made other arrangements today for our child, 'I'm sure you understand.'"

As one of the first *'pioneers of alienation'* Ira Turkat wrote a famous article entitled, *Divorce Related Malicious Mother Syndrome*. In the article Turkat defined criteria for mothers who denied regular visitation to the father. While Turkat (like many others) has redefined the issue of gender, many of his initial observations are worth revisiting and reviewing. In *Divorce Related Malicious Mother Syndrome*, Turkat states,

"Experts are in relative agreement that regular and uninterrupted visitation with the non-residential parent is desirable and beneficial for children, except in extreme circumstances (Hodges, 1991). In fact, some states, such as Florida, have laws written to reflect this view (Kean, 1990). Unfortunately, even when the father and children have legal rights to visitation, individuals with divorce related malicious mother syndrome continue to interfere with it.

A mother, who previously attacked her ex-husband physically during visitation transfers of the children, refused to provide the children when the ex-husband had the police attend to monitor exchanges.

When one divorced father arrived to pick up his children for visitation, the mother arranged for her and the children to be elsewhere so that the father could not visit with the children.

One mother had her physically intimidating boyfriend assault her ex-husband when he came to pick up his children for visitation." [1]

"The President of The Council for Children's Rights (Washington D.C.) notes that such alienation is considered a form of child abuse (Levy, 1992). Unfortunately, the police typically avoid involving themselves in such situations. Furthermore, unless the victimized father is financially capable of returning to court on an ongoing basis, there is little that can be done to prevent such mother's behavior. Finally, even when such cases are brought to trial, the courts are often inadequate in supporting fathers' visitation rights (Commission on Gender Bias in the Judicial System, 1992)."[2]

David Levy, President of the Children's Rights Council also points out some of the difficulties parents encounter when trying to gain access to their children. Of particular interest is his observation:

"The failure of many court orders to recognize or deal with the incidence of one parent deliberately preventing or discouraging access between the child and the other parent, even when it has been ordered."[3]

Fortunately, some states are actually penalizing parents for interrupting or blocking court-ordered parenting time. Idaho, Iowa and most recently Tennessee have laws that result in the loss of recreational, professional, and/or business licenses for interference with access.[4]

In England, a new law (2002) states, "Separated and divorced mothers who refuse to allow contact between children and former partners, risk being fined, ordered to attend parenting classes or even forced to seek psychiatric help, under proposals being considered by the Lord Chancellor's Department. Courts would also order mothers to do community service or to pay compensation to the fathers for denying them contact with their children."[5]

These changes in the law are definitely positive actions toward protecting a parent's right to have access to their children. The message is very clear and creates a true disincentive for blocking court ordered parenting time.

If you live in the other 47 states or other countries, consider including provisions in your parenting or marital settlement agreement that specifically address interruption or denial of access to your children. These provisions should include 'consequences' or 'disincentives' for *any effort* made by the other parent to interfere with or obstruct parenting time. Examples of such provisions may include:

➤ "If one party interferes with custody and the issue is brought to court, the interfering party pays for court costs;
➤ Time interfered with is cumulative and made up at a later date;

➢ Fines for interference

➢ Family therapy ordered by the court

➢ Three strikes and you are 'out' rule – meaning that if you bring three actions in front of the court for custodial interference (warranted) custody transfers to the parent being rejected;

➢ Any other provision you determine beneficial to you and repugnant by your ex-spouse." [6]

Guidelines for Documentation to Help Facilitate Change
When a Parent is Obstructing Visitation:

➢ *Strengthen the written custody agreement.* If your existing agreement does not specifically delineate the hours and days you have visitation (See Chapter 11: *Access, Schedules and Parenting Time*) then by all means petition or coordinate for a change in the documents to *clearly define* your custodial time. This is crucial!

➢ Agreements citing *'reasonable visitation'* are ambiguous and are not adequate in most divorce cases, especially when a parent is manipulative or vindictive.

➢ *Establish a 'neutral exchange' location.* Exchanging the children at a neutral location may help reduce some of the opportunities an alienating parent has to obstruct the child's visit with the other parent. Neutral exchange is explained in detail in chapter 14.

➢ *Document your efforts to see your child.* Start an organized written log of your efforts to see your children. The written log should include the date, time and a description of each situation.

    ➢ Date specific examples can be taken to a mediator, Special Master or an attorney to help you validate concerns to facilitate change.

➢ Do not enter into the legal and/or mediation arena with vague citations or examples. Vague examples might include, "Well once in a while I can't see my kids," or, "You know, it's not easy to exchange the kids." These examples will not be sufficient to facilitate the change you desire.

➢ *Bring a witness.* If you can, have a witness with you at all exchanges of the children. Anyone will do, a co-worker, a neighbor, or a family member. This puts some pressure on the other parent to comply with your rights to visitation.

➤ Usually, 'The nice little single mother down the street' does not want bad publicity. If the exchange occurs with only the parents present, anything goes and the recollection of the event will become nothing more that "He said, she said hearsay."

> ➤ If the situation has escalated and you are thinking about legal action, then the 'witness' should be someone the court would consider a 'reliable witness.'

> ➤ In other words, someone the court would view as reliable, credible and would consider their testimony or declaration. A neutral professional or reputable uninvolved party would be ideal.

➤ *Videotape your attempts to visit your child.* Video recordings may not be considered by the court, but there is no harm in taking a video camera to the exchange.

> ➤ A counselor or therapist can review the exchange and offer some assistance or guidance. It is often very difficult to reconstruct and describe an emotional exchange of your children to someone else. The video recording will help clarify exactly what happened at the exchange.

> ➤ Be sure to check on the legalities of videotaping or voice recording any situation before proceeding. There are privacy issues and crimes associated with voice taping someone without their knowledge. That is why videotaping may be the most appropriate method to document the exchange, if needed.

➤ *Consider Supervised Visitation.* In many states the courts may order that a child's visits and/or exchanges will be supervised.

> ➤ "The need for high-quality supervision has come to the attention of federal and state authorities." [7]

> ➤ "There are many different reasons and degrees of supervised visitation. Specifically for the issue of obstruction of visitation there is what the legal system refers to as *'exchange supervision.'*" "Exchange supervision is limited to the actual exchange of the child(ren) between one parent and the other. The rest of the visitation between the child(ren) and parent is unsupervised." [8]

> > *Do not let the pattern of obstruction continue,*
> > *without making a coordinated effort to stop it!*

(Endnotes)

[1] Turkat, I. D. (1995). Divorce Related Malicious Mother Syndrome, *Journal of Family Violence,* Volume 10, pp. 253-264.

[2] id.

[3] Levy, D. (Ed) (1993) *The Best Parent is Both Parents, A Guide to Shared Parenting in the 21ˢᵗ Century.* Norfolk, Virginia: Hampton Roads Publishing Company, Inc. p. 58.

[4] Children's Rights Council, Inc., Speak out for Children, Volume 15-No. 3/4, page 1, Fall 2000/Winter 2001.

[5] Gibb, Frances Legal editor and Frean, Alexandra, *The Times* (London) February 9, 2002, Printed in *Speak Out for Children* ,Summer 2002, Vol. 17, No. 2, (page 17).

[6] Promoting Responsible Fatherhood, Parental Alienation Syndrome Newsletter, Excerpt from Chapter 4(A) PAS PKG Seminars E-mail: brainwashing@execpc.com

[7] Center for Families, Children & the Courts; Research Update, A Publication of the California Judicial Council, Administrative Office of the Courts, March 2002.

[8] id.

14.

Neutral Exchange

How to Minimize Separation Anxiety for the Child and Parental Conflict at Exchanges

————————————

————————

Separation Anxiety
1. The normal fear and apprehension expressed by infants
when removed from mothers or approached by strangers.
2. Any similar reaction in later life caused by separation
from familiar surroundings or close friends or family. [1]

Carla Garrity and Mitchell Baris define *moderate conflict* in their excellent book *Caught in the Middle: Protecting the Children of High-Conflict Divorce.*

"Parents who fall in the category of moderate levels of conflict frequently function well as individual parents but are prone to fight and argue when they are face to face. Children from these families, therefore, benefit from transitions especially designed to minimize contact between the parents." [2]

It does not take much for a parent to invoke separation anxiety in a child before leaving to see the other parent. The younger the child, the easier it is for a malicious or vindictive parent to make the child sad or nervous. A parent may simply say, "I will be so worried about you while you are gone and I am so sorry that you have to go." "Just remember it is only for one night, then we'll be together again." Some parents will become very dramatic, even crying, when saying good-bye to their child, even for short visits to the other parent's home.

These malicious parents are trying to sabotage the child's visit with the other parent before the visit begins. Many children will arrive at the other parent's home in a sad or angry state of mind.

Take for example, the mother in New Jersey who would place a photograph of herself in her 3-year-old child's pocket before an overnight visit with the father. She would cry and tell her child to think of her while they were apart *(for an overnight.)* The child would arrive at the father's home clutching onto the picture in his pocket. When the father noticed his child's anxiety he asked the child what he was doing.

When the son produced the photograph of his mother, the father expressed that the picture should be in a safe place where it would not get lost or ruined. The son was very relieved to release the photograph. Once the picture was out of the child's pocket, he began to relax and enjoy his visit with his father. Interestingly, he never worried about the picture for the rest of his visit nor did he ask for it back when he returned to his mother.

In another example, the mother in New Mexico insisted on adorning her child with her jewelry before the child would visit with the father. In this case the mother would tell the child to hold onto the jewelry and think of her whenever the child was "scared or afraid of the father." (This child was being programmed to fear her father.)

Ironically, this mother refused her daughter's simple request to take her favorite teddy bear to the father's home for visits. The child would have benefited far more by having her teddy bear rather than her mother's jewelry. The teddy bear would have provided her with some security and continuity between the two homes. Unfortunately, for this child, the mother had a different agenda and the teddy bear was only allowed to reside at one home.

Ideas to Help You Identify and Cope with Separation Anxiety at Transitions

➢ Do you think your child is experiencing difficulty before, during or after an exchange?

   ➢ Make an effort to assess what kind of anxiety your child is experiencing.

   ➢ Write down examples of what you feel are signs and/or symptoms of the anxiety. (See the examples below)

   ➢ When a parent documents their observations about the child at an exchange it will help identify if there is a pattern to the child's behavior. Is the behavior an anxious reaction to the exchange?

      ➢ Documenting the child's symptoms also helps a parent 'remember' what they observed. Often, the exchange can be as upsetting to the parent as it is to the child. Documenting the experience will help when trying to describe the incident to others, such as a therapist or attorney.

   ➢ Try not to get mad or frustrated with your child at the time of the exchange.

   ➢ Try not to take the child's reaction personally, realizing they are experiencing difficulty they may not understand.

   ➢ Tell your child you understand it is sometimes difficult to go back and forth between the homes.

   ➢ Ask the child if there is anything you can do to make it easier for them, without changing existing rules or schedules.

   ➢ Begin to think about a way to facilitate a '*neutral exchange*' for your child.

   ➢ Work with your attorney, psychologist or parenting coordinator to figure out the best method to exchange your children between homes. The goal should be to establish an exchange procedure that will result in the least amount of anxiety or emotional trauma to the child.

Examples of Documenting Potential Anxiety.

8/1/03   Johnny is 10 years old. He is becoming very angry with me before he has to leave the house to go to his mothers. He now routinely tries to create a problem so there will be an argument. He will argue about anything.

10/15/02   Jeffrey is 8 years old. Every time he gets ready to go to his mother's house he asks if he can take a toy with him. It has been explained to him that this isn't the best idea, but every exchange he tries to convince me otherwise, usually ending in bad feelings. If I let him take the toy, it is never seen again at my home. If I don't let him take the toy, he is angry and mad. Sometimes he will literally stuff something in his pocket, "steal" it so he has something to take back. I don't understand it.

6/7/03   Mary is 12 years old and at the end of every visit she wants to wear a pair of shoes that she did not arrive with. She becomes very agitated and angry when I ask her to wear the shoes she was wearing when she arrived. She states she "doesn't like those shoes" and insists on wearing another pair of shoes from my home.

4/19/03   Adam is 3 years old. When I drop him off at his mother's house he starts up the driveway with his 8-year-old brother. Half way up the driveway Adam lies down, even if it is raining. He lies there until his mother runs down the driveway to pick him up. Sometimes when she picks him up he kicks and screams at her. It is awful.

The Preschool Child: Janet Johnston has done extensive research on children of divorce. In her excellent book *Impasses of Divorce* she states:

> "The preschool children were multi-symptomatic during transitions from one parent's home to the other. These symptoms were a major issue in the parental conflict and often a reason for the next fight. At least one parent (usually the principal custodian) found the child extremely difficult or distressed before or after visits, and cited the child's disturbed behavior as reasons for limiting or eliminating the contact with the other parent, who was seen as an inadequate caretaker. The other parent countered by claiming that the complaints were untrue or exaggerated (rationalizations for reluctance to share the child) or by blaming the first parent for inducing the child to behave in a disturbed manner.

❑   When Mrs. A found her three-year-old daughter curled up on the sofa, sucking her thumb, and talking in a regressed manner after the visit, she concluded that her ex-husband had been talking 'baby talk' to the child, and she cited this as evidence of his inappropriate fathering. Mr. A felt his daughter 'was upset because she had to interrupt the wonderful time we were having together and return to mother.'

After observing the children and receiving detailed weekly reports from parents and others (such as teachers and relatives), we became convinced there was validity to the claims that these preschoolers were distressed. They had a plethora of dramatic emotional, behavioral, and somatic responses, many of which seemed contradictory. For example, a child would be happy, even wildly excited about the visit, but would resist and cling when it came time to leave. Or they could be compliant and mature about leaving but return regressed, babyish, and difficult to manage. After a seemingly smooth and uneventful visit, they awoke in the night screaming with terror or wet or soil the bed." [3]

Johnston also found in her studies that the majority of preschoolers exhibited separation anxieties during transitions. Johnston states, "They cried and clung to whichever parent they were leaving, so they protested departing for the visits and resisted returning." [4]

Separation anxiety may be present in many different situations. Therefore, it is important to observe your child and make objective notes that will help identify the reason for their anxiety. It is also very important to realize that anxiety in a child before, during and after an exchange to the other parent is often a normal occurrence.

In the pre-school child, it is important to observe for any reactions to an exchange. Parents often describe a variety of ways in which the preschooler reacts to moving from one parent to the other. Preschoolers do not have the emotional maturity to understand their feelings, and they need extra support and understanding from both the receiving parent and the parent returning the child.

There are many ways the preschooler may manifest their feelings of anxiety before an exchange. Symptoms of anxiety for the preschooler prior to an exchange may include:

➢ Temper tantrums or behavioral problems (for no apparent reason)
➢ Crying or becoming overly agitated without being provoked
➢ Clinging to the parent they will be leaving (sometimes hours in advance of the exchange)
➢ Uncharacteristically quiet and withdrawn, or,
➢ Extremely hyperactive and overly excited

> ➢ Fidgeting with toys or other belongings

> ➢ Complaining of physical symptoms (stomach ache or a headache)

> ➢ Asthma or an allergic reaction may be present as a result of the tension

> ➢ Nightmares before or after the exchange

> ➢ Difficult or aggressive behavior

> ➢ Extremely tense and demanding

> ➢ Insecure (needing special attention such as wanting to sleep with the parent even though they have been sleeping in their own bed)

> ➢ Bed wetting

The School Age Child (ages 6 –12) may have an entirely different response to parental conflict, divorce and the exchange from one home to the other. Johnston describes her findings of the school age child as:

> "They [the school age child] develop different patterns of coping and defensive response to disputing parents, and they typically become more in-volved, even enmeshed, in the parental conflicts and play a significant role in the drama, thereby creating a family impasse." [5]

> "…the parents perceiving them to be more mature, drew them into the dispute, burdened their children with requests for support, comfort, and reas-surance of their own troubled emotions." "…Children were used as commu-nications channels between parents who refused to talk directly to each other. They carried messages back and forth….Like the proverbial Greek messen-gers, the children were blamed and punished if the message was not to the receiver's liking." [6]

Johnston's research found that the school age child was often caught in the middle, becoming the target of the angry exchange. Johnston also found that the school age child was "often symptomatic at the time of the transitions between parents." [7] Johnston describes the possible reactions for the school age child around the time of the transition as:

> ➢ Frequently stressed

> ➢ Often apprehensive

> ➢ Vigilant

> ➢ Quiet and withdrawn

> ➢ "Spaced out"

> ➢ "Zombie like"

> ➢ "Blocked out to the world" [8]

The Adolescent and Young Adult: To further the discussion on transitions, one must also consider the potential reactions the adolescent and young adult may have. Many parents of divorce find their adolescent children to be very unpredictable. Adolescents and young adults have much more independence and may opt not to visit one parent at all.

In divorce cases with high conflict, the adolescent may have learned how to manipulate and control both parents and their environment. Transitions for the adolescent may be more difficult due to social relationships and peer group activities. Parents should pay close attention to their adolescent children to differentiate whether the child is experiencing difficulty as a result of the transition, or if the change in behavior is related to normal adolescent development.

✶   ✶   ✶   ✶   ✶

The descriptions of the various reactions children may demonstrate before, during and after an exchange are included in this chapter to help a parent identify and document potential problems with separation anxiety and exchanges. It is important to remember that *both parents* may experience difficulty with the child at an exchange. The purpose of documenting the child's behavior is to identify the problem and explore alternatives to exchange the child in hopes of reducing their stress as it relates to the exchange and the transition from one home to the other.

Neutral Exchange

In Chapter 11 we discussed parental access, schedules and parenting time. Deciding on the best exchange location for your child is a very important decision and can make the difference between a smooth or a disruptive exchange. *Exchanges of the children must be clearly defined!*

➢ It is imperative that the written agreement addresses where and how the children will be exchanged. The exchange procedure should be described in detail, including specific days, times and locations of the exchanges.

➢ Try to use the child's school and extracurricular activities as the neutral exchange locations. This allows the child a buffer zone between homes (dropped off by one parent, picked up by the other)

➢ Decide where the children will be exchanged on non-school days.

- ➢ Summer camp or other extracurricular activities shall be treated as the same definition as 'school' for the purpose of exchanging the children during non-school months.

- ➢ Decide where and how the children will be exchanged in an emergency.

- ➢ Make every effort not to exchange the child at the home of the other parent.

- ➢ Choose a neutral location where the child can be supervised or occupied in a certain activity.

- ➢ Make every effort to assure that someone associated with *your* family transports the children to and from an exchange. (Parents, aunts, uncles, friends of the children, etc.)

  - ➢ Take your children to school on your scheduled days or have someone associated with *your* family take them to school.

- ➢ Pick up your children from school or have someone associated with your family pick them up from school.

- ➢ Avoid Sunday evening exchanges of the child during a custodial weekend. Whenever possible, the weekend should begin on Friday after school and flow through until Monday morning, when the child is delivered to school.

- ➢ Always opt for a smooth weekend and deliver or arrange for the children to be delivered to school from your home (in good spirits with their homework complete) on Monday morning.

(Endnotes)

[1] Webster's Encyclopedic Unabridged Dictionary, Thunder Bay Press, San Diego, CA, 1993.

[2] Garrity & Baris, *Caught in the Middle: Protecting the Children of High-Conflict Divorce*, 1994, New York, Lexington Books, page 52.

[3] Johnston, J. R. & Campbell, L. E. G. (1988). *Impasse of Divorce: The Dynamics and Resolution of Family Conflict*. New York: The Free Press, A Division of Macmillan. pp. 127-128.

[4] id., p. 128.

[5] id., p. 151.

[6] id., p. 152.

[7] id., p. 154.

[8] id., p. 154-155.

15.

Psychological Warfare and Games of the Child's Mind

———————————————

———————————

In previous chapters, we have explored some of the motivational factors and circumstances that can cause problematic relationships between separating and divorcing parents. Many of these chapters have touched on the psychological and emotional abuse of the child. Once the door is open to understanding the various factors that can affect a terminating parental relationship, the possibility of the malicious parent-child interaction becomes more feasible.

Understandably, it may be very difficult for some individuals to comprehend that a parent could be so destructive to injure their own child by using *psychological warfare* to hurt the other parent. However, brainwashing, stalking and the alienation of a child from the other parent are commonplace in the world of divorce.

Unfortunately, the methods to identify and deal with the damaging outcomes these psychological games have on families of divorce is practically nonexistent. The behaviors discussed in this chapter should be considered (by all entities) as *'psychological or emotional abuse of the child.'* These disturbing psychological games should also be considered *'psychological and emotional mistreatment of the parent'* who becomes the victim of these brainwashing campaigns.

The legal system needs to find a better way to identify and acknowledge that these psychological games are routinely present in families of divorce. To further that challenge, the legal system needs to make an effort to create mechanisms to help minimize these behaviors, even if it involves custodial sanctions for parents who knowingly involve their children in psychological warfare. Again, the high case loads in the family law courts (and the judges inability to spend the time to investigate these behaviors) gives the malicious parent a *license to condition and program* their children.

We will now explore some of the more common emotional games that parents willfully play, using their own child's mind. These games are intended to maintain control of the child, the other parent and the child's time with that parent. These games are very common in divorce and parents should be keenly aware of the negative and often traumatic effects these games have on children.

Much of our society, persuaded by current social influence, believes that a mother would not intentionally hurt her child. It is the *'maternal thing'* of this generation. In many cases, the excuse is given that divorcing parents are preoccupied with their own emotional pain, often becoming oblivious to the child being caught in the parental crossfire. This may be true in some situations, but I believe there is a very high percentage of parents who know exactly what they are doing when they engage their children in psychological warfare. It is also my opinion that these parents knowingly manipulate the child in an effort to align the child with them, get revenge and hurt the ex-spouse.

This type of psychological warfare and emotional abuse may also be defined as failing the *Solomon Test*: the mother who would rather kill her child than share the child with someone else. Essentially that is what these parents are doing. They are killing their children from within. *They are the parents who eat their young!*

These affected parents do not have respect for their children and have even less respect for the ex-partner. They may become obsessed with the divorce, and their ultimate goal (whether conscious or unconscious) is to control or destroy the relationship between the ex-partner and the child. Even the *ideas and preconceived methods* of destroying the parent-child relationship may contribute to the affected parent feeling avenged and powerful.

'...the younger the children, the easier it is to programme and/or brainwash due to their high level of innocence, suggestibility, and gullibility. A young child does not need to be present as an observer to believe that a parent has been injured if he or she sees the parent limping, wearing a sling or bandage, or crying after having just been with the mother or father. Many programmers are adept actors. Their level of anger may supersede any shred of sensitivity to the child's reaction and well being. These parents often believe that they are acting in the child's best interest, even if they have to orchestrate and lie." [1]

Only those parents capable of separating their identity and needs from the other parent, who recognize and overcome their anger and resentment after divorce, will be able to assess their participation in *the use of the child in psychological warfare*. As stated previously, it takes two people to dance. If one parent will not dance, that parent will be empowered to help diffuse the negative and damaging effects these psychological games may have on the child.

Children involved in *psychological warfare* may experience many negative long-term ramifications. As a result of the abuse, these exposed children may have a decrease in their self-esteem and self-confidence. They may also experience difficulty in developing their own sense of identity, often leading to a devalued view of themselves and others. Many times, children involved in parental psychological warfare will develop significant issues with child-power versus parent-power. This phenomenon is also described as a *hierarchy reversal*, whereby, a child suddenly becomes the parent, and the parent becomes the child. In the most severe cases of involvement, the child may demonstrate adverse behavioral problems and experience difficulty in school and social relationships.

LOYALTY GAMES

All the games described in this chapter involve *loyalty issues*, and all loyalty issues have a negative impact on children. When a parent engages a child in psychological warfare they *expect the child to take sides*, to make a choice between one parent or the other. When a parent is vindictive or wants revenge, almost any family subject (no matter how trivial) can become fertile ground for a loyalty issue.

✱ ✱ ✱ ✱ ✱

THE MESSENGER

'*The Messenger*' is the psychological game played when one parent asks the child to take a message to the other parent. Some examples of playing '*The Messenger*' may include:

> "Ask your Dad when he is going to pay for your school pictures. He said he was going to pay for them and he hasn't done it yet."

> "Ask your father how come your child support check has been late the last three months."

> "Tell your father that I can't afford to buy your soccer shoes this year so he'll have to buy them and then we can share them between the two houses."

> "Tell your father I have signed you up for lacrosse. He said he wasn't going to pay for it, but legally he has too."

> "Tell your father that Mark and I are going to Spain and ask him if he can have you the week of April 4th."

In these scenarios, the child is responsible for relaying the message to the other parent. The child is also responsible for taking care of the issue, rather than the parents. Most children do not know what to do with the information, and are often delivering a message that could have a great effect on *their life*. Imagine the 10-year-old boy delivering the message to his father about the soccer shoes. Not only is he involved, he is wondering if his father is going to pay for the shoes. "What if Dad doesn't pay for the shoes? "Mom says she can't afford them and if I don't have shoes, I can't play soccer."

If the parents do not converse about the children in a civil and businesslike manner, then a note or letter should be put in a sealed envelope, stamped and *mailed*. Children should not even be used to deliver written information to the other parent. Asking children to deliver an envelope is also involving them in the emotional game. All too often, the child as *the messenger*, gets shot and is caught in the crossfire of the parental interaction. The psychological impact of being the *messenger* can be devastating to a child!

THE MESSENGER – ONCE REMOVED

In this emotional game, a parent improvises their method of using the child as a messenger. These parents know it is inappropriate to involve the child by asking the child to verbally communicate a message to the other parent. However, they need and *want* the child to be involved in the divorce dynamics and the parental issues.

Take for example, the mother in Oklahoma who was manipulative enough to involve her children in parental issues without giving the impression of doing so, actually *camouflaging* her efforts to involve them. This mother always had an *issue* before the exchange of the children, and she would routinely write the father '*a note.*' Usually, she would sit down at the dining room table, located centrally in her home, and hand write a pleasantly toned note that usually had an underlying vindictive motive. Superficially, the letter appeared very cordial and pleasant. However, understanding the motive within the content often made the letter manipulative and toxic to the father.

The children in this family were old enough to read, and because of their mother's personality were more than curious about the interactions between their divorced parents. The mother incessantly involved the children in every issue. Sometimes the mother would even ask the children for their opinion of what she should do about the issue and what she should include in her note to the father. In this effort she was able to involve the children so that when the father read 'the note' the children would be able to voluntarily give their input, ideas and suggestions. Other times the mother would write her note and leave it openly on the table several hours before the scheduled transition between the homes.

This mother never mailed the letters, but instead asked the children to personally carry the letter and *"hand it to the father"* and specifically *"not to the stepmother."* The mother would also alternate which child she would choose to deliver the note to the father. This technique empowered each child at the time of an exchange, creating a 'point-child' for the issue that was to be delivered to the father.

For example, upon arrival to their father's home, these programmed children would hand the letter to him. "Oh, here's a letter from Mom. It's about changing the calendar again this summer so that we can go to Mexico."

This type of message affects everyone in both homes. The father will feel that he has to respond to the mother's request. The children are excited about going on a trip to Mexico, though they now know it will depend on whether the father agrees to the calendar change. The mother has succeeded in the delivery of her message and she now she has a formidable presence in the father's home at the onset of his custodial time.

Other times, when the mother was determined to make sure the children were involved in an issue she would send the note without an envelope. With this maneuver, the mother could prep the children. She might say to her young child, "Oh, I'm out of time to find an envelope, but here is a note for your father about why I don't want you participating in football any longer. You know the reasons. Will you be sure you hand it to him directly?"

By using her children as messengers the mother was able to keep her children engaged in the psychological warfare. For example, the mother knew that the father and son were enjoying a sport together and she was threatened by it. The nine-year-old son was now squarely in the middle of what he would consider a 'huge issue.' As the messenger, he was to deliver a note to the father, a message that may have a huge impact on the child's life. The child knew of his mother's disapproval of his participation in football, and was now in the position of handing the father a letter that could greatly affect his life.

This example clearly illustrates how a parent can knowingly manipulate a child. This mother had every intention of using her children as *messengers* to the father's home. In this case, the children were messengers throughout their childhood, and as young adults were unable to differentiate or understand appropriate boundaries.

I SPY

Parents play '*I Spy*' when they ask the child to spy and report back to them about the other parent. Typical spy games include a parent *prepping a child* to pay attention to certain details or events that happen during their visit with the other parent. When returning from the visit with the other parent, the spying parent will ask the child questions. They may even preface their questions with, "Now remember what we talked about last week, it is important for me to know what is going on at your father's. So:

"Who is Dad dating?"
"Who's car was that in front of you father's house on Saturday night?"
"Where did you go to dinner?"
"How many drinks did Daddy have at dinner?"
"Did your father's new friend come to his house yesterday?"
"How many times did your father talk about me?"
"What did your father tell you about the divorce?"
"Is your father still smoking pot?"

I Spy is a very complicated game for a child and often becomes a double-edged sword. The child feels pressured to spy on one parent and return with information to the other parent. These children soon learn they are betraying both parents. The child is betraying one parent when spying on them, and betraying the other parent if they do not return with the requested information. When the child plays *I Spy*, they often know the information they are reporting may be painful or make the spying parent angry. This game is very unfair to the child and places them directly in the middle of parental emotions and loyalty issues. The child's preoccupation with *fact-finding* also dilutes their ability to enjoy time with the other parent. Clawar and Rivlin state:

> "Children who spy on a parent have usually been set up to do so. It is not in a child's best interest to take on the role of obtaining information that could harm the child-parent relationship. The clandestine [secret] nature of spying and the information gathered usually elicits anxiety in the child." [2]

Clawar and Rivlin describe spying or a child becoming a conduit of information for one parent as:

> "In many instances, especially during the divorce process parents overtly request that a child spy on the other parent to retrieve financial or social information. It is not unusual for parents to find that they are harboring a spy who secretly examines the contents of a wallet; looks through the mail, checkbooks, papers, and documents; or eavesdrops and then reports back to the other parent. Most children do not like themselves for conducting such covert activities but feel that they must comply. These young rescuers are often able to be coerced because they are genuinely protective of a parent whom they believe will become, without their help, a victim." [3]

Take for example, the mother in Kansas who brainwashed and programmed her young son by telling him he had the '*best memory in the whole world.*' The three-year-old son was very proud of his '*good memory.*' The mother would reward her son for his *good memory* by giving him candy when he *remembered* juicy tidbits of information from his visit with his father.

The son became addicted to the emotional rewards he received from his mother. On one occasion at his father's home he proudly stated, "Mommy says I am so good. Mommy says that I have the best memory in the whole world! Mommy says I have such a good memory because I can remember everything that happens when I am with you. Last night I remembered that you had three beers (holding up three little fingers.) Daddy, do you think I have a good memory?"

"POOR ME"- THE VICTIM

'*Poor Me*' is the game a parent plays that burdens the child with the unfairness of the divorce (whether fabricated or not) and the attitude that everyone, including the child, should feel sorry for them and protect them.

"This is terrible."
"This is awful."
"What am I going to do?"
"How can I survive on this pittance?"
"Because Dad left me I can't do this and we can't do that."
"Of all people, how could this have happened to me?"

Playing the victim to a child and others sends the message, "The divorce was so unfair, every one should feel sorry for me. I've lost everything and I'll never be happy again. I can't do it on my own. Please help me."

Unfortunately, a child might believe the parent, especially if the child perceives that the lifestyle *has* changed for the *victim parent*. *Poor Me* often results in the child feeling sorry for the parent, and assuming the position of a caretaker. The switch of the child taking care of the parent, actually protecting the parent, is called *parentification*. Often, when one parent plays the victim they are perceived by the child as the good parent, the parent the child needs to take care of and protect. The other parent may not even know that *Poor Me* is being played, and soon becomes the bad parent in the eyes of the child.

The *female factor* contributes gainfully to the game of *the victim*. Therefore, mothers are often able to play the victim more convincingly than fathers. Many mothers use the *Poor Me* strategy to ingratiate themselves into the pity of their children, the children's friends and families, coaches, teachers and all others who might otherwise have been indifferent or neutral to the divorce situation.

Take for example, the mother in North Carolina who was so skilled at playing the victim that she easily convinced her child's baseball coach that the father was evil spirited, and a horrible father to her child. She portrayed herself as the victim of abuse and the poor innocent mother trying to raise her child to the best of her ability.

In front of the child, she would cry and tell the coach how awful things were for her and how she worried about the child when he was at the father's home. One year the coach gave the child, who was an average player on team, the Most Valuable Player Award. When confronted by the other team parents, the coach confided that he felt so sorry for the mother he thought this would make things better for her. He told the parents that by giving the child the MVP award, it would help "even things out and level the playing field" and would make life better for the child in the mother's home.

DENIGRATION AND CHARACTER ASSASSINATION

A parent plays *'Denigrate'* when they say negative things about the other parent in the presence of the children. This game is *very common* in families of divorce, as parents often go through a period of revulsion and hatred of the other parent during the separation process. If the hatred started during the tenure of the marriage, it often escalates out of proportion during the separation and divorce process. Some divorced parents take these emotions to extremes and want to share their desire to devalue and diminish the importance of the other parent.

In reality, the denigrating parent's perceptions of the other parent may be accurate or their assessment of the other parent's faults may be justified. However, *any criticism* of either parent is very difficult for a child to understand. When a parent demeans the other parent in the presence of the child it causes a process called *internal devaluing*. Internal devaluing occurs when the child feels they are being depreciated along with the other parent.

> ***Take for example,*** the mother in Connecticut who deliberately sat her children down before and after each visit with the father. Before the visit, the mother would *'remind'* the children of why their parents got divorced. "You need to remember that your father is an alcoholic and a drug addict and that is the reason we got divorced. He is not a good person and you need to be very careful when you are with him. Be sure that you stay together during your visit so that you can protect each other. I will be very worried about you while you are gone. You will only be there overnight, so I will see you right after school tomorrow. Remember, be careful. If I had my way, you would not have to go to your father's at all!"

It is important to remember that children have a love for both parents regardless of how the parents may feel about each other. A parent who makes derogatory or negative comments about the other parent, is actually making an attack on the child itself. Children involved in the game of *Denigration* are caught in the middle of their parent's feelings and their negative emotional expressions about one another.

KEEPING SECRETS - COHORTS IN SECRET-KEEPING

'Keeping Secrets' is the game played by a parent who is trying to control information. In *Keeping Secrets* the parent creates a covert alliance with a child. This secret alliance is very unhealthy for children. A child co-opted by a parent to play *Keeping Secrets* will not feel comfortable asking normal questions or discussing typical family issues with the other parent. These children often feel they have something to hide, and harbor even normal family or personal information as a secret. Of secrets, Clawar and Rivlin state:

> "Children are most comfortable with the ability to have free-flowing communication with parents and family members. Some parents strongly feel that any information regarding that parent's 'new life' is 'none of the other parent's business.' Children are admonished not to divulge even the most innocuous information. These secretive parents are often paranoid types, who 'pump,' or interrogate, their children for information while demanding secrecy about their own lives.
>
> As a rule, children find it burdensome to keep secrets, because part of being a child means being spontaneous." [4]

Take for example, the mother in Washington who convinced her children that whatever happened in her home was a secret, never to be told to the father. Her children were programmed and very practiced in keeping secrets from the father. The mother would confide in her children and then instruct them "not to tell."

When the father requested that the young children have a psychological evaluation, the mother refused, stating, *"her children* did not need therapy, *all three of them were perfectly normal."* The court disagreed with the mother, and ordered that the children were to have individual psychotherapy (of short duration) for the purpose of a baseline assessment.

The idea of therapy for *her children* was very threatening to the mother and she stepped up her efforts to keep *everything in her home a secret.* Therapy posed a unique twist to the mother's need for control. She would coach her children before therapy and interview them after their individual sessions, to determine what they had shared of their life with the therapist. Understandably, the children were very guarded in therapy and the therapists were aware that something was amiss.

One therapist recommended that the father go to the library and check out some children's books on *'Secrets.'* The therapist believed it would help the children have a better understanding of the meaning of secrets. The intent was to allow the children to explore secrets outside of the family conflict.

The father followed the therapist's recommendation and brought home several children's books about secrets. In particular, his two young twins became highly intrigued with the new books. The girls carried one book with them where ever they went, and repeatedly asked their father to read it *with them* and also *to them*.

One morning the twins announced to their father they were going to take the book to school. They said the teacher always asked the class to bring in books they liked. The twins clutched onto the book and said they wanted the teacher to read the book to the class. When the twins came home from school, they said the teacher really liked the book, but there wasn't enough time to read it today, so they left the book at school to be read tomorrow.

Two days later, the mother's custody time began, and the book went with the twins to the mother's home. Who would have imagined the book about secrets would have caused a rage of paranoia and anger in the mother? The mother was infuriated and accused the father of trying to brainwash the children about secrets.

That night the father came home to hear his young twins' voices on the answering machine. They were crying, disoriented and very upset. "Daddy, Daddy, can I hear you? Can I hear you? The secret wasn't worth it, the secret wasn't worth it!" In the back round, an adult voice could be heard, "Mary and Janet, get off the phone, you know the rules, your mother said no phone calls to your father's *ever*!" The telephone message ended.

Two days later, when the father had his next visit with his children, he asked the twins what had happened to the book and why had they called him from their mother's home. The twins both said they did not know what the father was talking about. He told them about the message and the twins both said, "Daddy, we didn't call you." He assured them that they did, and they repeated, "Daddy, we didn't call you, don't you think we would remember?"

Unfortunately, even the mental health professionals involved in this complicated case were unable to provide much help to the children in this family. The mother's ability to convince her children that she needed to keep secrets from the father undermined the father's ability to maintain a healthy relationship with his children. Even as a young adults, these children were unable to share simple experiences or aspects of their life with their father without being cautious and guarded with their information.

LYING

"I need you to tell your father a little white lie." Asking a child to lie to the other parent is another form of emotional abuse. Six- year-old Margaret stated to her father, "Mommy said I wasn't supposed to tell you. She told me it was OK to tell a 'little lie,' that I was sick and stayed home from school. But really, Daddy, I wasn't sick. I was fine. Mommy just wanted me to stay home with her because she didn't want to be alone and yesterday was her birthday."

Teaching a child to lie erodes a basic moral fiber in the child, and can create a lifelong dilemma. "If my parent asked me to lie, then lying must be alright." Yet, society, school, church and friends expect a different moral standard from the child. This contradictory message to children is confusing and can seriously undermine a child's perception of reality.

Again, the younger the child, the more susceptible they are to the game. A young child will comply with a parent's request to lie, because they innately trust their parent and will naively obey instructions.

Lying also teaches children to have a tremendous disrespect for the other parent. The child may mirror the attitude of the parent who lies. "If Mom thinks it is alright to lie to Dad, then why shouldn't *I*." A parent who lies to the other parent (or asks the child to lie) is adversely *modeling* for the child. The message to the child is that the other parent is not worthy of a truthful or meaningful relationship.

JUST LISTENING

Another game played frequently is *Just Listening* to telephone conversations between the child and the other parent. Many parents will actually tell the child what to say and how to respond when the other parent calls.

Take for example, the father in Nevada who had moved to a town several hundred miles away after divorce. As a live away parent, he called his children frequently for continuing contact. When the father would call, the mother would routinely listen to the conversation on the other telephone. She would then instruct the children on how to respond to the father's questions and comments.

Sometimes the mother would instruct the children to plead with their father to come home. 'Come home, Daddy. We miss you." "Daddy, when are you coming back?" The mother programmed her children intentionally to make the father feel guilty, and in doing so placed her children in the middle of the parental emotions.

Other times the mother would listen in silently to gather information about the father and his relationship with the children. The mother would then use the information later to rehearse for the next telephone call.

When parents '*listen in*' on private conversations between a parent and a child they are actually diluting the child's relationship with the other parent. Again, the child cannot be spontaneous, loving or open to share their lives, feelings and experiences freely with the other parent.

IT'S PLAY TIME!
LET'S REHEARSE WHAT WE ARE GOING TO SAY AND DO!

"Bad Daddy, Bad Daddy, Daddy You Are Bad!"

When a parent plays '*Let's Rehearse*' with a child, they are able to control the child's behavior through practice and careful preparation. These parents anticipate certain situations, and will prepare the child in advance to support their motives.

Often, these parents are very domineering and are seen by the child as being very powerful. As a result of this power, children will follow the instructions to comply with the rehearsing parent, to make them "happy." These children may say horrible things to the other parent (as a result of the rehearsal and preparation) and may not realize the emotional impact their statements will have.

Children may actually enjoy the game of *Let's Rehearse* at a young age. However, as the child grows older and matures, they have been taught that harmful and emotionally damaging interactions are 'appropriate,' 'normal' and 'nothing to worry about.' These children have been *trained* to exercise negative feelings and actions toward a loved one, and are then rewarded by the rehearsing parent for their '*performance.*' Essentially, through this type of brainwashing, the programming parent is in control of the child's emotions, as if they were dolls or emotional robots. These parents are actually using *play therapy* to involve their children in the psychological warfare.

Take for example, the mother in Alabama who would repeatedly discredit the father, telling their three young children negative things about him. After returning from a one week vacation with their mother the young children went to visit their father. They arrived at their father's house performing and singing, "Bad Daddy, Bad Daddy! Daddy you are bad!" The children sang their song repeatedly during the entire two-day stay with their father. They would dance and run around the house, away from their father, almost like a game of tag yelling and singing, "Bad Daddy, Bad Daddy, Daddy you are bad!"

When the father confronted the mother she merely smirked at him and said, "I don't know what you are talking about. Perhaps the children really feel that way. In fact, they must feel that way. Why else could they say it? Certainly you don't think I would say anything like that in front of the children, let alone make it into a song!"

Parents who engage in *Let's Rehearse* usually use many other brainwashing methods. If they have more physical time with the child, especially during the younger years, these parents are able to '*condition*' the child against the other parent. The coercion and brainwashing of children is easy, especially if there is continuous momentum and uninterrupted physical access to the child.

Take for example, the mother in Pennsylvania was able to orchestrate scenes at transitions. Before the father would come to the mother's home to pick up his child the mother would rehearse with the child to tell the father that he did not want to go with him for the overnight visit. When the father would arrive to pick up his son, the son would 'perform' his speech and tell the father he did not want to go with him. The mother would then act surprised at the child's mood and comment, and would support the child's request to stay home with her.

The mother would say to the father, "Well, I guess he really doesn't want to go with you today, it's too bad, but I can't *make* him go." "In fact, I'm not ever going to make him go or do anything he doesn't want to do." She would then take the small child by the hand and escort him back inside the house and close the door with the father still standing there.

Parents who play *Let's Rehearse* may view the ex-partner as *the enemy*, and fear that the child will show positive emotions toward the other parent. Until these parents feel they have regained control of the child's emotions, they may temporarily view the child as the enemy, as well. These parents need to control the child in an effort to maintain control of the current custodial arrangement and their relationship with the ex-partner. Some parents may feel threatened and the need to control the child originates in their effort to protect their custody arrangement or they may fear a change of custody could occur.

Take for example, the family in Arkansas that was ordered to submit to a psychological evaluation. The family was ordered by the court to see a psychiatrist to help them manage the post divorce conflict. The court might have had the best interest of the children in mind when ordering therapy, but this more scrutinized environment caused a threatened mother to take more drastic measures to control her children's mind, actions and responses to the father.

In this case, there was evidence that the mother was trying to control her children and brainwash them against the father. Before meeting with the psychiatrist the mother would make the children *practice* what they were going to say, and rehearse their lines before they would arrive at her office. These children had little chance to be honest or spontaneous with the psychiatrist because the mother had physical custody and drove them to and from the psychiatrist's office.

At one session the psychiatrist requested a meeting with the mother and father together, arranging for the children to arrive later in the session by the baby-sitter. Knowing in advance that the children would be delivered later in the session the mother used this opportunity to coach her children. She rehearsed with them how to walk into the room: "When you arrive at Dr. Carol's office, walk directly over to Mommy and sit in Mommy's lap and give her a BIG kiss to say hello. It is very important."

The children practiced what they learned and upon entering the office did exactly as the mother had instructed. The mother then held the small children in her lap, gloating with pleasure. But after a few minutes the children became restless, and it was obvious the mother was beginning to struggle to keep them in her lap. Fortunately, Dr. Carol was astute and observed the children's uneasiness.

When Dr. Carol encouraged the children to step down and play with the toys on the floor the mother held onto her children a little tighter, not allowing them to leave her lap. It became obvious she was losing control of the children and she stated, "What's wrong children, you must be nervous, we all know you want to sit with Mommy." The children paused, but the psychiatrist was able to encourage them off her lap and onto the floor.

This mother was threatened, and she was afraid her children would say hello or express affection to the father in the presence of the psychiatrist. Just prior to the meeting the mother had exposed her insecurities. She telephoned the psychiatrist to *'remind her'* that the children did not like the father and they were afraid of him. "The children are so afraid of their father that many times they do not want to go to the his house, even for a short visit. I don't know why I'm telling you this, I'm sure you'll be able to observe this at our meeting this afternoon."

THE INTERROGATOR

"Children perceive the adults with whom they converse as well-informed people who question them only to test their knowledge. Children find it difficult to understand how they could possess important information unknown to an adult. In response to an interview, children attempt to determine what the adult expects to hear and then answer accordingly. They exhibit what is known as acquiescence - responding 'yes' to questions in an attempt to satisfy the expectations they attribute to the adult interviewing them." [5]

Terence Campbell, Ph.D.

There are many ways in which a parent can interrogate children and receive information about their lives in the other parent's home. And again, the differentiation between basic information gathering and interrogation can become quite complicated. There is a broad spectrum that occurs between a normal conversation with a child about their 'other life' and actual interrogation.

Many parents are simply curious about their child's life when apart, and are hoping to share some commonality when talking to them about their time spent with the other parent. Other parents, however, may become obsessed with the information and what occurs at the other parent's home. This is when the game becomes emotionally dangerous. Therefore, it is important to make an effort to understand how and *why* parents gather information, the underlying reasons for 'needing to know' and how the information is actually obtained and then used.

Take for example, the three young children in Texas who have short visits with their father, usually an overnight visit one day during the week. The visits begin after the father's work, from 4:00 PM until 7:00 AM the following morning. The father's profession did not allow for much flexibility, so the exchanges occurred at the mother's home.

When the father would return the children to the mother's home in the morning she would sometimes greet all of them nicely at the front door, and other times she would not appear at all, leaving the front door slightly ajar for the children to enter on their own. Often, the children would enter their mother's home not knowing what to expect, the 'nice mother' or the 'scary and angry mother.' As a result, these children were often very apprehensive at the time of transitions.

Once inside her home, the mother would sit her small children down on the couch. She would then carefully place them next to each other and she would sit on the floor in front of them, on her knees, talking to them in a sweet and saccharin voice. She may not have been nice to them when they walked in the door, angry that the father had time with them. Now, however, when they were placed immediately on the couch, the mother was 'very pleasant,' and she made them feel comfortable, offering them a sweet treat and hot chocolate to celebrate their reunion. She needed something from her children. She needed information.

The mother would then begin to ask her young three children questions about their overnight visit with the father. She would ask them to describe, in detail, each and every thing that had happened in the previous 15 hours.

"Oh darling's, tell me what you and Daddy did last night? "Did you have a good time?" "Did you go out to dinner? "Where did Daddy take you to dinner?" "Did someone else go with you?" "Did you know that Daddy asked me to join you for dinner, but I had other important plans?" "Did Daddy have anything to drink last night?" "I thought so ...." "What time did you go to bed? "All of you?"

A parent may not be aware that the ex-partner is interrogating the children. In fact, children may not be aware that the questions being asked are inappropriate or harmful. How could young children be aware of the techniques of interrogation? Young children do not know about appropriate boundaries and do not have the knowledge or cognitive experience to understand that a parent would intentionally harm them.

In her excellent book, *Understanding the Borderline Mother,* Christine Lawson, Ph.D., describes the young boy who is slapped across the face by his mother.

"When young children are deliberately hurt by their mothers, their first instinct is to repress recognition of their mothers as the source of their pain. A toddler whose mother slapped him across the face looked at his mother and exclaimed, "Somebody hit me." The young child needs to preserve the image of mother as good in order to survive psychologically...." [6]

Children experience their parents for who they are. They do not have a form of reference or the emotional maturity to differentiate how they are being treated. As in the example above, children cannot consciously analyze or interpret why the mother was asking them so many questions, or why the subject matter, 'Daddy,' is so important to her.

The Interrogator is often very difficult to detect. Once a child is out of a parent's physical custody, there is really no way to know how they are being treated. As described by Lawson: *"The[borderline] witches children live in terror of her power. The look in her eyes strikes fear in their hearts. Words alone can shatter their souls."* [7]

Take for example, the father who lived in Virginia. This father paid very close attention to each of his four children's comments, and was able to identify that his ex-spouse was interrogating the children. When the children would visit their father they would state, "Mommy asks so many questions about what we do when we are with you."

When the children were young, the visits with the father were of shorter duration. During these years it was easier for the mother to question the children because she could ask, "What did you and Daddy do last night?" Information was very recent, and the children could recall it easily.

As the custody and visitation situation changed, whereby the father was given longer blocks of time with the children, it was more difficult for the mother to interrogate the children or receive accurate information. Instead of having one-night visits (making it easier for the children to recall facts) the interrogating mother had to change her tactics. This mother needed to broaden her realm of questioning, for example, she would ask:

"Now tell me, what was the *funniest* thing that happened at Daddy's house?"

"What was the *saddest* thing that happened?"

"Did anyone get in trouble when you were at Daddy's? Oh, how awful, how did Daddy punish you? Did he spank you? Were you sent to your room?"

"Who *cried* the most at Daddy's house? Why did you cry?"

"Who was the most *scared* at Daddy's? What was the *scariest* thing that happened at Daddy's?"

The fact that the mother actually changed her methods of interrogation validated her motive to uncover how her children's time was spent with their father. Even after years of divorce, this mother was compelled to interrogate her children. She actually designated their first day together (after parenting time with the father) as *"Let's Get Reacquainted Day."*

The father learned about this from his oldest son, who was now 13 years old. One day the son voluntarily remarked, "It's such a drag. Every Tuesday at Mom's, after our five days with you, we just go home after school. She won't even let us go to our practices or stay after school for special projects. She makes all of us stay together, and all we do is talk." Then he mumbled "about you."

The father asked, "Are you sure about this?" The son replied, "Yes, I'm sure, it's called *'Let's Get Reacquainted Day.'* Ask our coaches, we're never there on Tuesday. What's really weird is it seems like the only thing we talk about is you, and all the things we did at your house."

Essentially, these children were programmed and *required* to *'share'* with the mother the "most important and significant *'things'* that happened during their time with the father."

In another example, a father in Illinois discovered that his children were being interrogated when he was given the opportunity to review letters the mother had written to the children's therapists, school and extracurricular instructors.

When confronted about her methods of examining her children, the mother refused to admit it stating, "I could care less about what goes on at the father's home. Honestly, I don't even ask the children what they do there."

The letters revealed otherwise. It became obvious the mother was not only grilling and investigating her children about the father, but that she was actually *cross-examining* them during her interrogation. One child would give an account of what they recalled of their experience at their father's. The mother would then cross-examine the other child to determine if the information was accurate, or if the child was telling the truth.

In the last example, the children were put in the middle of a dangerously seductive vice. They learned that enjoying their time with their father was obviously not acceptable to the mother. Perhaps in an effort to downplay the events at the father's, or to 'save themselves from further grief,' one child would portray a vague story to the mother. The other child would observe the mother's unhappy response and would react by giving a more vivid account or having a *'better recall'* about the events that happened at the father's home. This example illustrates what some experts call a *"love triangle,"* when the reality of trust, honesty and emotions are clouded by manipulation and severe issues of loyalty. The relationship between the mother and each child was affected, as well as the relationship between the siblings.

In this scenario, the child providing the most information to the mother was *rewarded*. The child providing the *vague information* was consequently punished for (1) not telling the mother the truth (instilling guilt) (2) protecting the father (being disloyal) and (3) not being as loyal as the other child (second best and loser of the game).

BRAIN TWIRLING

All the examples above are considered *brain twirling*, but some of the emotional games are more overt than others. One of the best examples of ultimate *brain twirling* is *Opposite Day Game*. When playing *Opposite Day*, the parent instructs the child they can only say the word 'yes' or the word 'no.' The child is given the choice of whether they want to say *yes or no*. If there is more than one child playing the game with the parent, the children have to select the same word. Once the *opposite day word* is chosen, the parent and the children can begin to play.

Everything communicated during the game starts with a question. If the question is not answered with the word chosen (yes or no), the child is declared 'out' and can no longer play the game.

> ***Take for example,*** the mother in Mississippi who thoroughly enjoyed playing *Opposite Day Game* with her five small children. She enjoyed the game because she could manipulate her young children's minds, preparing and training them to have diminished emotional responses to others. In turn, the children enjoyed the game because nothing meant anything when you played, and there was always a *surprise* at the end of the game. Besides, it always seemed to make *"Mommy laugh."* Imagine you are 4 years old and you have chosen the word *"Yes."* Your mother is now going to ask you a series of questions:
>
> | | |
> |---|---|
> | "Is today Monday? | Yes. |
> | Is it sunny outside? | Yes. |
> | Is it raining outside? | Yes |
> | Is today Wednesday? | Yes |
> | Are we playing Opposite Day Game? | Yes |
> | Is Opposite Day Game fun? | Yes |
> | Do you like to play Opposite Day Game? | Yes |
> | Did you ask Mommy to play Opposite Day Game? | Yes |
> | Do you love Mommy? | Yes |
> | Do you want to live with Mommy? | Yes |
> | Do you think Mommy is the best Mommy in the whole world? | Yes. |
> | Do you like candy? | Yes |
> | Is this a fun game? | Yes |
> | Are you scared of Daddy? | Yes |
> | Is Daddy mean? | Yes |

Do you love Mommy?	Yes
Do you like Mommy's new friend?	Yes
Does Daddy spank you at his house?	Yes
Is Daddy mean?	Yes
Do you hate Daddy?	Yes
Do you hate Daddy's girlfriend?	Yes
Do you love Mommy?	Yes

When playing *Opposite Day,* a child will often hesitate about answering a question such as, "Do you hate Daddy?" Nevertheless, the game continues with the child nervously laughing when he answers yes. Soon, he has no feelings of the emotional impact of his statements, and he wants his treat at the end of the game.

This type of game is emotionally confusing to children, and they are taught to disregard and suppress their own feelings and emotions.

WHO LOVES ME MORE?

In the game, *Who Loves Me More*, children learn to fight for the affections of their parent. Small children are particularly vulnerable to this game. Parents who play this type of game are searching for the loyalty and love they are missing, and they need their children to prove their love.

A child can begin the game by grabbing playfully at their mother saying, "I love Mommy!" Another child then playfully grabs at the mother and says, "No, I love Mommy more!" At first, the children are laughing and glancing at each other playfully, anticipating with excitement what will happen next. The mother begins to applaud her children for their affections, as the children become more competitive, aggressive and excited as the game progresses.

Finally, the children's excitement and competitiveness intensify, until one child becomes so frustrated they begin to cry. The mother has ultimately received the attention and gratification she needed, and is reassured that she is loved by her children (to the point they will fight over her.) She is now able to be a *real* mother and provide *comfort and cuddles* to the injured child, and praise to the other child for being so loyal and strong.

Children may never overcome the emotional traumas of psychological warfare.

All the examples above are, and should be considered, emotional abuse.

Some Ideas and Suggestions to Help Diffuse the Effects of Psychological Warfare

➤ In all situations, try to remain as objective as possible allowing you to observe your child's response and reactions to certain events.

➤ Listen to your child carefully. Do not brush off alarming comments.

➤ Remember to document date specific interactions that concern you as a parent.

➤ Remember that these psychological games and experiences are emotionally painful, harmful and can be very confusing and frustrating to a child.

➤ Evaluate whether you (as a parent) are also contributing to, or playing an emotional game with your child.

➤ Evaluate if you are being drawn into the 'mind game' of the other parent.

> ➤ If you are drawn in, at any level, recognize your involvement and stop the unhealthy interaction as soon as possible.

➤ Observe the level of your child's involvement in 'the game.'

> ➤ Have they been rehearsed?
> ➤ Are they asking questions that reflect 'spying' or 'ease-dropping?'
> ➤ Are they making comments or asking questions that are inappropriate for their age?

➤ Be persistent in your attempts to have contact with your children, even if visits are un-pleasant or if psychological warfare is obvious.

➤ Establish an exchange location that is neutral. As discussed in Chapter 14, a parent's home may be a very powerful location to play a game.

➤ Talk to your attorney or mental health professional about different approaches to eliminate the power of the mind games.

➤ Talk to your child openly and honestly about how you feel when they say things that are hurtful, or when they act in ways that hurt you.

> ➤ This 'reality check' for children may help them understand that what they are being taught (or asked to do by the other parent) is not appropriate.

➢ Establish telephone guidelines between the two households. If your child is not able to talk to you privately and without interference from the other parent, then perhaps you can make arrangements with a third party to assist you. See Chapter 17 for different options regarding telephone and other communications with your child.

➢ If your family has engaged in psychotherapy, assure that appointments are scheduled equally between the homes and include appointments during your custodial time.

  ➢ This assures that you [or your designee] are driving the child to the appointment, eliminating some of the emotional pressure a child may experience before meeting with a therapist.

  ➢ Assure there is adequate time between a visit with the other parent and the appointment with the therapist. This allows the child time to 'debrief' or 'decompress' before entering the therapist's office.

  ➢ The goal is to allow the child to express their *own ideas and feelings* versus the rehearsed or brainwashed version they may be saying on behalf of the programming parent.

➢ If your work schedule does not allow you to drive the child to the appointment, then recruit someone close to you to help. A friend, grandparent, aunt or uncle can help you in situations such as this.

  ➢ Relying on the other parent for this kind of assistance may strengthen their ability to emotionally affect or brainwash the child, during your custodial time, on the way to the therapist's office.

➢ If your family is involved in litigation, request that the court appoint a mediator, parenting coordinator or a special master to intervene in your case. Ask for a list of professionals to choose from.

  ➢ Request that the individual has the appropriate credentials, and is familiar working with families of divorce involving parental alienation and high conflict situations.

  ➢ Do not be afraid to ask questions regarding how a divorce professional is viewed in the community, and what their outcomes involving family therapy and evaluations have been.

(Endnotes)

[1] Clawar, S. S., & Rivlin, B.V. (1991). *Children Held Hostage: Dealing with Programmed and Brainwashed Children*, Chicago, Illinois: American Bar Association, p. 91.

[2] id., p 96.

[3] id., p. 73.

[4] id., p. 81.

[5] Campbell, T. W. (1998). *Smoke and Mirrors: The Devastating Effect of False Sexual Abuse Claims*. New York: Insight Books, Plenum Press. p. 102., 1998, page 102.

[6] Lawson, C. A. (2000). *Understanding the Borderline Mother, Helping Her Children Transcend the Intense, Unpredictable, and Volatile Relationship*. Northvale, New Jersey: Jason Aronson, Inc. p. 139.

[7] id., p. 123.

16.

The Telephone and Other Communication Devices

Unfortunately, the telephone and other telecommunication devices can be used as an intrusive and manipulative way to bother a parent during their custodial time with the children. Unless closely monitored, the telephone, pagers and e-mail can significantly interfere with your relationship and *your time* with your children.

Except for the long distance parent, telephone calls, pagers and e-mail messages should be considered interruptions of *parenting time* and visitation with a child. The other parent should limit their communication to your home, and the communication should occur only in urgent or emergent situations. Your children *and you* have a right to the visitation free from interference from the other parent.

It is very important to acknowledge that the issue of communication is a very tricky one. Experts and the courts applaud frequent and uninterrupted telephone communication and access between a parent and child. Unfortunately, as we have seen in other sections of this book, the legal systems efforts to enhance better communication between a parent and child, simultaneously gives the malicious parent a license to interfere.

A malicious and interfering parent may use the telephone and other communication devices to intentionally interrupt the parenting time of the other parent with the child. The interfering parent may use these communication devices to:

➢ Dilute the time the child spends with the other parent.

➢ Grill and investigate how the child's time is being spent at the other parents home, making detailed inquiries about the child's time.

➢ Focus on small details when the child is visiting the other parent.

➢ Inquire if the child is 'alright' or 'scared' at the other parents home, asking, "Is everything okay, I just have a funny feeling?"

➢ Telephone at inappropriate times, such as early in the morning or very late at night, to disrupt the visit.

➢ Ask to talk with the child just before leaving for school, to make sure everything is all right. The parent may ask the child if they finished their homework, or did they need anything at school. The parent may even posture the question stating they will be near the school that day and could drop off anything the child needs.

➢ Ask to speak with the child just before bedtime. This interferes with the other parent's bedtime routine and can be very disruptive, especially to young children.

In their excellent book, *Caught in the Middle,* Garrity and Baris include telephone communication in their parenting plan considerations.

"Telephone access: Ordinarily children should be allowed to telephone each parent from the other's home and should be assured of privacy during these calls. Sometimes, however, numerous non-emergency calls to or from the other parent constitute an annoyance and are disruptive to the visits. When this occurs, the time and frequency of telephone calls need to be limited so as not to intrude on family life. They should not, for example, be made at mealtime or homework time or after the child's bedtime." [1]

A parent can easily use the telephone and other communication devices to manipulate or dilute a child's time with the other parent. It is important to realize that these parents may be unhealthy, and are often consumed by the need to have complete control of the child.

Take for example, the mother in Oregon who had the majority of custodial time with her child (70/30) yet she would continually make efforts to disrupt the father's visitation time with their child. The mother was able to dilute the child's visit with his father with the use of the telephone. She would tell the son (before his visit with the father) she was planning something very special when he returned to her home. She also told the son she *may be* calling him at his father's if she needed to confirm her special plans. In reality, the mother had every intention of calling the son at the father's home to interrupt his visit.

The mother would then call the father's house and leave the following message, "David is expecting my call. I told him I would call and let him know what day we are going to the Blazer's game next week. He needs to know this information because he wants to invite a friend. Please be sure to give him the message, as he is expecting my phone call. In fact, I need him to return my call so that I know he got the message and I can move forward with our plans."

In this example, if the father had the son return the telephone call, the mother's manipulative use of the telephone achieved the following:

➤ Interfered with the child's visitation time with the father.

➤ Deliberately crafted an incident to emotionally engage the child, even though he was physically at the father's home.

➤ Created a competitive scenario; the mother has something more fun to do than the father.

➤ Created unnecessary contact with the child as this could have easily been discussed and planned during the mother's custodial time.

On the other hand, if the father chose not to return the telephone call, the mother would be able to present a negative issue to her child during his next visit with her.

"Did your father tell you about the plans to go to the Blazer's basketball game? He didn't? Do you see how awful your father is? I told you I would be calling, and it was such a simple message. Now we can't go because I didn't hear back from you. It's all because your father is so angry with me and refuses to cooperate. I'm so sorry. I should have known he wouldn't tell you and purchased the tickets anyway. Now there aren't any tickets available."

There are now hurt feelings, anger, conflict and both the son *and* the mother can be mad at the father. Through the manipulative use of the telephone the mother created an alliance with her son and successfully diluted his time with his father.

What is a Parent to Do?
Fortunately, Parents Do Have Options!

The ground rules for the telephone, pagers and e-mail have been divided into the following separate *boundary levels*. These three categories pertain mostly to parents who share physical custody of the child with frequent visitation and parenting time. Ideas for *Live Away* parents are addressed later in this chapter.

Δ   Unlimited Telephone Contact
Δ   Problematic Telephone Contact
Δ   Restricted Telephone Contact

Ground Rules for the Telephone

❑ *Unlimited Telephone Contact*

Free unlimited telephone contact with each parent and no problems of manipulation or interference noted or suspected. Good luck and continue to keep up the good work!

❑ *Problematic Telephone Contact*

One or both parents are insisting on telephone contact with the child during the other parent's custodial time.

The telephone contact is disruptive to one or both of the households.
One parent may refuse to acknowledge there is a problem regarding the frequency and content of the communication with the child during the other parent's custodial time.

One parent is using the telephone to stay connected to the child and the other parent during visits, instead of allowing them to have uninterrupted time together.

Establishing Guidelines for Problematic Telephone Contact

❑ If one parent is determined to have telephone access with the child during the other parents visitation, follow Garrity and Baris' ideas of limiting the telephone access by delineating when the telephone calls can and will be accepted in *your home*.

❑ Explain the guidelines clearly to your children so that there can be no mistake or misinterpretation of the meaning and intent of the rules.

❑ If the other parent is difficult, and is having a hard time respecting the communication boundaries established for your home:

    ❑ Schedule a mediation session to discuss the guidelines with the other parent, with a follow-up letter of explanation.

    ❑ Write your own letter to the other parent in (non-angry terms) stating how you would like telephone access to be handled in *your home*, or,

    ❑ Have your attorney address the issue with your ex-partner, even making it a part of your settlement agreement or parenting plan.

❑ Monitor the use of the telephone closely for several months to assure that telephone access and communication with the other parent is acceptable and not disruptive in *your home*.

❑ Without infringing on your child's privacy, keep a journal of the frequency and duration of the telephone calls your child has with the other parent. Most importantly, observe and document (in brief notes) the emotional impact these telephone calls have on your child.

    ❑ Observe your child (as objectively as you can) after each telephone call, page or e-mail contact. Note your child's reaction to the call. Is your child sad, happy, overly happy, crying, giddy, nervous, hyperactive, angry or any other reaction?

    ❑ In the same log, document your personal feelings.

    "I wish she wouldn't call. The children are upset,"
    "Gee that's nice that we can do this with the kids," etc.

    [A sample telephone log is included at the end of the chapter]

❑ After two or three months review the log and analyze the nature, content and patterns that have developed regarding communication with the other parent in your home. If you do not think the telephone communication is productive, and that it is treading on your personal territory with the children, then you may need to make some changes.

 ❑ Review the log with an objective close friend, family member or counselor to get neutral feedback about your particular situation.

 ❑ Remember, once the pattern and practice of routine telephone calls is established it may not be easy to alter the *status quo.*

❑ *Do not* use the log for court proceedings.

❑ *Do not* use the log as a punitive device or share the content with your children.

❑ *Do not* use the log to retaliate against anyone in your family, including your child or your ex-partner. (To do so may result in losing your child's trust and confidence and may arm the other parent with a legitimate complaint about you.)

Even an ordinary and uncomplicated life can become hectic for individuals. The telephone/communication log is simply a method to assist in the assessment of appropriate boundaries and communication. The primary goal of the log is to evaluate the use of the telephone and other communication devices to help a parent manage life in their own home. The telephone log will help a parent determine if the telephone (or other communication device) is being used inappropriately or manipulatively by the other parent, to undermine visitation with the children.

❑ *Restricted Contact:*

Frequent telephone contact is wanted by other parent, but the situation is not comfortable for the children, the custodial parent or amenable to the visit.

The telephone contact from the other parent is disruptive and non-productive.

One parent is experiencing difficulty with the communication issue when the children are in their home.

Establishing Guidelines for Restricted Communication

❑ Continue or start a telephone log to help identify and narrow your concerns.

❑ Restrict the hours of telephone contact even more. Be more specific about the days and times the children will be available to receive telephone calls from the other parent. Be precise.

❑ Assess what time will be the least invasive in *your home* to receive a telephone call from the other parent. Carefully define the hours that telephone calls will be accepted. Delineate, "Judy should call between the hours of 5:00 and 6:00 PM."

❑ Use a mediator, counselor or attorney if you need help drafting an agreement. *Do not give up on your right to privacy with your children!*

❑ If you can afford it, install a second telephone line dedicated to the 'interfering parent' with an answering machine connected to that line.

❑ Review the substance of the telephone calls for validity and content.

   ❑ Was the telephone call urgent, necessary, or manipulative?

❑ Would it be *reasonable* to consider the telephone call 'deliberate interference?'

❑ Assess the situation and make a decision. Should the children return the telephone call to the other parent now, tomorrow morning or wait until the other parent's next visit with the children.

❑ Remember, you are monitoring the communication process for a good reason. You are trying to free your child emotionally, so they can enjoy themselves when they are with you, without unnecessary interruption of your visit.

❑ Assure the other parent understands your position and knows the guidelines regarding telephone and e-mail communication in your home.

❑ Explain that if there is truly an urgent matter, the children will return the telephone call.

❑ Non-urgent issues should be taken care of the next time the other parent has the child.

If *restricted contact* is necessary, the manipulative or vindictive parent may accelerate their efforts to increase the frequency of communication with the child. These malicious parents may sense the need for autonomy and independence by the other parent. Even the idea of the other parent's self-sufficiency may threaten the malicious parent, and may increase their need to intrude in the other parent's life.

A malicious parent may begin to *create* situations to justify and substantiate their need to telephone the child. For example, these parents may fabricate issues, claiming they are calling to '*relay an urgent message*' or need to '*coordinate information and activities*' for the child.

Remedies for efforts such as these are addressed in other chapters of the book. In short, be sure to talk to the other individuals involved in your child's life, such as coaches, teachers and instructors to ensure that information is being relayed accurately to both homes. This reduces the opportunities for the other parent to call your home to '*relay information.*' It also empowers you to be in control of the same information.

Summary of Ideas to Promote Efficient Use of the Telephone

❑ Turn all telephone ringers off at a certain hour (the hour that you designated) and turn the answering machine volume off. You can monitor for calls but it shouldn't be necessary. The other parent should only be calling during the designated times and for matters of importance.

❑ Restrict the hours the other parent can call the children. Assess what time will be the least invasive in *your home* to receive a telephone call from the other parent. Carefully define the hours that telephone calls will be accepted. Delineate, "Judy should call between the hours of 5:00 and 6:00 PM."

❑ If the other parent needs to telephone your home, instruct them to leave a detailed message, so that a return telephone call is not necessary.

❑ Some parents may portray their telephone call as urgent or emergent in an effort to receive a return telephone call. Be careful of this manipulative maneuver.

❑ Inform the other parent that if they do not leave a clearly detailed message, as requested, their telephone call *will not be returned*.

❑ Be careful not to react to a situation such as this, "Hi, this is Kate and it is very important that I talk to either you or one of the children right away. So call me back as soon as you can."

❑ The sense of urgency transmitted via the telephone can create a contagious reaction and often the curiosity is too luring to resist. Take your time and remember to ask yourself, "What could be so important that she couldn't have left a detailed message, especially when I specifically asked her to?"

✶   ✶   ✶   ✶   ✶

Establishing these simple boundaries for limited and restricted communication will help any parent maintain some autonomy in their own home. The same rules should apply to e-mail and pagers. Monitor the use of these devices, and assess if they are being used inappropriately to interfere with the child's time with the other parent.

Live Away Parents

If you are a live away parent, telephone communication can definitely work against you. Telephone calls can be restricted and manipulated so that you cannot have access to your children. In his article, *Divorce Related Malicious Mother Syndrome*, Ira Turkat states in Criterion 2B: Denying Uninhibited Telephone Access:

> "Given the physical absence of one parent, the telephone plays an important role in maintaining the bond between child and non-residential parent. Individuals suffering from Divorce Related Malicious Mother Syndrome engage in an array of actions designed to circumvent telephone access.
>
> A father calls to speak to this children as was told that they were not at home when in fact he could hear their voices in the background.
>
> When one father called to speak with his children, the mother put him on 'hold' informed no one, and them left him there.
>
> Knowing that the children's father was away on vacation, one mother encouraged them to leave several messages on his answering machine to call back immediately only if he would like some additional visitation time with his children." [2]

If you are one of these fathers there are ways to make communication work more to your advantage. Turkat continues:

> "Some fathers find the alienation attempts so painful and fruitless that they eventually are extinguished from calling their children; they simply 'give up.' Placed in a no-win scenario, the father's 'abandonment' (Hodges, 1991) unfortunately achieves the precise result aimed for by the individual suffering from Divorce Related Malicious Mother Syndrome." [3]

If you are a live away parent, there are ways to make communication work more effectively to your advantage. Examples may include:

❑ Be persistent in your intentions to have contact with your child.

❑ Think of alternative ways to communicate with your child.

❑ Keep an accurate, date noted log of your attempts to communicate with your child and the response from the other parent's home.

❑ Identify an individual, hopefully a mutual friend or family member, who will help you in your communication efforts with your child.

❑ Arrange with the school (or other neutral party such as a coach, church, family friend) a time to speak with your child (on a regular basis), assuring that your communication will not be interrupted, influenced or overheard.

    ❑ This solution provides a 'neutral setting' to communicate with your child. A setting where the obstructive parent cannot interfere with the content or duration of the conversation. The child will feel less burdened and may truly enjoy the 'space' provided to communicate with you.

❑ Assure that the 'neutral third party' understands the reasons for your efforts to communicate with your child. Explain the situation carefully to the third party to avoid further misunderstandings or alienation.

❑ When you see your child, explain to them simply and unemotionally the efforts you have made to talk with them and the difficulties (brushed over) that you have encountered.

❑ "Gee, you know it is really hard to get a hold of you at your Mom's house. Do you have any ideas on how we can communicate more often?"

    ❑ "Gee, you guys are so busy over there, let's think of a better way to talk."

Do not become a victim of the other parent's manipulation!
Work with your child to solve the communication problem,
and let your child be part of a constructive solution.

Most importantly, show your child that you really care!
Stay in touch!

Regarding the Telephone and Other Communication Devices

The communication policy with the children should be fair and equal when using the parallel parenting model. If one parent requests non-interference during their parenting time, the policy should also extend to the other parent's home. Therefore, each parent should respect the non-interference principle and the legitimate use of the telephone, pager or e-mail.

Establishing *appropriate boundaries* regarding communication between a parent and a child should be considered a positive proactive parenting strategy. However, it is important to remember that the courts and experts prefer free and unlimited contact between a parent and a child. In addition, the malicious and vindictive parent may create obstacles to confuse and prevent the implementation of necessary communication boundaries.

With this in mind, the boundaries defined regarding communication should be presented very carefully. This can be achieved by demonstrating a cooperative attitude regarding the policy of communication with the child. "Yes, I want my child to have open communication with the other parent, *and this is what will work the best in my home.*"

Setting appropriate limits facilitates communication with the other parent, and provides clear guidelines that best suit *your home* and *your lifestyle* with *your child.*

★   ★   ★   ★   ★

Guidelines and Examples for the Written Parenting Agreement may Include:

❑ Assure that the guidelines are equal and fair for both homes as it relates to your requests for privacy with the children.

❑ Both parents agree that it is important for the children to have uninterrupted time with each parent.

❑ Both parents agree that telephone contact, and contact with other communication devices, will be kept to a minimum during the other parent's custodial time.

❑ Both parents recognize and understand that these procedures are meant to enhance the parent/child relationship during each parent's parenting time. Both parents understand that these procedures are not intended to alienate a child from the other parent.

❑ Both parents will introduce these communication procedures into their normal family routine, *without being critical of the procedure*, or blaming the other parent for tying to interfere with access to the children.

❑ Both parents agree that if there is an urgent or emergent matter, then telephone communication will be necessary.

❑ An urgent or emergent matter is defined as:
    (Define) _____

❑ Each parent will ask the other individuals or entities involved in the child's life (schools, medical/dental offices, instructors, teachers, coaches) to notify *both homes* of information regarding the child (ren).

❑ Both parents understand that these routine communications between the other entities listed above are *not* of an urgent or emergent nature.

❑ Each parent agrees to leave a detailed message, if absolutely necessary, that does not require a return telephone call from the other parent. It should be noted that this should be a rare occasion.

❑ Both parents agree that if there is telephone communication between a parent and a child during the other parent's custodial time, that the telephone calls will be of appropriate content. For example, the parents agree they:

    ❑ *will not* tell the child how much they miss them.
    ❑ *will not* ask the child information about the other parent.

The Telephone and Other Communication Devices • 165

❑ *will not* ask the child about their plans with the other parent.

❑ *will not* discuss emotional issues that may upset the child.

❑ *will not* tell the child of plans they have made for when the child returns.

❑ *will not* tell the child disturbing or upsetting news.

❑ *will not* ask the child to call them back before they go to bed.

❑ *will not* create a situation whereby the child feels a need to call the parent back.

❑ other: _____

❑ If there must be communication between a parent and a child during the other parent's parenting time then these calls will occur:

❑ Example: _____

    (Every other day, every 3 days, one time per week, etc.)

❑ If there is to be communication between a parent and a child during the other parent's custodial time, then the following schedule for telephone communication will be used:

❑ *Father's Home:*

❑ Telephone calls will be accepted on: <u>Day of Week, Day of Weekend</u>

❑ Telephone calls will be accepted between the hours:

❑ _____ and _____ during the week (Monday - Friday)

❑ _____ and _____ on weekends (Saturday and Sunday)

❑ Telephone calls will be limited to _____ minutes/child.

❑ *Mother's Home:*

❑ Telephone calls will be accepted on: (from example above)

❑ Telephone calls will be accepted between the hours:

❑ _____ and _____ during the week (Monday - Friday)

❑ _____ and _____ on weekends (Saturday and Sunday)

❑ Telephone calls will be limited to _____ minutes/child.

❑ Both parents agree the guidelines above are to be strictly followed. If for any reason the guidelines above are not followed, then the parents agree that telephone communication may not be in the child's best interest and other arrangements will need to be made.

Sample Telephone Log

Date/time	*Reason for Telephone Call*	*Special Notes/Reactions*
Wed- 8/12	Mary called to tell the children how much she misses them.	Joey begins to cry.
Sun - 6/22	Mary calls to see what is going on. Mary tells Betsy she is going to get her a kitten as soon as Betsy comes home.	Betsy says she wants to go to her mother's now. She seems anxious and upset.

(Endnotes)

[1] Garrity, C. B. & Baris M. A. (1994) *Caught in the Middle: Protecting the Children of High Conflict Divorce*. New York: Lexington Books. p. 149.

[2] Turkat, I. D. (1995). Divorce Related Malicious Mother Syndrome, *Journal of Family Violence*, Volume 10, pp. 253-264.

[3] id.

17.

Illness, Parental Alienation and Munchausen by Proxy Syndrome

---

" The subjects all met the criteria for borderline or histrionic personality disorder."
Pope study, etc. al, (1982) [1]

"...some authors have referred to the 'delusional intensity of parental concern.'"
(Woolcott, Aceto, Rutt, Bloom & Glick, 1982)" [2]

"Munchausen by proxy syndrome is more a pathology of the parent-child
relationship than a pathology of self." [3]

Munchausen by proxy syndrome is a fascinating subject and surely one that cannot be described fully in this chapter. It is a genuine syndrome and may manifest itself in an unlikely candidate. The purpose of introducing this topic is to make parents aware of one aspect of parenting that may be easily overlooked during the different phases of separation and divorce.

When separated, parents are not physically present on a daily basis to view the care of their child in the other parent's custody. The examples in this chapter are presented to illustrate how seemingly normal parents may need their child to be ill to satisfy their own psychological needs, or to manipulate the child's time with the other parent.

In some cases, the stress of a separation and divorce may catapult a parent into a situation of Munchausen by proxy or parental alienation. These parents, *particularly mothers,* want and need their child to be sick. Loving and caring for children are considered basic natural instincts for human mothers. Sadly, some mothers exceed these basic parenting instincts, *needing the child to be sick*, so they can foster their own maternal instincts despite any reality of illness of the child.

Separation and divorce may intensify an affected mothers need to care for her child. For these mothers a change in the custody of the child, even sharing the child with the father two days a week, may trigger a strong emotional sense of loss. An affected mother may need to *'make up'* for the emotional time lost as the primary caretaker.

Take for example, the mother in Montana who was having a very difficult time managing the stress of her separation and divorce. This mother's anxiety and stress manifested itself as an inability to spend time alone. She would often tell her three small children they were sick so she could keep them home from school to be with her.

The children were too young to understand or know whether they were sick or not. They learned to enjoy missing school, and receiving the special attention bestowed upon them by their mother when they were 'sick.' In return, this mother was not faced with the ugly reality of being alone, and received the maternal gratification she desperately needed. This mother viewed her loss of custody several days a week as a "loss of precious time with her growing children." Keeping the children home from school fulfilled her needs to mother her children (on a part time basis) after divorce.

Unfortunately, as these children grew older they could not differentiate between a real illness or a "fake" illness as imposed on them by their mother. Because all three children had been involved, they were unable to observe illness between each other as a real or fabricated incident. These children had a difficult time in later years with their responsibility to school, work and social obligations.

Like their mother, the children had learned to cope with stress by 'creating' an illness or ailment to avoid stressful situations. Rather than having the confidence to pursue opportunities, these children would need to be sick or injured to avoid a possible failure. They had developed competing values: responsibility to self, school, work and society versus the need to stay home with their mother when she was lonely.

In this case the mental health professionals stated, "These are *'good children'* and to be *'good children'* they will comply with their mother's wants and needs." The underlying message to these *'good children'* was that their mother must know what is right, and we need to do what she wants (needs). Even when these children entered high school, the mother could persuade them to stay home with her when she was lonely or unable to cope with her life. She did this despite the negative impact this had on the children's academic progress and their personal growth.

Needing the child to be sick, and presenting the child for medical (or sometimes psychological) treatment, are indicators of a very complicated and severe emotional disorder defined as *Munchausen by proxy syndrome*. *Munchausen by proxy* is a very complex and multifaceted disorder. In another attempt to avoid criticism of being politically incorrect, it is important to note the following as described by Teresa Parnell and Deborah O. Day:

> "Because only a small number of documented cases have involved father or other caretakers as perpetrators, the term *mother* is used in this volume interchangeably with the terms such as *perpetrator* and *abusing parent*. Female pronouns are also used to refer to MBPS [Munchausen by proxy syndrome] perpetrators." [4]

Teresa Parnell and Deborah O. Day have done extensive research on Munchausen by proxy syndrome. They have published their work in their excellent book, *Munchausen by Proxy: Misunderstood Child Abuse*. Some of Parnell and Day's definitions of Munchausen by Proxy include:

> "…instead of an individual presenting him- or herself to a physician with false or induced symptoms, the individual (the parent) presented her child, thus a "by proxy " form of Munchausen was described…." [5]

> "…Specifically Munchausen by proxy syndrome, or MBPS, is a form of child abuse in which a caretaker fabricates or induces illness in a child. The caretaker then presents the child repeatedly for medical attention, all the while denying any knowledge of symptom origin. This form of child abuse can lead to physical and/or psychological damage to the victim, owing either to the direct actions of the perpetrator or to the intrusive medical procedures performed by doctors to diagnose the child's suspected illness. In 95% of cases, the child's mother is the perpetrator (Schreir & Libow, 1993A). [6]

"Mother-perpetrators' actions cover a broad spectrum, from misrepresenting symptoms (Giffin & Slovik, 1989) to tampering with lab specimens (Verity, Winckworth, Burman, Stevens & White, 1979), to actually creating symptoms of illness in their children." [6]

"The mother-perpetrator's chilling behavior often occurs against the backdrop of what is described as perfect, nurturing, self-sacrificing, and attentive parenting (Leeder, 1990). That a mother may deliberately harm her child in such a way, endangering a child's life and manipulating medical professionals, is, for many, unthinkable; the mere suggestion challenges a basic tenet of human motherhood. When expressed, these suspicions often engender passionate disbelief among physicians, nurses, and hospital administrators, who may rally to support the mother (Blix & Brack, 1988; Waller, 1983). Once this wave of resistance is partially squelched by confrontation of the perpetrator, the disbelief often extends to others who are drawn into the case, such as mental health professionals, child protection workers, attorneys and judges (Feldman, 1994; Sheridan, 1989; Waller, 1983; Zitelli, Seltman, & Shannon, 1987). When confronted, these mothers invariably deny or seriously minimize their actions in spite of evidence to the contrary. They are quite convincing, and the literature is replete with examples of their persuasiveness." [7]

In one example, a father in Wisconsin was not notified of his child's absences from school. During the divorce process the mother promised the father she would notify him if the child missed school. The father was unassuming, believed his ex-spouse and there was not a formal written agreement.

At the end of the school year, the father received his daughter's report card from her eighth grade teacher. He was concerned by the teacher's comments that the child was smart and had potential, but her absences from school were affecting her ability and opportunity to succeed at the level she was competent of achieving. It is important to note that no one at the school thought to notify the father about the child's absences, even though he had joint legal custody and regular visitation with his child.

Before confronting the mother about the absences, the father obtained his child's medical records for the past year. There was not one instance of a true illness, yet the mother had taken the child to the doctor (describing various symptoms and ailments) to get attention and to avoid criticism of her child's absences. "If I felt she was sick enough to take her to the doctor, then surely she was sick enough to miss school."

Unfortunately, in cases such as this, it is difficult to rally legal support. An attorney or judge may not take this type of situation seriously. Imagine the legal time and expense that could be spent investigating the medical records and the subjective testimony of the mother or the child. Ultimately, it was the mother's custodial time and she will argue that she "made a decision regarding her child's health that she felt was in their best interest."

In another example, a mother in Missouri programmed her 7-year-old daughter to lie to the father. Knowing the father might be suspicious of the daughter missing school, the mother involved the child in the Munchausen event.

When Maria got into her father's car she stated, "Mommy said I wasn't supposed to tell you. She said I was supposed to tell you that I was really sick and I had to stay home from school. But really, Daddy, I wasn't sick. I was fine. Mommy took me to the doctor because she said she would feel better if we went to the doctor. She said she needed to talk to the doctor. She said she needed to talk to the doctor about why I was sick....It was OK, though. I had to have a blood test, but they gave me a toy when it was over."

When confronted about the child's absence the mother stated that the child was in "agony" and could not possibly have attended school that day. Yet, the medical record stated:

" 10/15/03: Maria is here today with her mother. She has skipped into the office and has offered no complaints of her own. No fever and vital signs are normal. Mother states Maria has an upset stomach and could not go to school today. No negative findings. Child happy and appears in good spirits. Skipping out the door as she leaves."

✱ ✱ ✱ ✱ ✱

The examples in this chapter may seem minor when examining the full spectrum of illness, Munchausen by proxy and parental alienation. However, *any aberrant or unusual behavior between a parent and a child regarding illness should be investigated*. As noted by Parnell and Day:

> "Cases involving 'only one episode' or 'just exaggeration' can still be dangerous. The potential for (iatrogenic) harm exists any time a false medical history is provided to a physician. Additionally, *a mother's need to have a sick child*, combined with simulation of illness, can lead to actual physical illness in the child." [8]

> "As more cases are identified, understanding of the diverse and complex motives underlying MBPS is broadening. Clearly, more than one motive may be present, and motives may change over time." ..."In its simplest form, the motivation for the behavior may be stated as follows: the maintenance of a relationship with medical practitioners to meet a plethora of psychological needs." [9]

As we have discussed, *illness* presents many opportunities for a parent (if so inclined) to interfere with a child's access to the other parent, the other parent's right to be informed about the progress of the child and a child's right to attend school and extracurricular activities. For the gaming and manipulative parent, *illness* offers a myriad of opportunities to alienate the child from the other parent.

Many parents, particularly mothers, believe that the father is not capable of taking care of a sick child. This is one component of the proprietary perspective about parenting that many mothers may believe. Often, if the child is sick, the mother will not let the child go to the father's home, or she will insist that the child return to her home for '*the appropriate care.*' The child may only have a minor illness, such as a cold or general malaise, but the mother will insist on being the *only one* to care for the child.

Using the child's illness as the excuse to keep the child in their custody is often a camouflaged attempt to obstruct the visit with the other parent. In some situations, the child may play into the alienating parents efforts. In other situations, the child may not be aware that their visit has been cancelled due to the perceived illness, as minor as it may be.

Again, the message to the child is that one parent is superior over the other, the visit to the other parent is not important and that the child will have better care at the alienating parents home.

As discussed throughout this book, divorce situations may be viewed by many different standards. Some individuals, including professionals, may have extremely rigid views about divorce. To complicate things further, as noted above by Parnell and Day, there are many judgmental people in those professions that can directly affect your child's life. Often, these professionals are not educated about Munchausen by proxy or parental alienation, and therefore, may not understand a parent's need to be proactive on behalf of the child.

Therefore, it is paramount that parents monitor their child's attendance at school and extracurricular activities for aberrant or unnatural trends. In addition, safeguards should be in place to protect a child from unnecessary absences from their normal school, extracurricular or social activities. Without safeguards, it may be difficult to identify the problem or correct the negative effect this behavior could have on a child.

Considerations and Possible Solutions

In an effort to curtail aberrant behavior, there should be written parameters *defining illness*, including safeguards and procedures to protect the child. As in the second case described above, the child's opportunity to advance to a more distinctive high school was adversely affected by her school absences. In addition, the mother's approval of the school absences established a pattern of behavior for the child, resulting in negative consequences affecting her throughout her adult life. This is an example of what can happen without safeguards in place to protect the child.

It is important to define a procedure regarding child illnesses and school absences, and a written procedure should be included in a formal parenting plan or agreement. The effectiveness of the written procedure should then be monitored at certain intervals to determine if parents are being notified timely of frequent illnesses or attendance problems. An example of defining an illness may include:

➢ The parents agree the children should not be kept home from school for any other reason than illness. For the purpose of this agreement, "illness" is defined as the child having a fever over 100.5 and/or is nauseated *with* vomiting.

A copy of the written agreement should be given to the school and health care providers. This eliminates the possibility of misunderstanding or misrepresentation should the time come to ask for help in identifying a potential problem. The agreement should be kept with the child's medical and school records. This documentation will help clarify that illness and absence from school may be an issue for this child in the future.

Most importantly, the school staff should be informed about your concerns regarding your child's attendance at school. There should also be a procedure in place that guarantees you will be notified in the event of your child's absence from school. This can be achieved in several ways. Most schools have an appointed individual responsible for attendance records. You should establish a relationship with this individual and create an amicable arrangement for notification if your child is absent from school.

If you have an attentive and understanding school staff, they should offer to call you when the child is absent from school. Another alternative is to request that the school sends you a copy of the child's attendance record at monthly, bi-monthly or quarterly intervals. Sometimes the attendance record can be included with the child's report card or academic progress notes. This solution is sometimes the best. If absences are affecting a child's progress, the reports will arrive simultaneously and the parent is informed on a timely basis.

A word of caution: Some parents want to be notified immediately if the child has missed school. My opinion is to tread very carefully with this issue. The primary goal of monitoring attendance is to verify that your child is not missing too much school and that the reasons for absences are legitimate. Sometimes, even receiving the telephone call from the school the day of the absence can stir emotions, creating an overreaction or a need for immediate involvement to correct a perceived problem.

I strongly recommend beginning with the monthly or quarterly notification of attendance from the school. Should a pattern emerge that is of concern, then a more frequent notification policy can be established. Otherwise, parents may be at risk for the ever present opportunity for conflict, unpleasant conversations, needless probing or the other parent needing to talk to the 'sick child.'

In their excellent and informative book, *Munchausen by Proxy Syndrome,* Parnell and Day outline the School System Perspective on pages 269 - 273. They have published a list of indicators and state that the "list of indicators is intended simply to aid school personnel in determining whether particular cases warrant abuse reports and/or referral for medical review."[11] For the purposes of this book, the list below is reproduced in an abbreviated form.

Indicators for the School Professional

1. "School attendance problems.
2. Requests for hospital/homebound services.
3. Parent accusations that the school is making the child ill.
4. Parent presentation of extensive medical history file to explain child's illness.
5. Child reported to be too ill to come to school due to respiratory ailments.
6. Child reported to be too ill to come to school, but is involved in other activities.
7. Child appears to be suffering from impaired psychological development...
8. Unreasonable requests from a parent.
9. A symbiotic parent-child relationship.
10. Hysterical personality in a parent.
11. It appears that the parent wants to punish the school system.
12. Parent becomes hostile and threatens legal action.
13. The parent takes no real action to solve what she says are her child's problems.
14. The parent declares that 'other' professionals are in agreement with her regarding her child's condition, but fails to produce proof to substantiate her claims." [12]

Parnell and Day also state, "Finally, it is important for educators and others in the school setting to remember that Munchausen by proxy syndrome should not necessarily be ruled out simply because a child has a genuine previously diagnosed disorder. The presence of any of the indicators listed above should alert school personnel to take a careful look at the child's case." [13]

Parnell and Day follow their chapter on the school system perspective with a plan of action. I urge anyone dealing with a possible Munchausen situation to read their book and use it as a reference and resource.

Work with the school and health care provider staff and
make sure your child gets to school on time!

In closing, as with the use of children to stalk an ex-spouse, it is unfortunate there has not been significant research regarding the correlation between divorce and Munchausen by proxy. Regarding this issue, Parnell and Day note:

"In many cases of Munchausen by proxy syndrome, evidence of marital discord is uncovered at the time of suspicion. The stress inherent in removal of a child from the family, scrutiny by social service agencies, and involvement with the courts often places insurmountable strain on an unstable marriage. The perpetrator and spouse are then forced to acknowledge on some level the problems within the marital union. The spouse is also struggling with the deception of the perpetrator and her sometimes horrifying behavior. Additionally, separation from the perpetrator may be the only way for a father to regain custody of his child. In the population Deborah Day and I have studied, divorces have occurred in cases where the mother admitted the Munchausen by proxy allegations. The perpetrator's Munchausen by proxy syndrome behavior is likely to become an issue in the parenting plan. For instance, Florida has a shared parenting assumption, but Munchausen by proxy syndrome may certainly create an exception." [14]

I believe the indicators listed above should also be used to monitor attendance at extracurricular and other activities. There are many parents who may work with schools satisfactorily but may demonstrate some of the behaviors described above in the scope of their child's extracurricular activities. Perhaps, because of the social or legal influence of a school, a parent may not be *brave* enough to exercise Munchausen by proxy within the educational system. Yet, these same parents may demonstrate some of the characteristics described above to a less-threatening audience, such as, coaches, managers and instructors.

(Endnotes)

[1] Parnell, T. F. & Day, D. O. (Eds). (1998). *Munchausen by Proxy Syndrome: Misunderstood Child Abuse*. Thousand Oaks, CA: Sage Publication, Inc. p. 14.

[2] id., p. 18.

[3] id., p. 19.

[4] id.

[5] id., p. 5.

[6] Schreier, H.A., & Libow, J.A. (1993a). *Hurting for Love: Munchausen proxy syndrome*. New York Guilford.

[7] Parnell, T. F. & Day, D. O. (Eds). (1998). *Munchausen by Proxy Syndrome: Misunderstood Child Abuse*. Thousand Oaks, CA: Sage Publication, Inc. pp. 5-6.

[8] id., p. 26.

[9] id., pp. 17 - 18.

[11] id., p. 269.

[12] id., p. 269-273.

[13] id., p. 272.

[14] id., pp. 115-116.

18.

The Doctor and the Dentist
Participating in Your Child's Health Care

As discussed in the previous chapter, illness can pose many different scenarios for the divorced parent. While you may never experience the extreme of *Munchausen by proxy*, being informed of the dynamics surrounding a child's health or illness is very important. Health care is one of the *essential elements* in your child's life, and involvement in your child's health should be one of your primary goals.

If your attorney has not already helped you with this issue, you need to understand the importance of opening dialog and communication directly with your child's doctor, dentist and other health care professionals. These providers may include orthodontists, physical therapists, speech therapists, mental health or other practitioners your child may be seeing.

Establishing a relationship with these professionals in a positive and helping manner will open the door to a cooperative alliance. It is extremely important to avoid the temptation to tell *your side* of the divorce story, or expose hostile and angry feelings about your ex-spouse, even if you are mad. To do so may erode the primary goal of creating an alliance with these professionals. The main purpose of your relationship with these professionals is to provide an avenue to participate actively in your child's health care and general welfare.

Refraining from sharing your true feelings about the divorce does not mean avoiding the opportunity to share valid information with the professionals about your child's best interests, health and psychological welfare. To the contrary, any information that may assist the health care professionals to provide the best care to your child is important. The point is to be selective in your approach, relaying information that truly affects your child's health versus a natural tendency to co-opt or otherwise align people to see your point of view. Health care professionals should always remain neutral, and your input and information should help them to maintain that neutrality.

✶ ✶ ✶ ✶ ✶

Some mothers may claim they should be the only one to take the child to the doctor or dentist, truly believing it is the mother's role to do so. Parents should not be influenced or overcome by this misnomer! *Both parents* have a right (and should take the responsibility) to be involved in their child's health care needs, and fathers should not hesitate to take a child to the doctor or dentist, when needed. A father should not consent to being excluded from this important role and experience in a child's life.

When fathers participate in the child's health care, it gives the child confidence in their ability to parent and care for them. Imagine the unspoken message to children that the mother is the only qualified parent who can take them to the doctor or the dentist.

Sometimes, it may be best to delineate the responsibilities of each parents participation in the child's health care prior to complications. For clarity, the parenting agreement may state the "mother will be primarily responsible for medical visits" and the "father will be primarily responsible for dental visits."

The purpose for the division of responsibility of a child's health care is to create a separate but equal policy for each parent's involvement in their child's care. This type of policy may be established to eliminate duplicate visits and scheduling by the parents, streamline each parent's responsibility and to ensure the child obtains their regular check-ups and vaccinations without overlap and confusion. Under no circumstance should a parent be precluded from obtaining medical, dental or other health care services for a child, when necessary.

As we have illustrated throughout this book, many things can go awry quickly in a divorce situation. Clearly defining the responsibilities of each parent for the child's health care is very important. It is also crucial that the father assumes some of the responsibilities for this part of the child's growth and development. As we have stated in earlier chapters, it does not have to be the father who actually takes the child to appointments during his custodial time. It can be an aunt, uncle, neighbor, stepparent, close friend or grandparent. The key is to assure that your child has the care needed during your parenting time, to foster continuity and trust when the child is in your care.

Take for example, the mother in Massachusetts who would not allow the pediatrician to release her child's medical records to the father. In this divorce case, the father was trying to be proactive in his new parenting situation. He was making a conscious effort to organize a second home and establish a relationship with the child's health care professionals.

In this process, he wrote a cordial letter to the pediatrician's office requesting a copy of his child's medical records for his files. He enclosed a self addressed stamped envelope with his request, and offered to pay for the cost of copying the records. For whatever reason, the pediatrician's office immediately telephoned the mother to inform her that the father had requested the child's records.

The mother become very angry about the father's inquiry and request. In the heat of her anger she lied to the pediatrician's office, stating *she* had full custody of the child and did not give her consent to release the records to the father.

When the father called the pediatrician's office he was surprised to find the office staff angry with him. The office personnel informed him that "he did not have joint custody and they could not release the child's medical records to him!"

The father had to call his attorney for help. The attorney sent a letter to the doctor's office including a copy of the recorded judgement, documenting the joint custody status of the child. The attorney also included a copy of the state law, requiring the pediatrician to release the records to the father.

The father finally received the child's records but only after incurring additional legal costs, embarrassment, anger, aggravation and a hostile interaction with his ex-spouse. This episode also tainted the father's future relationship with the pediatrician's office staff, a relationship that would last for years to come.

This example illustrates how the mother had already '*co-opted*' the pediatrician's office staff to be sympathetic and protective of her. The office staff obviously knew her and believed her story, even though it was not true. To make matters worse, the physician's office staff was so '*motherized*' they were unable to deal professionally with the father, who truly had his child's best interest at heart.

This example also supports the recommendations made in this chapter regarding the possibility of negative experiences or difficulty in obtaining cooperation from the doctor or their staff. This type of biased and judgmental situation is quite common, and should not be overlooked. Immediate arrangements should be made to transfer the child's care to an office educated and supportive of dealing with families of divorce.

How to Address the Health Care of Your Child

➢ Be proactive in your child's health care!

➢ Investigate State Law in: 1) the state you reside, 2) the state your final divorce judgement was filed, and 3) the state your child resides (if different than yours). This can be done by asking an attorney or calling for free legal advise in the designated state.

➢ Obtain a written copy of your legal rights regarding your child's medical care, medical records and general medical information in each applicable state. Individual states have different laws and the status of your custody may change your rights, for example do you have shared custody, physical custody, legal custody, sole custody?

  ➢ Create a 'medical file' for each child.

  ➢ Include the written copy of your legal rights and your divorce decree in the file.

➢ If you do not already have your child's health care information, update your records and obtain the information from your ex-spouse. This information should include a complete list of all the names, addresses and telephone numbers of the health care providers the child has seen to date.

➢ If your divorce is not final, have your attorney include your child's health care information in your marital settlement agreement, parenting plan and legal judgement. This *is very important* information for every parent to have.

➢ It is preferable that all information regarding the child's health care providers is exchanged during the divorce proceedings and a means for communicating this information is clearly stated in the marital settlement agreement or parenting plan.

  ➢ Unfortunately, this element is often overlooked. If you can, try to establish that each parent is responsible to notify the other parent *in writing* of the names, locations, and telephone numbers of the child's health care professionals or any changes that take place. (See parenting plan at the end of this chapter.)

➢ Make a list of all of the names, telephone numbers and addresses of your child's health care providers. The list should be organized and easy to retrieve in case of an emergency or a need to contact a health care provider.

➤ Send a cordial letter to the physician's and/or dentist's office introducing yourself and informing them of your custody situation and how your time is shared with your child. This will alert the doctor and the staff of your interest in caring for your child. (A sample introductory letter is included at the end of this chapter)

➤ The introductory letter should include your request that the health care provider notifies you whenever your child is seen at their office. Ask them to make a note of this request in your child's chart, where it will be easily noticed. Let them know that as a two home family you would appreciate receiving a separate telephone call to each household informing you of:

1) the reason for the child's visit,

2) the doctor's findings and the diagnosis,

3) any medications that have been prescribed, including the name, dosage and frequency of administration, and,

4) follow-up treatment that is needed including follow up visits to the doctor's office.

Information, or lack thereof, may become a powerful tool for a malicious ex-partner. Make sure the health care providers inform you about your child directly. This does not mean that you have to personally talk to the doctor every time there is a medical visit, but rather a short message left on your answering machine by the office staff such as:

"Hello Mr. Jones, your daughter Nancy was seen today at our office for a sore throat. We have given her a prescription of Amoxicillin (antibiotic) that she needs to take 3 times a day for the next 7 days. We would like to see her in 3 days, and of course if she isn't feeling better in the next 24 hours please bring her in. She has an appointment for Thursday at 4:00, please call us if you have any questions."

This voice mail took less than 30 seconds to record and listen too. Now review the following example of how medical information can be used to manipulate and control a post divorce encounter.

> *Take for example,* the mother in New Mexico who 'simply forgot' to tell the father about the doctors visit when they exchanged their child after school. The father's telephone rang at 6:30 PM, just as he was sitting down with his daughter to eat dinner. "Oh, Dave, I'm so sorry, I forgot to tell you, Nancy has a sore throat and I took her to the doctor today and then *completely* forgot to tell you or to give you her medicine...
>
> Oh, while I have you on the line, I want to talk to Nancy and see how she is feeling... Now, do you want to come over here to pick up the medicine or shall I just stop by, on my way out to dinner with my new friend, Ted, and drop off the medicine at your house? ... Oh, don't forget to keep Nancy warm tonight, give her lots of orange juice and make sure she gets to bed early because Ted, our new friend, is taking us to the zoo tomorrow. ... Oh, and also, did you remember to mail the child support check today? I would really appreciate receiving it on time this month."

What is a father to do? He obviously needs the medicine for his child, and he needs to figure out how to exchange the medicine in a timely manner. The mother now wants to talk to Nancy to see how she is '*coping*' with her minor sore throat, *and* the mother wants to come over to *his* house!

This father's nice evening of visitation with Nancy has now been interrupted. His privacy is about to be invaded, and his ex-spouse has used this opportunity to let him know what her very important plans are for the evening and with her new friend tomorrow with his daughter. Pure manipulation! More important is the fact that Nancy's special time with her father has been interrupted, and she knows that her mother is coming over. This makes her time with her father not so special after all.

This episode could have been prevented very easily had the doctor's office notified the father in a timely manner about the medication and treatment of the child. The father would have had more options. Being informed would have allowed him to:

➢ Ask his ex-spouse for the medicine at the exchange, therefore it not being "forgotten,"
   -or-
➢ Ask the physician's office to provide two bottles of medications with labels and instructions so that the amounts of medication can be divided appropriately for the child's visitation schedule and safely administered by each parent.

Components to Consider for a Parallel Parenting Plan

❑ The parent primarily responsible for routine medical visits of the child:

> ❑ Mother
>
> ❑ Father
>
> ❑ Both

> ❑ The parent primarily responsible for routine medical care will make sure the child receives their annual examinations and vaccinations timely, and as recommended by the child's doctor.

❑ The parent primarily responsible for routine dental care of the child, including orthodontics and oral surgery.

> ❑ Mother
>
> ❑ Father
>
> ❑ Both

> ❑ The parent primarily responsible for the child's dental care will make sure that the child receives two dental examinations and cleaning each year, and that all follow-up and additional visits are scheduled and attended, as recommended by the dentist.

❑ Each parent will have input and open dialog with the child's mental health provider, if one is needed, or unless otherwise indicated by court order.

❑ Each parent will be given the name, address and telephone number of all health care providers for each child.

❑ This information will be provided at the beginning of each year unless a new health care provider is introduced into the child's care.

❑ If a new provider is introduced into the child's care, each parent will be notified in writing by the other parent within 48 hours of the name, address, telephone number and specialty of the provider.

❑ The health care information will be provided on the following form to help facilitate communication between the parents.

❑ Each parent will sign a general form and Authorization to Release Information to the other parent. (Sample below)

❑ Each parent agrees that an authorization for treatment of a minor will be given to all caretakers, relatives and important people in the child's life. (Sample attached)

❑ Our child's health care insurance will be paid by :

      ❑ Mother

      ❑ Father

      ❑ Both   (% Mother_____)

                     (% Father _____)

❑ Our child's health care insurance is:

    Name:_____

    Address _____

    Policy Number_____ Group Number: _____

❑ Each parent will be diligent in using providers that are part of the Health Insurance Network. For example, providers that are approved for the HMO or PPO health care plan.

❑ Each parent will be given a copy of the Health Insurance Plan so there will not be misunderstandings or confusion regarding the coverage, benefits and which providers can be used.

❑ Health care insurance information will be provided to each parent annually, unless there is a change in the insurance information during the year. If there is a change in the insurance information, the information will be provided to the other parent within seven days, in writing.

❑ Each parent will participate in the cost of the child's health care by contributing to the copayment for each medical visit as specified by the health care plan. For example:

    ❑ If the mother takes the child to the doctor, she is responsible for paying the $20.00 copayment required per visit.

    ❑ If the father takes the child to the doctor, he is responsible for paying the $20.00 copayment.

    ❑ The purpose of each parent contributing financially is to reduce the opportunity for the over-utilization or abuse of medical visits that may cause financial hardship if one parent is responsible for paying all copayment costs.

❑ All other out-of-pocket expenses, for example, expenses not covered by insurance such as deductibles or other non-covered benefits, (besides the regular office visit copayment), will be paid by:

    ❑ Mother

    ❑ Father

    ❑ Both   (% Mother_____)

                (% Father _____)

❑ In the event of a true emergency, and the other parent cannot be reached, the following individual we be notified on behalf of each parent:

❑ Father's Emergency Contact

    Name: _____

    Address: _____

    Telephone: _____

    Cellular: _____

    Relationship:_____

    Other info: _____

❑ Mother's Emergency Contact

    Name: _____

    Address: _____

    Telephone:_____

    Cellular:_____

    Relationship: _____

    Other Info:_____

❑ Both parents agree that _all medications_ will be correctly labeled, kept in child resistant bottles and out of the reach of the children.

❑ Both parents agree that the child will be registered with the doctor, dentist, hospital and all other health care providers using their full legal name and accurate date of birth.

★　★　★　★　★

Annual Health Care Information for _____

Name of the child (ren) _____ Year _____

Doctor: Name: _____ Degree:

Address: _____ Specialty:

City/Zip: _____

Telephone: _____

Dentist: Name: _____

Address: _____

City/Zip: _____

Telephone: _____

Orthodontist: Name: _____

Address: _____

City/Zip: _____

Telephone: _____

Mental Health: Name: _____ Degree:

Address: _____ Specialty:

City/Zip: _____

Telephone: _____

Eye Care: Name: _____ Degree:

Address: _____ Specialty:

City/Zip: _____

Telephone: _____

Other Provider: Name: _____ Degree:

Address: _____ Specialty:

City/Zip: _____

Telephone: _____

Our child's Health Insurance Carrier:

        Name: _____

        Policy Number: _____ Group Number: _____

        A copy of the insurance card is attached.

Special medical or dental concerns to communicate:

Allergies: _____

Symptoms: _____

Recurring Illnesses: _____

Other: _____

Routine Medical Information: The above information is complete and accurate to the best of my knowledge. I am providing this information to my ex-spouse, _____ as we agreed in our marital settlement agreement/judgment/parenting plan. Should any of these providers change (or a new provider is added to this list) notification will be sent to him/her by providing an updated copy of this form within 48 hours of the change. This form will be sent to: (address, city, state zip)   via US mail.

Emergency Medical Care: In the event of a life threatening emergency, I will notify him/her immediately with the name of the facility, doctor, addresses, telephone numbers and the description of the life threatening emergency. I will make this notification by telephone to the following telephone number (___) _____ or by facsimile to the fax number (_____) _____.

Per our agreement, we will make accommodations for each parent to spend individual time with our child in fair, *equal* and alternating increments, *without interference from the other parent*. We will ask for the health care staff's assistance in determining what the appropriate amounts of equal time should be spent with our child, so that we do not compromise our child's health care.

Other:

Signed: _____ (Father) Date: _____

Signed: _____ (Mother) Date: _____

Sample Introduction Letter to Health Care Providers

(Date)

(Name of Doctor/Dentist)
(Address of Doctor/Dentist)
(City, State Zip)

RE: (Name of child)

Dear Dr. _____:

    As you may be aware, my wife, <u>(name of ex-spouse)</u>, and I separated last year and we are now divorced. <u>(Child's name)'s</u> health care is very important to me and I want to make sure you have my current information in his/her chart.

    <u>Child's name</u> mother and I have <u>(legal status, e.g., joint physical and legal custody)</u> and <u>(child's name)</u> spends <u>(child's days and weekend schedule)</u> with me. I have attached a copy of our final Judgement for your records.

    I would appreciate your office notifying me whenever <u>(child's name)</u> is seen in your office. With this letter I authorize you and/or your staff to leave a detailed message on my voice mail, <u>(voice mail number)</u>, regarding any care that <u>(child's name)</u> receives. I would appreciate knowing the date, time, reason for his/her visit, any medications and follow-up care that may be required. If there is any thing I can do to assist in this communication process, please let me know.

    <u>(child's name)</u> health insurance carrier is:

        (Name of Insurance Carrier) (Address of Insurance Carrier)

        (Policy Number) (Group Number)

    I have enclosed a copy of the front and back of the insurance card for your records.

I am responsible for (Name of Child)'s medical finances and my billing address for statements and general correspondence is as follows:

(Your Name)

(Your Address)

(Your City, State & Zip)

(Your Home Telephone Number) (Your Fax number) (Your e-mail address)

(Your Cellular Telephone Number) (Your Office Number)

Thank you for your consideration. If you have any questions or need additional information, please do not hesitate to call me.

Sincerely,

(Your Name)

Sample Release of Information Form

I, _____, hereby authorize any and all information regard-

ing my child, _____, to be released to _____ .

Signed _____ Date: _____

Relationship to child: _____

Sample Authorization for Treatment of Minor Form

(I) (We), the undersigned, parent(s)/guardian(s) of _____, a minor, do hereby declare that the care of said minor has been entrusted to:

_____

(Name of individual, group, organization or school)

and that any adult member thereof is hereby authorized to act as agent for the undersigned to consent to any consultation, x-ray examination, anesthetic, dental, medical, psychological or surgical diagnosis or treatment and hospital care which is deemed advisable by and is to be rendered under the general or special supervision of any currently licensed dentist, physician, surgeon or other health care provider licensed under the provisions of the Medical Practice Act.

This consent authorizes the above health care providers to provide treatment as necessary at an off-site location, office of said provider or at a hospital.

This consent is being provided in advance of any specific diagnosis, treatment, or hospital care being required and is given to provide authority and power on the part of the aforesaid agent to give specific consent to any and all such diagnosis, treatment or hospital care which the aforementioned physician or other health care provider, in the exercise of his/her best judgement may deem advisable.

By signature of this consent, the undersigned hereby indemnifies and holds harmless _____, from any financial responsibility for so acting and the undersigned hereby agrees to pay the reasonable and customary charges for any x-ray examination, anesthetic, medical or surgical diagnosis or treatment or hospital care provided to said minor pursuant hereto.

This authorization shall remain in effect until _____. (date)

Signed: _____   Date: _____

Relationship to Minor: _____

Sample Log Regarding Health Care

Keep track of all unnecessary expenses or any situation that concerns you regarding your child's health care. Include this information in your Journal. Just a quick note stating the date, incident and the dollar amount, if appropriate.

Date	Incident	Dollar Amount
Example:		
10/15/97	Asked Susan for the names of the child's dentist/doctor. She refused to give me the information. Had to call attorney.	$ 100.00
	Legal Letter had to be written.	$ 55.00
09/02/98	Legal costs incurred re: Susan's refusal to authorize the pediatrician's office to release medical records to me	$ 150.00
	Letter from attorney, response and discussion.	

19.

An Emergency or Not?

Often, even emergency situations need to be defined clearly. When a parent is determined to stay emotionally connected to the other parent, they can easily draw them into their emotional arena by declaring an *emergency situation* for a child. While it may seem hard to believe, this is a very manipulative maneuver and can be quite alarming and disruptive to the unsuspecting or unassuming parent.

Receiving a telephone call from an ex-spouse informing you that there is a medical emergency involving one of your children can catapult the absent parent into an emotional frenzy and feeling of helplessness. The immediate and natural response of parental concern is coupled with an overwhelmingly strong need to be involved.

Take for example, the mother in Washington D.C., who called the father following a very heated and traumatic custody hearing. The court's decision had ruled against the father about significant custody issues. The mother called the father immediately after she returned home from court, and left the following message. "Oh, John, we need to talk immediately. Leslie has become dreadfully ill, and I need to talk to you as soon as possible. Please call me as soon as you get this message."

The father was devastated by the day in court and the judge's rulings and punitive demeanor. He was confused and disenchanted. His attorney tried to console him but agreed that the decision seemed harsh and biased. In contrast, the mother left the courtroom gleeful and gloating over her most recent victory.

The mother called the father claiming there was an emergency, but she did not state the nature of the crisis. The father did not want to return the telephone call, but there was an "*emergency*" regarding his daughter.

When the father returned the telephone call, he realized there was not an emergency at all. The mother had manipulatively alarmed the father to initiate contact with him. There was nothing wrong with the daughter. The mother had created a false emergency so the father would have to talk to her. She needed the direct interaction with the father to hear his reactions to the court rulings, to determine the level of his anger and loss, and to gloat further about her victory.

In another example, a mother in Minnesota insisted on being present during any '*emergency*' involving her child. For this divorced family, there was not a clear definition or understanding of an '*emergent*' or '*urgent*' situation. This mother was successful in her attempts to interfere with the father's custodial time, claiming an emergency about minor illnesses.

She would routinely come to the father's home, during his custodial time, to "make sure the child was being *appropriately* cared for." This mother would often claim an 'emergency situation' about a common cold, a minor laceration or similarly normal childhood illnesses or accidents.

This mother believed that any declaration of an 'emergency' entitled her to arrive at the father's home, unannounced, at any time of the day or night. One time she came to the father's home at 11:30 PM stating she "*felt* there was an emergency and she had stopped by just to make sure everything was all right."

Fortunately, there are legal remedies to help diffuse situations such as these, and again, they require a proactive legal plan. The best cure to discourage potential problems regarding *'emergencies'* is to establish a clear, written definitions for the words 'urgent' and 'emergent.' It is also best to establish clear written guidelines regarding *parental communication and conduct in the event of a true emergency.*

Components to Consider for a Parenting Plan

❑ Define an *"emergency"* clearly.

    ❑ A true emergency is defined as "a threat of loss of life or limb." Exactly that, the child is in a situation of imminent or possible death, or of losing an arm or a leg. (NOT a tooth!)

❑ Clearly define how each parent will be notified in the case of a true emergency.

❑ *The following guidelines should be used when communicating with the other parent about a "child related emergency."*

    ❑ *State the name of the child if you have more than one.* "This emergency call is regarding Johnny."

    ❑ *State the nature of the emergency in specifics.* "Johnny was in a car accident this afternoon and he has a skull fracture."

    ❑ *State the child's condition as clearly as possible.* "Johnny has been in and out of consciousness for the past 90 minutes. The hospital has listed him in 'critical condition.' Johnny will be in surgery at 4:00 PM."

    ❑ *State where the child is, including the name of the hospital, the town, the address and the telephone number.* "Johnny is at Modern Hospital, in Modern Town, on Modern Drive. The hospital telephone number is _____.

    ❑ *State who is seeing the child medically/professionally.* "I have met Dr. Jones. He is the neurosurgeon doing the surgery."

    ❑ *State when the best time for the other parent to visit the child will be.* "I know you will want to see Johnny before surgery. When you get here I will take a break so you can spend time with him alone."

    ❑ *State any other details that will help the other parent to feel in control of the situation even though they are not physically present.*

A very effective alternative is to ask the hospital personnel to make the telephone call for you. They are trained professionals and will be able to discuss the child's illness with the other parent objectively and knowledgeably.

❏ This solution allows the 'off-site parent' to ask pertinent questions about the child's condition, and receive informed answers from the health care staff.

It is very important that each parent *understands and respects* the boundaries of the other parent and their need for privacy when visiting with the child in an emergency situation! Each parent has a special and unique relationship with the child. Stressful situations induce strong emotions, and an emergency setting *is not the place to reignite post-divorce parental emotions and interactions.*

The medical professionals in the hospital can help manage the '*family traffic,*' and the visits with the child. It is important to adhere to hospital policy, and respect that *each parent* will want to spend special time *alone* with the child.

Do not overlap parental visits and bedside conversations. If you are both present at the hospital, take one-hour shifts at your child's bedside with 5-10 minute intervals of *free time and 'space'* between the visits. The purpose here is to minimize direct contact between the parents, and to maximize each parents personal time with the child. If the child is imminently ill, then the alternating visiting time should be of shorter duration, still leaving corridors of time and *space* between each parent's visit.

Unfortunately, some parents will not acquiesce. These parents will insist on being with the child at all times, dominating the hospital room and controlling the emotional environment. Parenting agreements that clearly define '*emergency situations,*' including guidelines for appropriate parental conduct, will help ease the strain prior to any unfortunate event involving a child. An emergency situation is *the worst time* to be negotiating time to spend with your child. Plan ahead, and if possible, agree on the guidelines outlined below.

A parent should contact the nursing supervisor on duty if they need intervention regarding their right to visit the child, free of interference from the other parent. This parent should explain to the nursing supervisor that they would like to spend some time alone with their child. If necessary, a parent can get a doctor's order so the nursing staff can enforce the request for private visits with the child. Also, there is usually a social worker or psychologist on duty at hospitals, who may be able to help define and enforce the 'in-house' boundaries regarding visitation with the child at the hospital.

Take for example, the mother in New Jersey who would not agree on the meaning of an *'emergency.'* She also would not agree to spend any time out of the hospital room if her child were seriously injured, sick or dying. She stated, "If he (the father) has so much hatred that he cannot see beyond himself and stand *with me* at *my side* during *my child's* death, then he should not be there at all."

Fortunately, the parenting coordinator who worked with this family was seasoned, and did not agree with the mother. This divorce case *revolved* around the mother's unwillingness to allow the father any special time with his child, even when the child was in his custody. The mother continually asserted the position that she had a right to be wherever she wanted, when it came to the business of her child.

The parenting coordinator had practical insight, and created a policy for the family regarding medical emergencies. First, the parenting coordinator defined urgent and emergent situations. Then she defined 'custody,' as it would relate to an emergency. For example, the non-custodial parent was defined as "the parent who does not have physical custody of the child when the 'emergency' occurs."

The policy stated that the parent who was not with the child at the time of the emergency (the non-custodial parent) would be notified as soon as the child was medically stabilized. If the child's life were in imminent danger, then the parent would be notified immediately.

Visitation at the hospital (by the non custodial parent) would occur after the child was medically stabilized. If the child's life were in imminent danger, the visitation would occur immediately for the non-custodial parent. In any case, visitation of the child would be arranged so that both parents were not visiting the child at the same time.

As crazy as it may seem, it is vital that parents decide how they will conduct themselves in the event of a true emergency. Even skilled professionals may have difficulty handling their emotions and reactions in extreme circumstances. Divorced parents may have great difficulty managing the emotional upheaval that can encompass an emergency situation. Guidelines established *before* such an unfortunate circumstance will help diffuse potential chaos in the midst of an emergency situation.

Components to Consider for the Parenting Plan or Agreement

❏ An emergency is defined as: "A threat to our child's life or loss of a limb."

    ❏ Other: _____

    ❏ _____

    ❏ _____

❏ The child will always be admitted to the hospital or other emergency facility using their *full legal name and date of birth.*

❏ Both parent's full legal names will be listed on the admission form when the child is admitted to the hospital, surgical center or urgent care facility.

❏ Both parent's emergency contact information will be included on the hospital admission form.

❏ The parent admitting the child to the hospital or other emergency facility will notify the facility of the divorce, and will ask that both parent's contact information is clearly visible in the child's medical record.

    ❏ The emergency contact numbers for *the mother* are:

        ❏ Telephone: (home)_____ (work) _____

        ❏ Cellular #: _____

        ❏ Other Number:_____

    ❏ In the event of a true emergency, and the mother cannot be reached, the following individual will be notified on her behalf:

    ❏ Mother's Alternate Emergency Contact Information

        Name: _____

        Address: _____

        Telephone: _____Cellular: _____

        Relationship: _____

❑ The emergency contact numbers for *the father* are:

    ❑ Telephone: (home) _____ (work) _____

    ❑ Cellular #: _____

    ❑ Other Number: _____

❑ In the event of a true emergency, and the father cannot be reached, the following individual will be notified on his behalf:

❑ Father's Alternate Emergency Contact Information

    Name: _____

    Address: _____

    Telephone: _____ Cellular: _____

    Relationship: _____

❑ In the event of a life-threatening emergency, each parent will notify the other immediately with the name of the facility, doctor, addresses, telephone numbers and the description of the life-threatening emergency.

    ❑ Each parent will make this notification by telephone, using the telephone numbers listed above.

❑ In the event of an urgent or life threatening situation, each parent will make accommodations for the other parent to spend individual time with the child in fair, equal and alternating increments, *without interference from the other parent.*

❑ The parents will ask for the health care staff's assistance in determining what the appropriate amounts of equal time should be spent with the child, so that they do not compromise or interfere with their child's health care.

20.

School Information
Participating in Your Child's Educational Experience

School functions and activities
often pose difficult situations for families of divorce.

As with the health care providers and extracurricular activities, the best strategy for the divorced parent is to take a *proactive role* in your child's life. While it seems logical that school administrators and teachers should be versed in divorce politics, it is often not the case. Therefore, do not assume that your child's school will act as a neutral entity in your divorce.

A malicious and manipulative parent can move quickly through the school hierarchy, establishing themselves as the better, or *more fit* parent. In addition, school environments are often fertile grounds for gossip. The school setting offers many potential opportunities for a vindictive parent to create problematic situations and relationships for the unassuming parent.

It is important to realize that your child's school environment and academic experience span the majority of their minor life. Primary school and middle school (kindergarten through 8th grade) occupy approximately *7 to 10 years* of your child's life. This means their friends and families, teachers, administrators, school coaches and instructors are all involved in your child's growth and development for almost a decade!

If a negative impression is established, especially in such a socially fertile environment as a school, it is very difficult to overcome the harm that can be incurred. *'Damage control'* often becomes the primary survival technique, and is usually not very effective within the school atmosphere. Surely, not the way to enjoy your child's educational experience.

Take for example, the divorced mother in Texas who viewed her child's school as a competitive environment. This mother wanted to be perceived as the 'better parent,' and she used the parent body at her child's school to fulfill her goal. For this mother, there was not room for two 'good parents.' She desperately needed to be the 'favored parent' among her child's classmates, teachers and school families.

This mother began her scandalous rumors about the father immediately after her child began kindergarten. Once the child was enrolled, she began manipulating the father's opportunities for involvement at the school, specifically not forwarding school notices regarding activities and events.

The father began to realize there were many school activities and functions that he was unaware of. He began to ask questions and discovered there were many activities from which he had been excluded. It wasn't until years later that people would approach the father and tell them of the horrible things the mother had said about him. On one occasion, the mother had actually solicited the other parents into taking a 'poll' about the father! Many of these confessing parents admitted that they had distanced themselves from the father, because of the mother's influence and comments about him.

It took the father more than five years to regain social composure with the school officials, teachers, families, coaches and instructors. In this case, the malicious ex-spouse had initiated a negative, rumor-based brainwashing campaign that had a *'domino effect'* on the father's ability to participate actively in his child's educational experience.

Interestingly, it took the mother only a few months to begin the process of destroying the father's reputation, yet it took the father years to recover from the damaging effects.

As with extracurricular activities, discussed in chapter 21, the school setting can pose many different scenarios for the divorced parent. While you may never experience the extreme case of alienation of a parent from the school and school activities, being informed of the dynamics than can occur is, again, very important. Education is one of the essential elements in your child's upbringing, and your involvement in your child's educational experience should be one of your primary goals.

It is imperative to establish open communication with the child's teacher, school administrators, principal, and the staff in the school office. This relationship is very important, even if you are living far away from your child. Establishing a relationship with the school personnel in a positive and helping manner will open the door to a cooperative alliance with these professionals. Remember, it is important not to convey angry and hostile feelings regarding the divorce. The main purpose of your relationship with these professionals is to provide an avenue to participate actively in your child's education, personal growth and development.

Beware of the parent who is not forwarding copies of school reports and information to the other parent.

Many mothers will claim they should be the primary source for school information and communication. These parents may attempt to persuade the school not to release the child's school records, report cards and other academic information to the other parent. The underlying message to the child is that the father does not care about the child or their educational experience. This manipulation of information devalues the fathers input, if any, to the child.

Some parents have actually claimed they have full custody (when they do not) in their efforts to screen information from the other parent. Other parents do not want a parent involved in any school activities, and will control the flow of information to achieve their goal.

Fortunately, the incidents of parents attempting to obstruct information from the other parent about the child and their educational experience have caught the eye of legislatures and other politicians. There are now many states who have laws and regulations requiring schools to provide information to *both parents*, even if they are divorced.

All parents should have a right and responsibility to be actively involved in their child's education. Do not allow the school or your ex-spouse to exclude you from your child's educational experience. Be sure that you know your rights regarding this issue. Investigate state law and research your rights to communicate with the school and have access to your child's school records and academic performance.

Your child's confidence in you will be augmented by your active involvement and interest in their school activities. Whether you live locally or at a distance, being informed of what is happening at your child's school means that you care. Children are very attuned to how much their parents know, and when you ask your child meaningful questions about their school activities, you are creating and/or maintaining an important bond with your child.

Assure that your child is aware of your interest and involvement in their school activities during your parenting time. This promotes the feeling of continuity and trust when the child is in your care.

Some Ideas on How to Stay Connected

➢ Ask your child about their personal progress in their classes and about any special interests they have in the subjects they are studying.

➢ Learn your child's teacher's names (by subject) and refer to them frequently.

➢ Get to know your child's teachers personally. Fortunately, for the long distance parent, an effective personal relationship can be fostered with a teacher or coach, via telephone or e-mail.

➢ Review your child's school calendar and incorporate current academic activities in your conversations with them. This is relevant whether the child is in your custody or if you are a live-away parent.

➢ Ask your child about their field trips and any special projects they are currently involved with.

➢ Volunteer to drive on school field trips (during your custodial time.)

➢ Participate in as many school activities and volunteer opportunities as possible (during your custodial time.)

➢ Children usually enjoy sharing their day-to-day school experiences. Being informed of the current school calendar, activities and special projects gives you the opportunity to share this important aspect of your child's life with them. (Even if you are a live away parent.)

How to Address the Educational Experience of Your Child

➤ Be proactive in your child's educational experience!

➤ Assure that your child is registered with the school using their full legal name and their correct date of birth.

➤ Investigate the State Law in 1) which you reside, 2) your child resides (if different) and, 3) where your divorce decree was filed.

> ➤ You can do this by asking your attorney, or,

> ➤ Call for free legal advise (in the applicable state) to help you discover your rights regarding information about your child's education.

➤ Be specific regarding your child's education, including your rights to copies of their report cards, basic communication of educational records and general school information.

➤ Identify your rights for your particular custody situation, for example, joint custody, physical custody, legal custody or sole custody.

➤ If you do not already have the information regarding your child's school then obtain the information from your ex-spouse immediately.

> ➤ This information should include a *complete* list of all the names, addresses and telephone numbers of the schools your child has attended including past and present institutions.

➤ If your divorce is not final, have your attorney include this information in the judgement, marital settlement agreement or parenting plan. This is very important information for you to have!

➤ It is preferable that all information regarding the child's education and related activities is exchanged during the divorce proceedings, including a means for communicating this information in the future.

➤ The method for communicating this information should be stated clearly in the legal agreement or parenting plan.

➢ Unfortunately, the importance of this element is often overlooked during the divorce process.

  ➢ Assure there is a clause in your agreement that guarantees each parent is responsible to notify the other parent (in writing) of any change in the child's school or academic experience.

  ➢ This information should include the reason for the change of schools, the name, address and telephone number of the new educational institution.

  ➢ The information should also include the name of the child's teacher and the principal or lead administrator of the school. (See parenting plan at the end of this chapter.)

➢ Make a list of all the names, telephone numbers and addresses so that you have it organized and easy to retrieve in case of an emergency or if you need to contact the school for any reason.

➢ Keep a written log of any situation that concerns you regarding your child's academic experience. This documentation will support your efforts to make appropriate changes in your custody arrangements, if needed.

➢ Send a cordial letter to the school and your child's teacher introducing yourself and informing them of your custody situation and how your time is shared with your child.

  ➢ This will alert the school staff of your interest in caring for your child. (Sample letter included at the end of this chapter)

➢ This introductory letter should include the specific request that the school notifies you of your child's academic progress on a regular basis. For example, report cards, progress notes, involvement in school activities and absences.

➢ Inform the school that as a two home family you would appreciate (and need to receive) separate notices and copies of report and progress records, school bulletins, activities and invitations.

➢ Provide the school with self-addressed, stamped envelopes to facilitate your request. (Usually the home room teacher can help with this necessary communication.)

It is important to remember that information, or lack thereof, is a very powerful tool. Assure that you are informed directly by the school!

Components to Consider Regarding Your Child's Education for a Parenting Plan

❑ The child will be registered in school using their full legal name only and correct date of birth.

❑ Each parent will be given the name, address and telephone number of all schools attended for each child.

❑ Each parent will have input and open dialog with the child's school, unless otherwise indicated by court order.

❑ Each parent will be listed on the school record with their current legal name, address and contact numbers, including telephone, fax, cellular telephone, employer, employer address, and telephone number.

❑ Each parent will be listed in the school directory with his or her pertinent information listed above.

❑ Each parent will be listed on the school registration information to be contacted in case of an emergency.

❑ The parents will abide by the guidelines for conduct outlined in the Health Care section of this agreement regarding emergencies.

❑ Accurate school information will be provided to each parent at the beginning of each academic year. This notification will occur annually, unless a new school is entered during the middle of regular school sessions.

>   ❑ If the child enters a new school (during the academic year) each parent will be notified (in writing) by the other parent within 48 hours of the name, address, telephone number, teacher name, administrator name (Principal) and the reason for the change of schools.

❑ To help facilitate communication between the parents, school information will be provided to each parent on an *Education Information Form*. (Included at the end of this chapter.)

>   ❑ The *Education Information Form* will be completed annually and provided to each parent.

>   ❑ The *Education Information Form* will be completed during the annual school registration process and will be mailed to the other parent via U.S. Mail, along with copies of the other school registration information.

❑ This information will be mailed within 7 days of the required school registration, or 7 days from the beginning of school.

❑ '*Special concerns*' will be completed on this form so that each parent is notified in writing of the other parent's concerns as they relate to the academic experience of the child.

    ❑ The inclusion of this information on the *Education Information Form* eliminates one parent trying to usurp the other by providing 'important information' to the school without the other parent's knowledge.

    ❑ The written communication of special concerns will help minimize the opportunity for nonproductive communication between the parents that can arise regarding general concerns of the child.

        ❑ The *special concerns* information will be given to the school and each parent at the beginning of the school year.

        ❑ The school should then assume responsibility to update the parents regarding the alleged concerns, if needed.

❑ Each parent will sign a general form of Authorization to Release Information to the other parent. (Sample below)

❑ The parents will alternate attendance at the parent/teacher conferences,

    ❑ Father will attend the _____ semester/quarter conference.

    ❑ Mother will attend the _____ semester/quarter conference.

        ❑Fall/Winter/Spring/Summer

        ❑Other Arrangement _____

   OR

    ❑ The parents will schedule individual meetings with the teachers to receive updates regarding the child's academic progress.

❑ Each parent will receive copies of report cards and any other academic notices regarding the child.

❑ *Important information from the conferences, aside from the school progress report sent to each parent,* will be forwarded (via US mail) to the other parent, within 7 days of the conference.

   ❑ *Important information* should be clearly defined and completed on the school update form (Included at the end of this chapter.)

   ❑ The purpose here is to eliminate the opportunity for conflict that can easily arise regarding academic progress, such as, "The teachers have said,"

> "Joey is not studying enough at your house."
>
> "His work is always late during your custody time."
>
> "His tardiness is unacceptable when he is at your house."
>
> "His work is sloppy and not proofread at your home."

❑ Our child's tuition for education will be paid by:
   ❑ Mother
   ❑ Father
   ❑ Both   (% Mother_____)
              (% Father _____)

❑ Each parent will participate in the cost of the child's education by contributing to purchase of:
   ❑ Textbooks
   ❑ Outdoor Education Expenses
   ❑ Uniforms
   ❑ School Supplies
   ❑ General Registration Expenses
   ❑ Hot Lunch
   ❑ School Insurance
   ❑ Parent Organizations
   ❑ Other
      ❑ These additional educational expenses will be paid by:
         ❑ Mother
         ❑ Father
         ❑ Both (% Mother_____)
                (% Father _____)

If you are having trouble accessing your child's academic records or school information:

A. U.S. law, the Federal Education Rights and Privacy Act, commonly known as FERPA, protects student rights, especially the privacy of the student and his or her record.

This law (also known as the Buckley Amendment) defines who has access to the school record. The record is available to parents and anyone else "'in parental relation' to the child (hereafter referred to as parents)." [1]

To check on the current status of this information you may contact:
Family Policy Compliance Office
U.S. Department of Education, Room 3017
Federal Building No. 6
400 Maryland Avenue, SW
Washington, D.C. 20202-4605
1-800-USA-LEARN
www.ed.gov

There are also several states that have laws stronger than this federal law, such as Texas and Iowa, which state that the non-custodial parent also has access to medical records from doctors as well as school records. Currently, the federal government does not grant access to medical records.

Annual School Information Form
(To be Completed by Each Parent with a Copy to Each Parent)

(__Year__) Education/School Information for _____ _____

                                         _____ _____

                                         Name of child (ren)   (Grade in School)

❑ School: Name: _____

        Address: _____

        City/Zip: _____

        Telephone: _____ Fax: _____

        Principal's Name: _____

        Teacher's Names:

                Home Room: _____

                Language: _____

                Math: _____

                Science: _____

                Music: _____

                Social Studies: _____

                P.E.: _____

                Humanities: _____

                English: _____

                Other: _____

                Other: _____

❑ At the father's home the following individuals may be contacted for school information:

    1. (name of individual)   (relationship to child)   (Telephone #   )

    2. (name of individual)   (relationship to child)   (Telephone #   )

    3. (name of individual)   (relationship to child)   (Telephone #   )

❑ At the mother's home the following individuals may be contacted for school information:

    1. (name of individual)   (relationship to child)   (Telephone #   )

    2. (name of individual)   (relationship to child)   (Telephone #   )

    3. (name of individual)   (relationship to child)   (Telephone #   )

Our child's Health Insurance Carrier:

    Name: _____

    Policy Number: _____ Group Number: _____

    A copy of the insurance card is attached.

Special Concerns:

Special Concerns that either parent would like to communicate to the school:
These concerns include the following:

Known Allergies:
Known Medications the Child is taking:
Other knowns:
Potential Learning Disabilities:
Potential Needs for Special Education:
Potential Psychological Concerns:
Potential Needs for Special Diets:
Recurring Illnesses:
Specific observations the parent would like the school to make:
Other:

School Information: The above information is complete and accurate to the best of my knowledge. I am providing this information to my ex-spouse, _____
as we agreed in the legal marital settlement agreement/ judgment/parenting plan.

Should any of the information change or a new school is added to the list he/she will be notified by providing an updated copy of this form within 7 days of the change. This form will be sent via US mail to:

(Address of the other parent)   _____

                            _____

Any progress reports, aside from what the school sends to each parent, shall be communicated on the following form.

Signed: _____ Date: _____

Sample Introduction Letter to Educational Institutions
Schools, Academies, Summer Educational Programs, etc.

(Date)

(Name of School Administrator)
(Name of Child's Home Room Teacher)
(Name of School)
(Address of School)
(City, State Zip)

RE: (Name of child)

Dear: _____: (Name of Administrator/Teacher):

As you may be aware, my wife, <u>(name of ex-spouse),</u> and I separated last year and we are now divorced. <u>(Child's name)</u> educational experience is very important to me and I want to make sure you have all of my current information for his/her record.

<u>Child's name</u> mother and I have <u>(legal status, e.g., joint physical and legal custody)</u> and <u>(child's name)</u> spends <u>(child's days and weekend schedule)</u> with me. I have attached a copy of our final Judgement for your records.

I would appreciate the school notifying me of <u>(child's name)</u> progress in school by sending me copies of all school report cards and interim progress reports. I would also appreciate the school sending me all notices sent home to parents regarding school activities, plays, recitals and parent/teacher conferences.

If needed, this letter authorizes you and your staff to leave a detailed message on my voice mail <u>(voice mail number),</u> regarding any communication that is necessary as it relates to <u>(child's name)</u> academic performance and other school activities.

I would also like to inform the school that the following individuals can receive information on my behalf, should the school not be able to contact me, and there needs to be communication regarding my child. These individuals include:

1. _____

      (Name of individual)   (Relationship)

2. _____

      (Name of individual)   (Relationship)

(page two)

I am enclosing some self addressed stamped envelopes to assist in the communication process. If there is anything I can do to assist in this effort, please let me know.

In addition, I am responsible for (Name of Child)'s educational finances and my billing address for statements and general correspondence is as follows:

(Your Name) _____

(Address) _____

(City, State & Zip) _____

(Home Telephone Number) _____

(Fax number) (e-mail address)_____

(Cellular Telephone Number) _____

(Office Number)_____

Thank you for your consideration. If you have any questions or need additional information, please do not hesitate to call me. I look forward to a productive and meaningful relationship with (Name of School.)

Sincerely,

(Your Name)

Sample Authorization for Treatment of Minor Form

(Most schools use a similar form for school registration)

(I) (We), the undersigned, parent(s)/guardian(s) of _____, a minor, do hereby declare that the care of said minor has been entrusted to the faculty and members of the administrative staff of: _____(Name of individual, group, organization or school) and that any adult member thereof is hereby authorized to act as agent for the undersigned to consent to any consultation, x-ray examination, anesthetic, dental, medical, psychological or surgical diagnosis or treatment and hospital care which is deemed advisable by and is to be rendered under the general or special supervision of any currently licensed dentist, physician, surgeon or other health care provider licensed under the provisions of the Medical Practice Act.

This consent authorizes the above health care providers to provide treatment as necessary at an off-site location, office of said provider or at a hospital.

This consent is being provided in advance of any specific diagnosis, treatment, or hospital care being required and is given to provide authority and power on the part of the aforesaid agent to give specific consent to any and all such diagnosis, treatment or hospital care which the aforementioned physician or other health care provider, in the exercise of his/her best judgement may deem advisable.

By signature of this consent, the undersigned hereby indemnifies and holds harmless _____, (Name of school) from any financial responsibility for so acting and the undersigned hereby agrees to pay the reasonable and customary charges for any x-ray examination, anesthetic, medical or surgical diagnosis or treatment or hospital care provided to said minor pursuant hereto.

This authorization shall remain in effect for the academic year _____. (Year)

Signed: _____ Date: _____

Relationship to Minor: _____

Sample Release of Information Form

I,_____, hereby authorize any and all information regarding my

child,_____ , to be released to _____ .

Signed _____ Date: _____

Relationship to child: _____

(Endnotes)

[1] *Speak Out For Children, Fall - 1990, NextStep Publications*, 1485 3rd, Astoria, OR 97103, handout at
   seminar, (503) 325-8828

21.

Extracurricular Activities

Extracurricular activities for your children may prove to be one of the most challenging issues of your separated or divorced status. Extracurricular activities include all the activities in which your child participates outside school and family life. Extracurricular activities include participation in individual and team sports, enrichment activities such as arts, music, ceramics and group activities such as Boy Scouts, Indian Guides, church activities, school plays and any other activity or interest your child may pursue.

Extracurricular activities comprise a large percentage of your child's time and incorporate important social and developmental phases of your child's life. There are many complexities to the *extracurricular factor* following divorce, and because of these complexities this chapter is divided into the following four categories:

➢ Extracurricular Activities:

  ➢ Choosing and Supporting Your Child's Activities
  ➢ Parental Attendance and Boundaries at Events
  ➢ The Mechanics of Autonomy
  ➢ Equipment Shuffling

It has been my personal observation that fathers can be somewhat clueless when it comes to a mother's intentional and aggressive interference with extracurricular activities. Generally, I suppose that men do not think like women, particularly when it comes to the manipulation and control of children.

When Ira Turkat first published his article, *Divorce Related Malicious Mother Syndrome,* he accurately summarized the dilemma of parental interference surrounding extracurricular activities. One of Turkat's criteria for a malicious parent was *"Denying Participation in Extra-curricular Activities."* In his very insightful article, Turkat states:

> "An integral part of the process of maintaining one's bond with one's child is to participate in activities that one did before the parents separated. School plays, team sports, and religious events are just some of the types of activities of importance. Malicious Mothers frequently engage in maneuvers designed to prevent participation in these activities.
>
> One father was deliberately given the wrong date and time for an important event for the child. The child was asked by the mother, 'I wonder why your father didn't want to come see you today?'
>
> One mother refused to provide the father with any information about any extracurricular activities in which the children were engaged.
>
> Prior to a child's soccer game, one mother told many of the team parents disparaging falsehoods about the visiting father. When he came to watch his son's soccer game, many of these parents looked at him with angry eyes, refused to talk with him, and walked away when he moved toward them.
>
> Malicious Mothers who engage in such behaviors rarely have to face penalties for such actions. Judges, attorneys, and policemen cannot involve themselves in every instance of blocked parental access. Furthermore, most fathers cannot afford the financial requirements involved. As such, the cycle of access interference perpetuates itself…" [1]

In addition to Turkat's criterion, there are many other methods a malicious parent can use to disconnect the other parent from the child and the child's extracurricular activities. These undermining techniques, as with Turkat's examples above, can be extremely damaging to the child and the child's relationship with the other parent. Other examples may include:

♌ One parent will not participate or take the child to an event or practice in which the other parent enrolled the child.

✎ One parent will deliberately schedule another activity for the child that interferes with an activity the other parent has enrolled the child. The new activity takes precedence and overlaps, coincides or occurs at the same time as the activity the other parent enrolled the child. The message to the child in this scenario is: "The other parent is not important. His ideas are not important, and you do not need to worry about what he schedules you for."

✎ One parent (without the other parent's knowledge) will telephone an instructor, and inform him that he/she "has been fired" and should no longer go to the other parent's home for lessons or instruction. The malicious parent then tells the child that the instructor has been fired, and they will no longer be having lessons at the other parent's home. Here, the message to the child is that there are no boundaries between the parent's homes, and that one parent in is "control" of the other parent's home and activities.

When discussing *boundaries for extracurricular activities* it is important to evaluate the importance of both parent's participation in the child's activities. To keep things in perspective, it is important to remember that parents from intact families (still married) do not always attend every event of their children together! Many families have other children participating in separate activities; and parents may have other interests, activities or obligations they must be present for. Therefore, it is often a natural occurrence that only one parent attends a child's event. Observe the field, gymnasium or concert hall and you will often notice that parents of intact families are often not present at the same event.

Here again, when one parent is having difficulty dealing with the loss of the marital relationship, they may focus on their own psychological needs. These parents may insist on being present *at every child related activity*. It is important to observe which parent is having difficulty 'sharing the child' regarding this important aspect of their lives. Carefully evaluate the motivation behind a parent's refusal to 'miss an event' or allow the other parent to have 'special time' with the child.

These observations may help identify which parent will fail the Solomon Test, as it relates to alternating the child's experiences equally and fairly. It will be easy to identify the parent who insists on maintaining contact with the other parent through extracurricular activities and special events.

Choosing and Supporting Extracurricular Activities for Your Child

As we discussed in Chapter 8, The Child's Health, Education and Welfare, extracurricular events are one of the essential elements of parenting your child after divorce. Therefore, it is important that you and your ex-spouse establish a mechanism to choose activities in which your child will be participating.

In the example given below, each parent will choose an activity in which he or she would like the child to participate. These activities are called the *'core activities.'* The core activities are defined as the primary activities (chosen by the parents) to benefit their child's growth and development. In addition to the selection of the core activities, the number of core activities needs to be defined. In the example below, to illustrate fairness, the child will have two core activities, one chosen by the mother and one chosen by the father.

The Core Activities

❑ Each parent will choose a *core activity* for the child.

❑ The *core activities* will take priority when scheduling the child for other non-core activities.

❑ Each parent understands that the *core activities* might change with each season.

    ❑ For example, the core activity in the fall may be soccer, winter may be basketball and in the spring may be swimming.

    ❑ Generally, once a child finds a special interest, the activity they choose will be consistent from year to year.

❑ Communication regarding extracurricular choices should be made early enough in the year to facilitate try-outs, sign-ups, and other team related activities.

❑ As with the calendar negotiation, it is best to have an annual agreement instead of ongoing discussions about potential activities.

❑ The agreement should state that unless there are changes in the choice *of core activities*, the agreement will continue until amended and agreed to by both parties.

Core Activities

❑   *Core Activity A:* _____ chosen by mother for <u>(season defined)</u>.

   ❑   This activity meets _____ days per week for _____ hours per day.

      ❑   Scheduled instruction or practice days and times are:

      ❑   Day of week: _____ Time (From to) _____

      ❑   Location: _____

   ❑   The cost of this *core activity* is _____ per month.

      ❑   Payment for this *core activity* will be made by:

         ❑   Mother

         ❑   Father

         ❑   Both

            ❑   % Mother ___% = $ _____ / month

            ❑   % Father ___% = $ _____/month

   ❑   Payment for transportation to this *core activity* will be paid by:

      ❑   Each household individually

      ❑   Mother

      ❑   Father

      ❑   Both

         ❑   % Mother ___% = $ _____/ month

         ❑   % Father ___% = $ _____/month

   ❑   Payment for the equipment for this *core activity* will be paid by:

      ❑   Each household individually

      ❑   Mother

      ❑   Father

      ❑   Both

         ❑   % Mother ___% = $ _____ / month

         ❑   % Father ___% = $ _____/month

❑ Payment for an additional set of equipment (so that equipment will not have to be transferred between homes) will be paid by:

    ❑ Each household individually

    ❑ Mother

    ❑ Father

    ❑ Both

        ❑ % Mother ___% = $ _____

        ❑ % Father ___% = $ _____

❑ Payment for an additional uniform (so that each home can function independently and items will not be lost, forgotten or misplaced) will be made by:

    ❑ Each household individually

    ❑ Mother

    ❑ Father

    ❑ Both

        ❑ % Mother ___% = $ _____

        ❑ % Father ___% = $ _____

❑ *Core Activity B*: _____ chosen by the father for <u>(season defined)</u>.

    ❑ This activity meets _____ days per week for _____ hours per day.

        ❑ Scheduled instruction or practice days and times are:

        ❑ Day of week: _____ Time (From to) _____

        ❑ Location: _____

    ❑ The cost of this *core activity* is _____ per month.

        ❑ Payment for this *core activity* will be made by:

        ❑ Mother

        ❑ Father

        ❑ Both

            ❑ % Mother ___% = $ _____ / month

            ❑ % Father ___% = $ _____/month

❑ Payment for transportation to this *core activity* will be paid by:

    ❑ Each household individually

    ❑ Mother

    ❑ Father

    ❑ Both

        ❑ % Mother ___% = $ _____

        ❑ % Father ___% = $ _____

❑ Payment for the equipment for this *core activity* will be paid by:

    ❑ Each household individually

    ❑ Mother

    ❑ Father

    ❑ Both

        ❑ % Mother ___% = $ _____

        ❑ % Father ___% = $ _____

❑ Payment for an additional set of equipment (so that equipment will not have to be transferred between homes) will be paid by:

    ❑ Each household individually

    ❑ Mother

    ❑ Father

    ❑ Both

        ❑ % Mother ___% = $ _____

        ❑ % Father ___% = $ _____

❑ Payment for an additional uniform (so that each home can function independently and items will not be lost, forgotten or misplaced) will be made by:

    ❑ Each household individually

    ❑ Mother

    ❑ Father

    ❑ Both

        ❑ % Mother ___% = $ _____

        ❑ % Father ___% = $ _____

❑ Both parents agree that the above two activities are important to _____ .

(Name of child)

❑ Both parents agree to support each activity, to the best of their ability, at least two days per week, whether it is practice, lessons, etc.

Other Activities

❑ *'Other activities'* are defined as any other activity, *besides the two core activities,* agreed upon by both parents as stated above.

❑ *Other activities* will be chosen between the parent and the child in each home.

❑ *Other activities* will not interfere with the *core activities.*

❑ Payment for any *other activity* will be the responsibility of each individual house-hold. For example, if the mother chooses another activity, in addition to *the core activities,* then she will be financially responsible for that activity unless other-wise decided and clearly stated in a written agreement.

❑ Both parents can participate in the *other activity,* however, the financial responsi-bility will be clearly defined. The parent's attendance at the *other activity* will be the same as the agreement regarding the *core activities.*

The written agreement or parenting plan regarding extracurricular activities needs to incorporate the financial responsibility for the payment of the equipment and uniforms associated with the activity. The agreement may also include which parent will pay for the cost of transportation to the activity. While it may seem like overkill, the financial responsibility for these portions of the extracurricular agreement should be clearly defined to avoid potential confusion or conflict.

Take for example, the written divorce agreement (New York) that stated, "The Husband and Wife will each choose an extracurricular activity for the child. Each parent agrees to participate in the selected activities to the best of their ability. Husband agrees to pay the child's expenses for these extracurricular activities, provided that the parties can agree on their selection. In no event shall the Husband be obligated to assume the cost of any extracurricular activity to which he has not agreed."

As agreed, the mother and father each chose a core activity for the child. And, as agreed, the father paid the expenses. Soon after the selection of the activities, the mother decided she wanted to add another activity for her child. She said many of the child's friends were participating in the new activity, and the child wanted to attend.

The father said he thought it would be all right, but that he was already paying for the other two core activities. He told the mother that if she wanted to pay for the new activity, he would agree to drive the child to the additional activity one day per week, during his parenting time.

The child had participated in the new activity for approximately four months, when the father received a bill in the mail stamped "Past Due." The father telephoned the mother and reminded her that he agreed to "*drive*" the child to the activity, and she had agreed to be financially responsible. He reminded her that he was already paying for the other two *core activities*.

The mother became very angry with the father's refusal to pay for the new activity, and filed a motion with the court citing the original agreement. The mother argued that the father agreed to "drive the child to the activity" therefore, he "agreed to the activity," and should be required to pay.

The court agreed with the mother, resulting in the father having to pay the past due bill and for continuing participation in the new activity. He was also required to continue to pay for the other two agreed upon activities.

The mother then chose to write a 'letter of clarification' to the staff of the new activity. She attached the new court order and stated, "As you can see, per court order, my ex-husband John, *is* responsible for the payment of this bill. Please bill him directly from now on, and let me know immediately if payment is not made promptly. I will not hesitate to seek help from the court again to make sure you are paid. I have attached a copy of the court order for your records. Thank you for all of your help, understanding and assistance to help me continue this important activity for my child."

Fondly, Mary (the only parent who really cares about this child.)

This example is included to illustrate how quickly a situation can change from amicable and agreeable to malicious and deceitful. It is paramount that your intentions for participation in extracurricular activities, and the limits of your financial responsibilities are clearly defined. Here, the divorce agreement was too vague in its intent and wording.

This example also illustrates how easily a malicious parent can manipulate an opportunity to confide in a child or co-opt extracurricular instructors. In this case, the mother used this opportunity to create anger between the child and the father. She chose to tell the child the father had refused to pay for the extracurricular activity. The next time the child saw the father she was angry with him. The mother also confided in the extracurricular staff, who in turn treated the father poorly when he attempted to participate in the new program. Ultimately, this mother succeeded in ruining the extracurricular experience for everyone, including her child.

In this case, the wording of the agreement (regarding the payment for extracurricular activities) was damaging to the child in the future, as it diminished the likelihood of cooperation between the parents regarding extracurricular activities. From the father's perspective, he wanted the court to modify the extracurricular portion of the agreement. He believed the mother had sufficient financial resources to finance additional extracurricular activities of her choice for the child. Unfortunately, the court would not modify the agreement.

This case illustrates how a liberal and undefined agreement, established at the beginning and chaotic state of the divorce process, can cause problems for parental agreements in the future. The parents in this case experienced difficulty throughout their child's youth in choosing activities and sharing the extracurricular experience of their child without tension and ongoing resentment.

Extracurricular Activities: Parental Attendance and Boundaries

Parental attendance and boundaries at your child's events are extremely important to consider before "testing out the field" in front of your child and others. As described above, even choosing or innocently signing your children up for an activity, can create loyalty issues that are significantly traumatic to your child.

As a general rule, assume the stricter the better when defining the agreement regarding joint parental attendance at extracurricular events. Strict boundaries can be altered or loosened if mutual respect for the *custodial parent's* space and the child's psychological wellbeing is demonstrated on a consistent basis after divorce. However, if limits are not established in the beginning, it is very difficult to create and implement them once a minimal amount of time has passed and the boundaries are unclear.

In their excellent book, *Caught in the Middle: Protecting the Children of High Conflict Divorce*, Carla Garrity and Mitchell Baris explore, "The (parenting) agreement might need to restrict joint attendance at school functions, recitals or sporting events, dividing them fairly between the parents ahead of time." [2] Garrity and Baris also state,

> "Some events, however, cannot be duplicated or divided. In the case of children's recitals or special school programs, parents should agree to keep away from each other if there is a chance they will argue. All too often, we hear children talk about looking forward to performing in the school play but fearing that their parents will spoil the occasion by fighting in front of their friends and teachers. Parents who cannot maintain some physical distance from each other at school events should agree to divide them, even though this means missing some of the milestone events of their children's lives. During the regular season, it will be easy enough to alternate attendance at games or athletic matches; play-off and championship matches, however, pose a harder challenge, especially as the children probably will want both parents to attend. Here again, if they cannot do so without conflict, they will need to divide up these events as well." [3]

It is important to note that physical distance alone, between the parents, may not be enough to protect the child from psychological pressure and loyalty issues. Children are very sensitive, and may have trouble when both parents attend an event and are in such close proximity. This is especially true if the child knows the parents do not get along.

Guidelines need to be specific and explained in detail to the parents regarding their conduct at joint events. Remember, it takes only *one parent* to spoil the atmosphere and the tone of an encounter. If one parent cannot abide by the guidelines, then joint attendance is not feasible and should not be recommended.

One way to establish a clear and fair guideline is for parents to agree on the designation of a '*custodial parent of an event.*' The *custodial parent of the event* can be defined in several ways. The underlying rule is that the parent who has custody of the event, has custody of the child *during the event.* The *custodial parent* can be defined as:

➤ the parent taking the child home from the event,
➤ the parent who has the child for the week,
➤ the parent who is out of town and is present specifically for the event, or,
➤ other designations that may be appropriate for your particular situation.

These detailed guidelines should also include a time limit by which the non-custodial parent should leave the event.

Take for example, the mother in Georgia who refused to leave the premises following events during the father's custodial time. In this case, the parents had agreed in a non-binding mediation (no written agreement) that the 'non-custodial parent' would leave the extracurricular location (following an event that occurred during the other parent's custodial time) within five minutes. The non-custodial parent would also limit 'good-byes' and 'congratulations' to the child to a brief 1 - 2 minutes. In respect of this parent/child interaction, the parent having 'custody of the event' would 'stand clear,' to allow the other parent space to say good-bye and give praise and love to the child.

This verbal arrangement seemed very fair, and for several years the agreement was very effective in supporting boundaries at events involving both parents. The child experienced both parents participating and enjoying the events without tension, conflict or loyalty issues.

But something changed, and the mother decided she would no longer honor the definitions or the agreement of the 'shared environment.' Instead, she began to interfere aggressively when the father had custodial time of an extracurricular event. This change in the mother's attitude, and her contrived actions, adversely affected the child. The physical distance between parents was violated, and the emotional pressure at the events began to loom clearly over the child.

The mother told the father that her child *"wanted her there* and that she had every right to be at the events without *rules!"* To make her point clear, the mother began dominating the pre and post event activities intentionally. She insisted that her child, child's friends and parents were attentive to her, often creating scenes of loud laughter and an exaggerated exuberant attitude. The mother would then look over gloatingly to the father, while he maintained the physical distance on which they had agreed.

In this case, the child's right to participate and enjoy their activity (free of *emotional baggage)* was not honored, and ultimately the child was caught in the middle of the parent's disagreements. Instead of being able to enjoy activities as a normal child, the child was repeatedly involved in parental disputes and burdened with loyalty issues at the extracurricular events.

Guidelines for Parental Attendance and Boundaries at Extracurricular Events

Once the parents have decided on the selection of the child's core activities, including the payment for equipment and transportation, they should then address and define the guidelines for joint attendance at the activities. Initially, this may be another difficult task, but once the guidelines are clearly defined it will significantly reduce the opportunity for conflict and awkwardness when both parents attend an event simultaneously.

❑ The *non-interference* policy should remain a priority at all events!

❑ Approach the agreement with a *'separate but equal policy'* for each parent's involvement in the child's activities.

❑ Every effort should be made to establish guidelines and boundaries for both parents as equally as possible.

  ❑ Assume that the stricter the agreement the better.

❑ Parents rarely consider setting limits. Rather, they flounder through unpleasant experiences, increasing conflict and opportunities for debate.

  ❑ Remember that boundaries can be relaxed if good parental behavior patterns are demonstrated over time.

❑ Setting clear limits and boundaries (in the beginning) helps build constructive boundaries for both the parents and the children.

❑ It can be very difficult to redefine boundaries when a minimal amount of time has passed, and destructive behavior patterns have emerged.

❑ Secure a written agreement regarding attendance and boundaries at extra-curricular events. Be as specific as possible.

❑ Separate attendance at extracurricular activities, without interference from the other parent, may well be the best arrangement.

➢ Positive outcomes of separate attendance:

    ➢ Reduces the opportunity for stressful situations, including loyalty issues for the child and unnecessary interaction between the parents.

    ➢ Reduces the child's potential involvement in parental issues, conflict and discomfort, and allows the child to enjoy *their* sport or activity free from *emotional baggage.*

    ➢ Allows the child to concentrate on their sport or activity. Trying to interact with both parents at an event may add emotional pressure on the child and distract them, hampering their ability to enjoy and/or perform their activity to the best of their ability.

    ➢ Allows the parents to enjoy the activity with reduced anxiety. The environment will be more conducive to a relaxed and non-stressful situation. The parent attending the activity will be able to visit with the other parents, without interference or loyalty issues.

➢ Clearly define which events require both parents to attend, for example, *special or one-time events.*

➢ *Special events* may be defined as those events that occur only once such as a one night only performance or an end of the season championship game.

➢ The parents will strive to alternate events in a fair and equal manner.

➢ Define which parent will be the *custodial parent of the event*, understanding that the parent's will alternate events in a fair and equal manner. Examples for the parenting plan might include:

    ➢ The custodial parent (the parent who the child is scheduled to be with that day and night) will attend the performance.

    ➢ Each parent will respect the custody time of the other. If it is one parent's night to attend the recital, the other parent will stay away.

    ➢ The parent who has 'custody of the location or event,' will stay for the 'post game wrap up,' 'post-recital ceremonies,' 'post-church etiquette,' etc.

    ➢ The non-custodial parent (the parent who does not have 'custody of the event') will attend the dress rehearsal, student performance, or whatever alternate performance is available to attend.

Special and One Time Events

❑ Clearly define '*Special*' and "*One-Time Events*'
❑ Examples of special and/or one time events may include:

    ❑ Religious events

        ❑ Confirmations
        ❑ Bah/Bar Mitzvah's
        ❑ _____ other

    ❑ Graduations

        ❑ Pre-school
        ❑ Elementary school
        ❑ Middle school
        ❑ High school
        ❑ College
        ❑ Graduate or specialty schools
        ❑ _____ other

    ❑ Plays/Recitals/Chorus/Performing Arts/Science Fairs/etc.

    ❑ Sporting events:

        ❑ Play-offs and championship games. Play-off and championship games are defined as:

            ❑ Post season play-off and championship games
(This *does not* include regular season games, or tournaments played during the regular season.)

            ❑ Regional, state or national events such as 'State Cup,' 'Nationals,' 'Olympic Development,' 'State Competitions,'
or _____ (other) _____

❏ If both parents must attend an event, establish guidelines for parental conduct, including guidelines for honoring physical 'parental space.' For example:

  ❏ The parent designated as the 'non-custodial parent of the event' will say a brief hello/good-bye to the child and leave '*promptly.*'

  ❏ 'Promptly' is defined as within 5 minutes of the end of the event, the final bell, final curtain call, end of performance, etc.

  ❏ The parents will remain 20 yards apart at all times (or other reasonable *clearly defined* distance.)

  ❏ There will be no direct communication between the parents at the special or one time event.

  ❏ Any communication should be made away from the event, and as defined in the communication section of the parenting agreement.

  ❏ The mother and her guests will sit on the _____ side of all events.
                                (right or left)

  ❏ The father and his guests will sit on the _____ side of all events.
                                (right or left)

When parents can agree to abide by guidelines such as these, it frees the child to participate and enjoy *their event* without emotional complications. *Remember, these events are about the child, not necessarily the parents!* The child observes and experiences both parents participating and attending *their special event.* The potential for conflict and unnecessary interference is significantly reduced, and the parent's attendance at the events appears to be civil. A child will build confidence in *both parents,* observing them attending events simultaneously, even though there may be no direct communication between the parents at the event. The child is supported, and both parents are able to participate in a very important aspect of the child's life.

The best case scenario is that the child does not know of these parental arrangements, and that the boundaries "just happen" naturally. Some parents, however, insist on involving the child in the parental boundary issue. Unfortunately, this effort to 'confide' in the child only dilutes the effectiveness of the guidelines.

Other Solutions to Attending Activities Separately

➢ Offer to videotape an event that can be shared with the other parent. This strategy has multiple advantages.

➢ The child observes and experiences their parent's cooperative efforts about the events (at least on the surface.) One parent is videotaping the child's event for the other parent. It also allows the absent parent the opportunity to share the event with the child in a different format, when they are together.

➢ Watching a video with the child presents the unique opportunity to view the event from a different perspective, especially for the child. The child watches their own performance and can share the event retrospectively with the parent.

➢ Use the opportunity of viewing the videotape to improvise and create a fun experience for the child. Fast forwarding and reversing of the video makes for a spontaneous comedy, and instills energetic enthusiasm in most children. Viewing oneself as a child works miracles on their self-esteem, even if they made mistakes. Use this time to your advantage to build a positive rapport with your child.

Guidelines for Maintaining Autonomy at Your Child's Extracurricular Activities

Hopefully, you will succeed in creating a written agreement for the selection of the child's activities, which parent will attend the activities and specific guidelines for parental conduct if both parents attend the same event simultaneously. Now is the time to enjoy your child's life and their extracurricular activities, free from interference by the other parent.

The following guidelines are listed to assist parents in creating autonomy with the new family structure, and to promote a special parent/child relationship as it relates to the child's activities.

Communication with Instructors, Coaches, Managers and Tutors

➢ It is very important to establish a positive rapport with all personnel involved in your child's extracurricular activities.

➢ Introduce yourself and get to know your child's coaches and instructors, despite which parent enrolled the child in the activity.

➢ This begins the process that enables a parent to take a proactive role in the child's activity. It is important to note that many parents may attempt to *co-opt* the coaches and/or instructors.

> ➤ Introducing yourself at the beginning of the season may help diffuse any damage that can be caused by any negative co-opting efforts of the other parent.

➤ Offer to go to coffee or lunch with the coach, instructor and/or manager. (If your schedule permits)

> ➤ Get to know the coach or instructor and let them know you are a willing and supportive parent. Use this meeting to your advantage, offering your help, support and your willingness to volunteer.

> ➤ *Do not* use the meeting to trash your ex-spouse.

> ➤ Let the coach or instructor know that you are supportive of your child and the activity.

> ➤ Tell the coach that you would like to order (and pay for) two (2) complete uniforms for your child.

> ➤ Explain to the coach that having two uniforms will make life much easier for your child.

➤ Requesting a duplicate uniform at the beginning of the season (during registration or sign-ups) eliminates many opportunities for unnecessary communication, confusion or potential conflict with the other parent.

> ➤ Malicious parents may use the exchange of uniforms as a means to communicate unnecessarily or to sabotage visitation time.

> ➤ There is nothing worse than realizing at the last minute that your child's uniform was not exchanged with the child. This leaves you vulnerable to calling the ex-spouse to ask for the uniform (or even one soccer sock) that is necessary for your child to participate in their activity. You are also at risk for appearing non-supportive, incompetent and unprepared for your child's activity.

> ➤ The request for an extra uniform may cost an additional fee, but it is well worth the expense. Arriving at a practice or a game without a uniform is humiliating to your child, and may cause a serious misunderstanding with the coach or instructor.

> ➤ Most individuals, including coaches and instructors, may not understand your situation or your inability to 'share items' with your ex-spouse. To others, the basic sharing of a uniform would seem an unlikely issue to create conflict.

➢ Ironically, the *simple issues* are often the ones a malicious ex-spouse may use to their advantage. Often, the simpler the issue the better, when trying to co-opt the coach or instructor. For example, a malicious parent may say to the coach, "Now you can finally understand. Their father is so unreasonable, he can't even share the uniform." Hence, the stage is set to undermine the other parent and create loyalty preferences with the extracurricular staff. *Eliminate the possibility!* If you can afford it, order a second uniform or whatever is needed to equip your child for their extracurricular activity.

➢ Financial concerns for additional equipment, instruments, uniforms and other extracurricular paraphernalia.

    ➢ If cost is truly an issue, and it is not possible to have separate equipment or uniforms at each home, then clearly define how the equipment will be shared between the two households.

    ➢ Children living in two homes become accustomed to *'shuffling'* items back and forth between households. It is not the best scenario and the fewer items that need to be transferred between homes, the better. Parents can assist their child in *'shuffling,'* or they can manipulate the need for certain items at the other home to a malicious advantage.

➢ Establish a procedure (at the onset of the activity) to minimize the opportunity for a parent to use the equipment to increase interaction or interference with your parenting time.

    ➢ For example, if the equipment, instrument or uniform does not arrive with the child for your parenting time, identify a neutral third party or location where the other parent 'who simply forgot' can deliver the items.

    ➢ Some parents elect to use the coach or instructor of the activity to act as the neutral party.

    ➢ These individuals can also assume the responsibility for calling the 'forgetful parent' and ask them to deliver the items when needed. Again, this eliminates the potential for individual interaction with the other parent, especially if they have maliciously created a situation to increase contact and perhaps conflict.

        ➢ Musical instruments can be delivered to the music teacher at any time other than when you or your child will be present.

        ➢ Equipment can be delivered to the coach or manager at any time other than actual practice or game times, when you and/or your child will be present.

➤ *Assure that the location for delivery of the 'forgotten items' is not the same location that you or your child will be.* The 'forgotten items' are often used as a very convincing way to have interaction with the other parent or child during 'non-custodial days.' It may take several attempts, but if the neutral exchange of the items does not result in the desired parent-to-parent or parent-to-child contact, then the manipulative ex-spouse will usually abort this method and try something else.

Communication About Extracurricular Activities

➤ Ask the coach's for assistance to assure that all communications (written, via telephone or e-mail) made regarding the sport or activity (including schedules and practices) is communicated to *both households.*

➤ Some malicious parents will tell the coaches and instructors there is not a need to inform the other household. These parents may portray that they communicate regularly with the other parent, and it is only necessary for the coach or instructor to make one telephone call.

➤ These parents need to have control of all the information, and may use the information to control the other parent's involvement in a particular activity.

➤ *Communication with both homes regarding extracurricular activities is paramount, and should occur whether or not it is your parenting time!*

➤ Emphasize to the instructors or coaches the importance of good communication with both homes.

➤ Communication with both homes eliminates potential stress for the child, who is often told it is his/her responsibility to "pass along information" as *the messenger.*

➤ Children *should not* be responsible for retaining trivial information such as change of location for practice or change of time for a game.

➤ Provide the coaches and instructors with your telephone number, address, e-mail, fax and cellular numbers.

➤ *Be persistent and stay informed!*

➤ Monitor the situation to ensure communication with the coach and/or the instructor is occurring to your satisfaction.

➢ If there is a lack of communication, call the coach, instructor or team manger and tell them what happened in specifics, redefining your commitment and interest in your child's activity.

In the beginning, you may not realize the importance of separate information and communication for your household. Being informed about your child's activity is paramount in keeping your life simple and free from post divorce conflict and confusion. Compare these two scenarios:

Scenario # 1: You have not seen Jayne in seven days. Jane gets into the car during an exchange and says, "Hi Dad. Oh, you need to know that my practice schedule has changed from 3:30 to 5:30 and we are now practicing at South Field instead of West Field. Mom said to be sure to tell you because you probably don't know what's going on."

As the other parent, you are already informed because the coach communicated with you timely. Your response to Jayne, "Hey, cool, I know all about it. Your coach is good about telling both your Mom and me what is happening. You do not need to worry about that. Everyone is working together to make sure you don't miss a thing."

The situation is diffused. You are relaxed and poised and express no anger or anxiety. Your child also gains confidence in the fact that you really *do* know, and care about, what is going on.

Scenario # 2: You do not know what is happening. The coach is not communicating with you. Jayne gets into the car during the exchange and says, "Hi Dad. Oh, you need to know that my practice schedule has changed from Monday and Wednesday at 3:30 to Tuesday and Thursday at 5:30 and we are now practicing at South Field instead of West Field. Something to do with field maintenance or something. Mom said to be sure to tell you because you probably don't know what's going on."

There is really no way to prepare for the surprise of hearing this information during the first few minutes of an exchange. As we have discussed, tension is typically higher at exchanges, and children often blurt out information they must give you as soon as they see you. Now, you are out of control of the basic information. You have no knowledge to base your reaction on. You may fall into the trap of reacting negatively in front of your child. Feeling "left out of the loop" your impulsive response may be, "Why wasn't I told?" "Why can't that stupid coach let me know what's happening?" "I can't take you Tuesday, you know that!"

You may experience some anxiety, anger or resentment, and now your child is emotionally involved in the situation. They probably like their coach or instructor. They may wonder why you are not informed, or they may just assume that only Mom knows what is happening. At least, that is how it may feel to a child. "Life is chaotic with my dad, organized and informed with my mom."

Taking a proactive roll in this type of situation can only work to your advantage. Place the responsibility for appropriate communication on the coach, manager or instructor. Monitor your communications with these individuals carefully. If there is confusion, express your concern calmly, emphasizing your need for *their support* to ensure your child will be able to participate and be successful in the activity.

In closing, it is important to remember this is not a popularity contest. Your request for current information regarding your child's activity is *entirely reasonable*! If the coach and/or the instructors are not willing or able to comply, then maybe you should reconsider your child's involvement in the activity altogether. After all, extracurricular activities are for *enrichment and enjoyment*, and should not become a convenient avenue to alienate or ostracize a parent from a child's activity.

Stay neutral and stay informed!
Be prepared to offer solutions, as a family of divorce!
Persevere for fairness and equality in all your child's activities!

(Endnotes)

[1] Turkat, I. D. (1995). Divorce Related Malicious Mother Syndrome, *Journal of Family Violence,* Volume 10, pp. 253-264.

[2] Garrity, C. B. & Baris M. A. (1994) *Caught in the Middle: Protecting the Children of High Conflict Divorce.* New York: Lexington Books. p. 59.

[3] id., p. 148.

22.

Passports, International Travel and Jurisdiction
Parental Kidnapping and Child Abductions

———————————

———————————

As with the chapter on stalking, this chapter cannot possibly include all the legal and psychological ramifications of parental kidnapping. This chapter is included to give the reader a brief overview of the progress made by Congress to protect the rights of children and parents who may be victims of a child being abducted by the other parent.

While the guidelines presented are specific and researched, they are not inclusive of preventing a kidnapping, or securing the return of a child. Assure that you and your attorney have thoroughly researched parental kidnapping, and that all your legal separation and divorce agreements address jurisdiction, the penalties for kidnapping and interfering with parental access.

Of special interest, is the fact that parents who kidnap have many of the same characteristics and motives as parents who brainwash or program and alienate their children from the other parent. These same characteristics also align with the personality traits of an individual who may also become a "stalking parent." The ultimate alienation of a child is to kidnap them (taking them to another state or country) where the intent is the child will never be able to have contact with the other parent again.

While more research is needed, it behooves any parent having trouble in the relationship with a former partner, to be informed of parental kidnapping and their rights to have access to their children.

Hence, when preparing legal agreements, all parents (and attorneys and judges!) should recognize the possibility of the parental abduction of a child. Again, in the beginning phases of separation and divorce the possibility of parental abduction might initially seem absurd. However, it is a reality to thousands of families each year. In fact, according to the Center for Missing and Exploited Children, 750,000 children are abducted each year (2100 per day) and more than 300,000 of those kidnappings are parental abductions!

In the government booklet, *International Parental Child Abduction*, published by the United States Department of State; Bureau of Consular Affairs, 1995, they state:

> "You and your child are most vulnerable when your relationship with the other parent is broken or troubled; the other parent has close ties to another country; and the other country has traditions or laws that may be prejudicial to a parent of your gender or to aliens in general." [1]

Attorneys Should Pay Close Attention to a Parent's Concerns.

In her article, *Parental Kidnapping: Prevention and Remedies*, Patricia Hoff outlines some of the common predictors of child abduction. Hoff explores the involvement and responsibility of attorneys in protecting children from kidnapping. She states,

> "If a client expresses concerns about a potential abduction, the lawyer should ascertain the basis for these concerns. The likelihood of an interstate or international abduction may be increased where there is evidence that a parent:

> ➢ has previously abducted the child or threatened to do so;
> ➢ lacks strong ties to the child's home state;
> ➢ has friends or family living out of the state or abroad;
> ➢ has a strong support network;
> ➢ can earn a living almost anywhere, or is financially independent;
> ➢ recently quit a job, sold a home, terminated a lease, closed a bank account or liquidated other assets;
> ➢ has a history of marital instability or a lack of parental cooperation; or
> ➢ has a prior criminal history. [2]

Hoff further states, "When there are risk factors present that indicate a heightened risk of child abduction, the lawyer should request safeguards from the court that are appropriate to the facts and circumstances of the case. These my include, but are not limited to:

> ➢ restrictions on removal of a child from the state or country;
> ➢ supervised visitation;
> ➢ specific visitation schedules;
> ➢ passport restrictions;
> ➢ obtaining reciprocal order from a foreign court;
> ➢ writs ne exeat; and
> ➢ bonds." [3]

It is interesting to note that Hoff cites in Section 4 of her article, The judge's view of safeguards: Prepare to meet a high burden of proof.

"Very few judges have extensive experience with parental kidnapping cases and may be wary about ordering protective measures absent a strong showing of the likelihood of flight."

"...All available evidence of the predictors set forth above, as well as others known to the parent who fears an abduction will occur should be presented. International abduction is possible, the lawyer should discover the foreign jurisdiction's custody law in order to educate the judge about the difficulties the client would encounter if faced with having to recover the child from abroad."[4]

There is also now an excellent online resource available for family law judges and lawyers at www.travel.state.gov. Once at the U.S. Department of State, Office of Children's Issues site, click on Resources for Judges on International Parental Child Abduction. This internet site offers many valuable tools for family law judges and attorneys.

A Brief History and Explanation of the US Child Abduction Laws

State Laws

"*Civil*: Before 1968, parents who abducted their children in the course of an acrimonious separation or divorce stood an excellent chance of being rewarded with custody. Any court before which the abductor-parent appeared had the legal authority to issue a custody order based solely upon the abductor's physical presence in the state with the child.

The inherent unfairness to the left-behind parent and the psychological harm to the child in being shifted from home to home, and the inefficiency and judicial expense wrought by repetitious litigation over child custody in sister states, ultimately led to the promulgation and eventual adoption by all 50 states and the District of Columbia of the Uniform Child Custody Jurisdiction Act (UCCJA).

The UCCJA governs when a court has jurisdiction to make a custody determination, limits the right of state courts to modify sister state custody orders, and requires recognition and enforcement of custody orders." [5]

"The UCCJA is primarily a jurisdictional statute that addresses when a court has subject matter jurisdiction in a custody case, whether a court should exercise jurisdiction and whether it must enforce or can modify the decree of another State.

The UCCJA stipulates that any of the following four bases could be used to establish a State's jurisdiction:

➤ The State is the child's 'home state.'

➤ The child has 'significant connections' with the State.

➤ The State has emergency jurisdiction.

➤ The State assumes jurisdiction when no other State has jurisdiction or when another State has declined jurisdiction because it is in the best interests of the child for the first court to assume jurisdiction.

Specific sections of the UCCJA are designed to prevent simultaneous proceedings, including:

➤ Section 6, which requires a stay of proceedings and inter-court communications when there are simultaneous proceedings in different States.

➤ Section 9, which requires that an affidavit be filed providing information about past and current custody proceedings, together with addresses of the parties and the child.

➤ Section 16, which requires that certified copies of custody orders be filed in the child custody registry of the court where the order is to be enforced." [6]

"*Criminal*: Every state now has criminal penalties for parental kidnapping (also referred to as 'custodial interference') and nearly all states have established missing children clearinghouses to assist in the location, recovery and return of missing and parentally abducted children."

Information on state missing children clearinghouses may be obtained by contacting the National Center for Missing and Exploited Children, 1-800-843-5678.

Federal Laws

The Parental Kidnapping Prevention Act (PKPA):

"This federal law (28 U.S.C. & 1738A), enacted in 1980, gives priority to the home state basis for subject matter jurisdiction. Its purpose is to resolve conflicts between two States in favor of the home state when one claims jurisdiction based on significant connections and the other claims jurisdiction based on home state. The PKPA requires courts to enforce and not modify custody orders of sister States that exercised jurisdiction consistently with the Act.

The PKPA also clarifies that warrants for unlawful flight to avoid prosecution (UKAP) can be issued in parental kidnapping cases. The Federal Bureau of investigation (FBI) can investigate interstate and international parental abduction cases in which a UFAP warrant has been issued. Finally, the PKPA allows 'authorized persons' to use the Federal Parent Locator Service to locate an abducting parent and parentally abducted child." [7]

Special Note: "The law does not permit parents to initiate inquiries on their own behalf: parents are *not* 'authorized persona.' In order to use the services of the FPLS for parental kidnapping and child custody cases, a parent should contact an authorized person in his or her state of residence."

"Authorized persons" may include:

➢ state court judges
➢ police officers and prosecutors
➢ state officials and state attorneys
➢ FBI Agents and U.S. Attorneys

To further clarify The Parental Kidnapping Prevention Act (PKPA), 28 U.S.C. 1738A; 42 U.S.C. 653-655; 663; 18 U.S.C. 1073 note, the federal Fugitive Felon Act, 18 U.S.C. 1073, applies to state felony parental kidnapping cases.

"This latter provision allows for the issuance of an Unlawful Flight to Avoid Prosecution ("UFAP") warrant upon the request of a state prosecutor when an abductor-parent has been charged with a state felony offence and FBI assistance is needed to locate the absconding parent. If the FBI locates the abductor-parent, the federal charges are dropped and extradition and prosecution under state law proceeds." [8]

Hague Child Abduction Convention:

"In 1988, the Hague Convention on the Civil Aspects of International Child Abduction came into force in the United States upon enactment of federal implementing legislation, the International Child Abduction Remedies Act, 42 U.S.C. 11601-11610.

The Convention calls for the prompt return of wrongfully removed or retained children to their country of 'habitual residence.' Once returned, substantive decisions about custody and visitation can then be made." [9]

According to the United States Central Authority, Office of Children's Issues, the Hague Convention governs only cases involving countries that have become parties to it. Information regarding the status of countries participating in the Hague can be obtained at http://www.travel.state.gov and then click on International Parental Child Abduction. As of February 1, 2004 the following countries (and the effective dates) are party to the Hague Convention:

Argentina	06/01/91
Australia	07/01/88
Austria	10/01/88
Bahamas	01/01/94
Belgium	05/01/99
Belize	11/01/89
Bosnia-Herzegovina	12/01/91
Brazil	12/01/03
Burkina Faso	11/01/92
Canada	07/01/88
Chile	07/01/94
China	
Hong Kong *(Special Admin. Region)*	09/01/97
Macau	03/01/99
Columbia	06/01/96
Croatia	12/01/91
Cypress	03/01/95
Czech Republic	03/01/98
Denmark	07/01/91
Ecuador	04/01/92
Finland	08/01/94
France	07/01/88
Germany	12/01/90
Greece	06/01/93
Honduras	06/01/94

Hungary	07/01/88
Iceland	12/01/96
Ireland	10/01/91
Israel	12/01/91
Italy	05/01/95
Luxembourg	07/01/88
Former Yugoslav	
Rep. of Macedonia	12/01/91
Malta	02/01/03
Mauritius	10/01/93
Mexico	10/01/91
Monaco	06/01/93
Netherlands	09/01/90
New Zealand	10/01/91
Norway	04/01/89
Panama	06/01/94
Poland	11/01/92
Portugal	07/01/88
Romania	06/01/93
Slovak Republic	02/01/01
Slovenia	04/01/95
South Africa	11/01/97
Spain	07/01/88
St. Kitts & Nevis	06/01/95
Sweden	06/01/89
Switzerland	07/01/88
Turkey	08/01/00
United Kingdom	07/01/88
Bermuda	03/01/99
Cayman Islands	08/01/98
Falkland Islands	06/01/98
Isle of Man	09/01/91
Montserrat	03/01/99
United States	10/25/80
Venezuela	01/01/97
Yugoslavia, Federal Republic of	12/01/91
Zimbabwe	08/01/95

In her excellent article, *Parental Kidnapping: Prevention and Remedies*, Patricia Hoff states, "Countries that have ratified the Hague Child Abduction Convention no longer pose the same problems as non-Hague countries do in regard to obtaining the prompt return of abducted children. However, if children are removed to, or retained in, non-ratifying countries, traditional enforcement problems must be overcome." [10]

Unfortunately, according to the Report on Compliance with the Hague Convention and the Civil Aspects of International Child Abduction, published by the United States State Department, 2001,[11] even children traveling to Hague countries are not always protected as hoped. In their 2001 report The Department of State disclosed,

> "This report identifies those countries that the Department of State has found to have demonstrated a pattern of noncompliance or that, despite a small number of cases, have such system problems that the Department believes a larger volume of cases would demonstrate continued noncompliance constitut-ing a pattern. It recognizes that countries may demonstrate varying levels of commitment to and effort in meeting their obligations under the convention. The Department considers that countries listed as noncompliant are not taking effective steps to address deficiencies.
>
> As discussed below, the Department of State considers Austria, Hondu-ras, Mauritius and Panama to be noncompliant using this standard, and Mexico to be not fully compliant. The Department of State has also identified several countries of concern that have inadequately addressed some aspects of their obligations under the Hague Convention. These countries are The Bahamas, Columbia, Germany, Poland, Spain, Sweden and Switzerland." [12]

Therefore, all possible precautions should be taken by any parent who is truly concerned about parental kidnapping!

A note of caution: "Criminal charges may have a distorting effect on the operation of the Hague Convention and may even prove counterproductive. With the Hague Convention, the emphasis is on the swift return of a child to his or her place of habitual residence where the custody dispute can then be resolved, if necessary, in the courts of that jurisdiction. As a rule, therefore, it is advisable to await the outcome of return proceedings under the Convention before deciding whether to initiate criminal proceedings against the other parent. *Some courts have denied return of children solely because the taking parent would be arrested if they accompanied the child home.* Many of these courts, U.S. and foreign, have held that the arrest of the parent would expose the child to psychological harm (Article 13(b))." [13]

The Criminal Justice System Response

"Federal laws mandate a role for law enforcement in the reporting of missing children, including parentally abducted children. State laws and procedures relating to missing children and to the crime of parental kidnapping vary widely." [14]

The Missing Children Act of 1982

"To promote the involvement of law enforcement in the location of missing children, the U.S. Congress passed the Missing Children Act of 1982, Public Law 97-292, 28 U.S.C. & 534 (a). This law requires the FBI to enter information about missing children into the National Crime Information Center (NCIC), a computer data base under the authority of the Federal Bureau of Investigation (FBI), which enables law enforcement agencies across the country to gain access to descriptive information about a particular missing person or fugitive.

Under this Act, local law enforcement officials can enter information on a missing child into NCIC (dependent on State Laws). The FBI is required to do so if local low enforcement does not." [15]

"The National Center for Missing and Exploited Children (NCMEC), a private nonprofit organization, receives Federal funds to serve as a national clearinghouse and resource center. NCMEC:

➢ Provides technical assistance in parental abduction and other missing children cases.
➢ Maintains a toll-free hot line (1-800-843-5678).
➢ Provides legal staff to consult with civil attorneys and prosecutors in child abduction cases.
➢ Serves as a national resource center on missing children.
➢ Works closely with State missing children clearinghouses." [16]

The National Child Search Assistance Act of 1990

"In the past, may State statutes and local law enforcement procedures required a waiting period before a child could be declared "missing" and an investigation started. Such delays made recovery of children more difficult.

To address this problem, Congress passed the National Child Search Assistance Act of 1990, Public Law 101-647, 42 U.S.C. &5780. This law:

> ➤ Prohibits law enforcement agencies from maintaining policies requiring waiting periods.

> ➤ Requires that information about missing children be entered immediately into NCIC and that NCIC entries be made available to the appropriate State missing children's clearinghouse." [16]

State Criminal Laws Relating to Parental Kidnapping

"All states have enacted criminal parental kidnapping statutes, most frequently termed 'criminal custodial interference' laws. These laws vary regarding whether parental kidnapping is designated a felony or a misdemeanor. In many States, parental abduction becomes a felony only after the child is transported across State lines.

The criminal liability of unwed parents, joint custodial parents, and sole custodial parents who abduct their children and prevent the other parent from having access to the children varies from State to State. In addition, in some States there is no criminal violation if the abduction occurs prior to the issuance of a custody order." [17]

Therefore, it is imperative that you and your attorney investigate the State law (in which you and your children reside) and that an issuance of a custody order is filed with the court as soon as possible!

The Creation of Clearinghouses

State Missing Children Clearinghouses

Most....."States and the District of Columbia have official State missing children clearinghouses, most of which were established by statute and exist within a State criminal justice agency. Clearinghouses vary in their resources and functions. Broadly described, these functions include:

> ➤ Providing public education and information.
> ➤ Communicating and coordinating with parents, attorneys, law enforcement, and other agencies.
> ➤ Helping locate and recover parentally abducted children.
> ➤ Serving as State contact under the Hague Convention in international abduction cases." [18]

Ideas and Suggestions for
Safeguarding Against Parental Kidnapping

❏ Thoroughly investigate your state law regarding jurisdiction.

❏ Be sure to investigate the state law in which you reside <u>and</u> the State law in which your children reside, if different.

❏ Thoroughly investigate your state law regarding law enforcement in the reporting of missing children, including parentally abducted children. State laws and procedures relating to missing children and to the crime of parental kidnapping may vary widely. [19]

❏ Assure that your legal custody agreement clearly delineates jurisdiction!

❏ Assure that your legal custody order is enforceable.

❏ "Do not proceed without a valid custody determination that is entitled to enforcement nationwide pursuant to the Parental Kidnapping Prevention Act (PKPA, 28 U.S.C. 1738A (a) (1980)." [20]

❏ "If a custody determination is made by a state court consistent with the PKPA's provisions, the resulting custody order is entitled to full faith and credit in all states and cannot be modified except as provided for in the federal law. 28 U.S.C. 1738A (d)." [20]

❏ *Assure that your attorney is familiar with (and has researched) all laws regarding parental abduction and child custody!*

❏ ***"Expressly state the basis for the exercise of jurisdiction and supporting jurisdictional facts.***

> ❏ At the bottom of the first page of the order, in **BOLD FACE UPPER CASE LETTERS**, state the penalties for violating the order.

> ❏ For example, **'VIOLATION OF THIS ORDER MAY SUBJECT THE PARTY IN VIOLATION TO CIVIL AND/OR CRIMINAL PENALTIES.'**

> ❏ Judges should advise the parties while they are in court about the consequences of non-compliance. See, e.g., Louis R. B. v. Terry B., Fam. Ct. Del., New Castle 1993 (Del. Ch. LEXIS 122) (March 24, 1993) (Court strongly advised both parties that one could be prosecuted if the child was not made available as ordered.)" [21]

Passports

❑ One effective strategy is to make sure that the child's passport is retained by a neutral, professional third party. Ideally, this should be an attorney. (An attorney can be held professionally liable if they release the passport without following appropriate procedures.)

    ❑ This policy should be in place and included in the settlement agreement whether or not there is a concern of parental abduction.

❑ The neutral professional third party cannot release the passport to either parent without the express written consent of both parents, including but not limited to:

    ❑ Dates of Travel   ❑ Places of Travel

    ❑ Itinerary of travel including lodging and specific airline and verified flight information.

    ❑ Proof of round trip ticket purchase (in full) from the traveling parent.

❑ While these guidelines are intended to help protect a child from international kidnapping, they are not full proof. For example, if the child has dual citizenship, as discussed below, a parent may be able to take the child out of the country with the procurement of a passport from the other country.

Consider Creating an Extraterritorial Custody Agreement (ECA)

❑ The Extraterritorial Custody Agreement, sample attached, is signed and acknowledged by both parents that the child is traveling out of the country with one parent.

❑ The attached example of an ECA is included as an example only. In no circumstance is the example of the ECA intended to replace an attorney or to provide legal or other type of advice. The ECA is presented here to provide the reader with some insights to the seriousness of parental kidnapping.

❑ In theory, the ECA states the rights of the non-traveling parent and reconfirms the child's legal jurisdiction including the superior parental rights of the non-traveling parent. For example, the traveling parent agrees *without duress* that the non-traveling parent is:

    ❑ A fit and loving parent to have the care, custody and control of the children.

    ❑ Provides the children with a loving and nurturing home in their legal jurisdiction.

    ❑ It is in the children's best interest to continue and enjoy the benefits of such a close and continuous association with the non-traveling parent and their family.

❑ The children currently enjoy all the material benefits of a superior standard of living in their current living arrangement with the non-traveling parent, including the benefits of a superior education and extracurricular activities.

❑ The Children have resided in _____ since _____(date) and have extended family and close friendships.

❑ Under no foreseeable circumstances would it be in the best interests of the child to be removed from the regular custody of the non-traveling parent and their family.

❑ That for the purpose of returning the children to _____ (county, State) USA, the non-traveling parent's rights with respect to the children are superior to those of the traveling parent, and for this purpose, the non-traveling parent shall be deemed to have <u>sole</u> custody of the children.

❑ The ECA outlines the time period for travel and establishes legal procedures to follow if the traveling parent does not return the children, e.g., within 48 hours of the scheduled return travel plans.

❑ The failure of the traveling parent to provide notice within the agreed upon time is the basis for the non-traveling parent to seek to establish rights in the foreign country.

❑ Before travel to a foreign country, each party designates a legal representative in the foreign country to act on their behalf should the traveling parent refuse to return the children to their legal jurisdiction and to the other parent.

❑ The signed extraterritorial custody agreement should be filed with the court of the child's legal jurisdiction.

Passport Policies Relating to Children: United States Department of State

Summary

❑ "...a parent or attorney may request the Office of Children's Issues to place the child's name in the Children's Passport Issuance Alert Program (CPIAP) lookout system. Under this system, the Department of State will notify the requesting parent or attorney that a passport application is being filed for the child. In these cases, if the Department has on file a court order granting sole custody to one parent, or restricting the child's travel, the passport would be denied." [22]

❑ The parent should contact the Office of Children's Issues, SA-29, 4th Floor U.S. Department of State, Washington D.C. 20520; Toll Free Phone within the U.S. 1-888-407-4747 (8 a.m. - 8 p.m.) Telephone: (202) 736-9130, Fax: (202) 736-9133." "All requests must be in writing, and include the child's full name, date of birth, place of birth, social security number, address and phone number of the requestor. [22]

❑ It is vitally important that parents with concerns about parental child abduction consider CPIAP as an abduction prevention measure. [22]

❑ "A parent who has a court order of sole custody, an order forbidding the child's departure from the jurisdiction or a similar order, may have the lookout entered and if a passport is applied for, it may be denied based upon the order.

❑ If an abducting parent is the subject of a federal criminal warrant, his or her passport may be revoked by the passport office if the warrant and the parent's name, date and place of birth, and whereabouts are provided to the Department." [24]

Directory and Resources for Abducted Children – As of 02/01/04

Office of Children's Issues
SA-29
U.S. Department of State
2201 C Street, NW
Washington D.C. 20520
Toll Free: (888) 407-4747
Telephone: (202) 736-9130
Fax: (202) 736-9133

Requests for certified copies of a child's passport application can be obtained from:

Department of State
Passport Services
Office of research and Liaison, 5th floor
1111 19th Street, NW
Washington, D.C. 20522-1705
Telephone: (202) 955-0447
Fax: (202) 955-0288

Office of Children's Issues
Internet Address: http://travel.state.gov

This web site also includes Country-Specific Abduction flyers.

National Center for Missing and Exploited Children (NCMEC)
Charles B. Wang International Children's Building
699 Prince Street
Alexandria, Virginia 22314-3175
Telephone: (703) 274-3900
Fax: (703) 274-2200
Internet address: http://www.missingkids.org
24-hour hotline for emergencies: 1-800-THE-LOST
1-800-843-5678

Federal Parent Locator Service (FPLS)
The FPLS can be accessed through local and State Child Support Enforcement Offices.
The names of those offices are available in telephone books and from the address below.

Office of Child Support Enforcement
Federal Parent Locator Service (FPLS)
370 L'Enfant Promenade, SW
Washington, D.C. 20201
Telephone: (202) 401-9373
Internet Address: http://www.acf.dhhs.gov/

For ABA Publications
American Bar Association (ABA)
750 North Lake Shore Drive
Chicago, IL 60611
Telephone: (312) 988-5555

The Office of Children's Issues, Internet Address: http://travel.state.gov, has Country-Specific Abduction flyers. These Country-Specific Abduction flyers provide current information about a participating country's specific child abduction policies and procedures. Each Country-specific flyer may contain information, such as:

➢ General Information about the country.

➢ Hague Convention Status.

➢ Who qualifies to apply under the Hague Convention.

➢ The Central Authority for the country, what the role of Central Authority and how they can be contacted, including the Department name, address, telephone and fax numbers.

➢ A description of the attachments/documents required by the country to be filed with the Hague application form, and instructions on how to obtain an application form. For example, each Country-Specific Abduction flyer may describe how to provide:

    ➢ documentation to support the child's "habitual residence."

    ➢ information regarding the location of the child.

    ➢ documentation to support "evidence of rights of custody."

    ➢ photographs of the child and of the taking parent.

    ➢ original or certified true copy of the child's birth certificate.

    ➢ original of certified true copy of marriage certificate and divorce decree, as appropriate.

    ➢ original or certified true copy of any court orders relating to access, custody or guardianship of the child.

    ➢ an affidavit or sworn statement from the left-behind parent that clearly explains what access is sought.

    ➢ where to send the completed Hague application and the supporting documentation.

    ➢ other useful non-essential documents.

The Office of Children's Issues also reminds applicants that "as of March, 2002 the State Department is experiencing considerable delays of three to four weeks in the delivery of regular mail due to mandated irradiation against harmful substances. They strongly recommend that Hague application packages be sent by courier such as FedEx, DHL, Express Mail, etc., to ensure prompt delivery." [22]

The flyers may also include a brief overview of the Country-specific judicial procedure, including:

> ➢ What to expect during an initial case processing.
> ➢ How the return decision is made.
> ➢ How long the process takes.
> ➢ Is it necessary to retain the services of a lawyer in the other country.
> ➢ How to find a lawyer in the other country.
> ➢ What costs the 'left behind parent' may incur during the recovery process.
> ➢ How decisions can be appealed.
> ➢ Explanations of any 'conditions for return of the child' under the Hague.
> ➢ Criminal remedies, with explanation that filing criminal child abduction charges in the U.S. against a taking parent may jeopardize a Hague Convention case. (Country specific)

Example of "Evidence of Habitual Residence"

"Evidence in an Affidavit or sworn statement from the applicant that clearly explains the habitual residence of the child and the circumstances surrounding the wrongful removal or retention of the child. If the application is not made within 12 months of the removal or retention, an explanation for the delay in making the application is required." (Australia 2004).

Other relevant information for "evidence of habitual residence" may be included to give the court a proper understanding of the situation. Additional information may include: information about where the child lived, who the child lived with, whether the parents were living together or apart; if living together, the nature of the relationship between the child and the applicant; if living apart, where the child lived and the nature and extent of contact between parents and child; any periods of time spent out of the requesting country, time spent in school, name of the school, child's grade in school, the child's routine prior to the removal or retention; child's relationship with other family members; whether the applicant had any knowledge of the abducting parent's intentions; what actions the applicant took on learning of the removal or retention; what arrangements the applicant can make for the return of the child (to accompany the child back home, to pay for airfares, etc.) (Country Specific Abductor Information - Australia 2002)

Example of "Evidence of Right of Custody"

An Affidavit of Law from a lawyer/attorney, that clearly explains the applicant's rights of custody at the time of the removal or retention as defined in Article 3 of the Conventional. Alternatively, a copy of the relevant Statute, Civil Code or Applicable State Law at the time of the removal or retention may be sufficient. Note: It is not necessary to obtain a post-abduction court order of sole custody to apply for assistance under the Hague Convention. Obtaining such as order may actually complicate your case. (Country Specific Flyer - Australia and Canada, 2004.) [22]

Information on Dual Nationality

"The concept of dual nationality means that a person is a citizen of two countries at the same time. Each country has its own citizenship laws based on its own policy. Persons may have dual nationality by automatic operation of different laws rather than by choice. For example, a child born in a foreign country to U.S. citizen parents may be both a U.S. citizen and a citizen of the country of birth.

A U.S. citizen may acquire foreign citizenship by marriage, or a person naturalized as a U.S. citizen may not lose the citizenship of the country of birth. U.S. law does not mention dual nationality or require a person to choose one citizenship or another. Also, a person who is automatically granted another citizenship does not risk losing U.S. citizenship. However, a person who acquires a foreign citizenship by applying for it may lose U.S. citizenship. In order to lose U.S. citizenship, the law requires that the person must apply for the foreign citizenship voluntarily, by free choice, and with the intention to give up U.S. citizenship.

Intent can be shown by the person's statements or conduct. The U.S. Government recognizes that dual nationality exists but does not encourage it as a matter of policy because of the problems it may cause. Claims of other countries on dual national U.S. citizens may conflict with U.S. law, and dual nationality may limit U.S. Government efforts to assist citizens abroad. The country where a dual national is located generally has a stronger claim to that person's allegiance.

However, dual nationals owe allegiance to both the United States and the foreign country. They are required to obey the laws of both countries. Either country has the right to enforce its laws, particularly if the person later travels there. Most U.S. citizens, including dual nationals, must use a U.S. passport to enter and leave the United States. Dual nationals may also be required by the foreign country to use its passport to enter and leave that country. Use of the foreign passport does not endanger U.S. citizenship. Most countries permit a person to renounce or otherwise lose citizenship.

Information on losing foreign citizenship can be obtained from the foreign country's embassy and consulates in the United States. Americans can renounce U.S. citizenship in the proper form at U.S. embassies and consulates abroad." [25]

An excellent resource regarding Parental Abductions is the publication, *Family Abduction: How to Prevent an Abduction and What to Do If Your Child is Abducted.* This publication is produced and distributed by the National Center for Missing & Exploited Children, the Office of Juvenile Justice and Delinquency Prevention (Office of Justice Programs, U.S. Department of Justice) and in cooperation with the ABA Center on Children and the Law (A program of Young Lawyers Division, American Bar Association.) The publication can be obtained by calling the National Center for Missing & Exploited Children - 1-800-THE-LOST, (1-800-843-5678) or by ordering online at www.missingkids.org.

Another excellent resource is *A Family Resource Guide on International Parental Kidnapping.* "This guide provides practical, detailed advice about preventing international kidnapping and increasing the chances that children who have been kidnapped or otherwise wrongfully retained will be returned." [26] This publication can be obtained from the Juvenile Justice Clearinghouse (JJC). Copies can be ordered online at http://puborder.ncjrs.org/ or by calling JJC at 1-800-638-8736.

endnotes)

[1] United States Department of State, Bureau of Consular Affairs. (1995). *International Parental Child Abduction.* p. 1.

[2] Hoff, Patricia M., *Parental Kidnapping: Prevention and Remedies.* Chicago, Illinois: American Bar Association, Center on Children and the Law. Parental Abduction Training and Dissemination Project.

[3] id.

[4] id., p. 13.

[5] id.

[6] U.S. Department of Justice, *Obstacles to the Recovery and Return of Parentally Abducted Children,* Research Summary, A publication of the Office of Juvenile Justice and Delinquency Prevention, March 1994, page 2.

[7] id., p. 3.

[8] Hoff, Patricia M., *Parental Kidnapping: Prevention and Remedies.* Chicago, Illinois: American Bar Association, Center on Children and the Law. Parental Abduction Training and Dissemination Project, id., p. 2.

[9] id., pp. 2-3.

[10] id., p. 14.

[11] U.S. Department of State, The Office of Children's Issues, *Report on Compliance with the Hague Convention on the Civil Aspects of International Abduction,* April 2001.

[12] id.

[13] International Parental Child Abduction, http://www.travel.state.gov/Int'lchildabduction.html, 2001, Office of Children's Issues, Department of State, Washington D.C. 20250-4818.

[14] U.S. Department of Justice, Obstacles to the Recovery and Return of Parentally Abducted Children, Research Summary, A publication of the Office of Juvenile Justice and Delinquency Prevention, March 1994, page 3.

[15] id.

[16, 17] id., page 4.

[18, 19] id., page 5.

[20] id., page 3.

[21] Hoff, Patricia M., *Parental Kidnapping: Prevention and Remedies.* Chicago, Illinois: American Bar Association, Center on Children and the Law. Parental Abduction Training and Dissemination Project, page 5.

[22] Department of State, Office of Children's Issues, *Fact Sheet on Passports for Family Law Judges and Lawyers,* www.travel.state.gov.

[23] U.S. Department of State, The Office of Children's Issues, Report on Compliance with the Hague Convention on the Civil Aspects of International Abduction, April 2001.

[24] Palmer-Royston, Sharon, United States Department of State, Washington D.C., Passport Policies Relating to Children, Summary.

[25] http:www.travel.state.gov/dualnationality.html.

[26] National Center for Missing & Exploited Children. www.missingkids.org.

PART FIVE

THE RESOURCES

23.

Glossary of Terms

-A-

Abuse - a behavior that causes physical, mental or emotional harm. [3]

Acting In - a behavior in which children turn their social-emotional problems inward as a way of coping with the programming/brainwashing. [1]

Acting Out - a behavior in which children direct their social-emotional problems onto the external environment - other people, institutions, or objects - as a way of coping with the programming/brainwashing. [1]

Active Participant - a child (or any other person) who is aware of the intent of the programmer/ brainwasher and actively participates in the process. [1]

Adversarial Divorce - Divorce where parties involved have conflicting interests and function more as enemies rather than individuals who are working together toward a fair (acceptable and affordable) settlement. [2]

Adversary system - The system of resolving disputes where the two sided compete instead of cooperate. [3]

Affidavit - A written statement made under oath and filed with the court. [3]

Alienation - one result of a programming/brainwashing process that leads to the estrangement of the child from the other parent. [1]

Alignment - a process whereby a child begins to side with a programming/brainwashing parent. [1]

Alimony - Periodic or lump sum support payments to a former spouse. Currently referred to as spousal support. See also Spousal Support. [3]

Allegations - The claims made by one side in a lawsuit. [3]

Ally Syndrome - techniques employed in order to get the child to side with one parent against the other. [1]

Alternative dispute resolution - A collection of techniques that settle a dispute without a trial. [3]

Appeal - A request to a higher court to review a decision made by a lower court.

Appraisal – Procedure for determining the fair market value of an asset when it is to be sold or divided as part of the divorce process. [2]

Arbitration - A form of alternative dispute resolution where the two sides submit the dispute to a third party, who makes the decision. [3]

Assets – Cash, property, investments, goodwill, and other items of value that appear on a balance sheet indicating the net worth of an individual or a business. [2]

- B -

Best interests of the child - The legal standard used to guide decisions about child custody and child support. [3]

> A discretionary legal standard used by judges when making decisions about custody, visitation, and support for a child when the parents are divorcing. [2]

Bias - An inability of the judge to make an impartial decision. [3]

Birthright - the feeling that many women have that because of their special biological linkage to the child, they have special rights and power in regard to that child. [1]

Brain Twirling - a technique of confusion whereby the programming/ brainwashing parent sets up two contradictory programmes; the first is to love and the second is to have disdain toward the other parent. [1]

Brainwashing - the actual selection and application of particular techniques, procedures, and methods employed as a basis for inculcating the programme. [1]

Burden of Proof - The standard by which a case is decided. The duty to prove a fact in dispute.[3]

- C -

Child as parent's best friend- a detection factor that is revealed by adults (and their children) who do not employ parental direction, guidance, and authority but always remain tin the mode of a peer to the child. This has the effect of undermining any authority or discipline that may be exercised by the other parent who wishes to exercise appropriate role prerogatives of an adult (parent). [1]

Child Custody - The right to raise the child and/or to decide how the child is raised. [3]

Refers to matters concerning the living arrangements and right to make legal decisions for a minor child following a divorce. See also Legal Custody and Physical Custody. [2]

Child Support - The money one parent pays the other for the care and welfare of the children.[3]

The amount of money paid by a non-custodial parent to the custodial parent for a child's' day-to-day expenses and other special needs. Custodial services are also considered a form of child support.

Child Support (and alienation) - an economic issue that may serve as a social basis for programming and brainwashing whereby one parent wishes to obtain financial gain. [1]

Child Support Guidelines - A mathematical formula used to calculate how much money one parent should pay the other. [3]

A series of mathematical formulas that calculate a range of child support money to be paid. Guidelines are based upon traditional custody and visitation arrangements. They do not address equitable financial responsibility when there is shared physical custody or split custody (each parent has physical custody of one or more of their children). Congress has mandated that states adopt child support guidelines and support enforcement procedures.[2]

Clarity - the degree to which a mental health label is understandable to professionals, the court, and parents. Also can refer to the understandability of a programme. [1]

Clean Hands Doctrine – A legal concept hereby a person's complaint against his/her spouse may be discounted by the court if the plaintiff ere regarded as having acted in a way this morally or legally wrong. [2]

Coaching behavior - a detection tool that is revealed by prodding behavior on the part of programming and brainwashing parents; it is most readily observable when children take statements out of context and, secondarily, use adult language. [1]

Coalitions - another term for multiple programming/brainwashing whereby siblings, grandparents, aunts, uncles, friends, and others participate in a programming and brainwashing process with one parent. [1]

Coercion of Ideas - forcing a child to have ideas that mirror those of the parent and are often damaging to the child. [1]

Cohort - the attempt that programming/brainwashing parents make to have an ally in the child for all their own views of the past marital relationship and their present fears. [1]

Collusion Technique - a technique whereby programming and brainwashing parents attempt to coordinate with the child on their negative views and opinions of the other parent. Children who have participated in this technique often speak in terms of "us" versus "him or her." [1]

Collusive - the incorporation of the child into the belief patterns and thoughts of the programming/brainwashing parent. [1]

Common-law division of property – Method of dividing marital property based upon who holds legal title of ownership. Most states that originally followed this rule now use "equitable distribution." Mississippi is the only state that strictly follows this method of dividing property upon divorce. [3]

Community property – Method of assigning ownership of assets and responsibility for debts acquired during the marriage equally to both spouses. If the court feels that "equal" division is unfair, most community property state courts have the discretion to use "equitable distribution."[3]

Comparative martyr role - an extreme form of the good versus bad parent; the programming/brainwashing parent portrays him- or herself as the innocent victim. [1]

Competitive - when one parent competes with the other parent, usually involving the child, so that the competitive parent can "win" a particular situation.

Compliance - the fourth stage of the programming/brainwashing process where the child begins to demonstrate that he or she shares the attitudes, beliefs, opinions and, ultimately, the behavior that the programmer/brainwasher desires. [1]

Conciliation - A form of alternative dispute resolution where a neutral person helps the parties settle their dispute. [3]

Conditional Love - love that is based on the child's acceptance of the programmer/brainwasher's ideas, values, and opinions concerning the other parent. [1]

Conflict - Conflict is created when parents have opposing views, clash and disagree about the decisions regarding the divorce and their children. When parents clash, disagree, fight or contend they are in conflict.

Conflict Oriented - When a parent, sometimes only one parent, needs conflict to continue the relationship with the other parent. Some people are difficult and need conflict in their lives. These individuals are "conflict-oriented."

Confusion - a technique (and/or a result) whereby contradictory information, ideas, emotions, and values are presented so as to induce a lack of clarity, commitment, or direction on the part of the child. It occurs when a child has a reality base (the father demonstrates love), but is contradicted by the programmer/brainwasher ("your dad never loved you") [1]

Contempt of Court - Behavior intended to obstruct a court order. [3]

Continuity and family history - an argument most often employed by women that state that they have had the majority of contact and upbringing experience with the children, and that, therefore, they should continue in this role; it can serve as a basis for programming/ brainwashing. [1]

Contradictory techniques - techniques that involve sending two opposing messages to a child. The common result is confusion/ambivalence. [1]

Co-opting - When an individual tries to *co-opt* another, they are trying to convince or persuade the individual to assume their point of view, take their side, or align with them to support their cause. The mother 'co-opted' the therapist to dislike the father.

Co-parenting - Is the term used to represent two separated or divorced parents who are cooperating in the parenting of their children when not living together. Co-parenting indicates that the parents get along and make joint amicable decisions about their children, communicating on a regular and non-conflicting basis.

Core Activities - A term used in extra-curricular activities. A core activity is one of the primary activities chosen for the child. There may be one, two, or three 'core activities' chosen for the child. These 'core activities' are activities that will take priority over other activities scheduled in the child's daily routine.

Credibility - believability of a person's opinions and statements of fact... [1]

Custodial Parent - The parent who is primarily responsible for raising the children. [3]

The parent with whom a minor child resides or who makes legal decisions for the child (solely or jointly with the other parent) following a separation and divorce. In joint custody, each parent is considered the custodial parent when the child is with that parent. [2]

- D -

Dangling love - as aspect of conditional love whereby programming and brainwashing parents hold out the reward of affection and caring until the child conforms to the attitudinal and behavioral characteristics toward the other parent that they desire. [1]

Denial - refusing to accept the fact that programming/brainwashing is taking or has taken place; denial may be conscious or unconscious. [1]

Denial-of-existence syndrome - a series of techniques used to deny or to not acknowledge the social existence of the other parent. [1]

Deposition - An oral statement made under oath. [3]

Deprogramming - treatment procedures and techniques employed in order to correct, neutralize, modify, clarify, terminate, and/or reduce the impact of programming/brainwashing on the child. [1]

Desire to create the "new" family - because women are viewed as family creators, they are more likely to focus on a new unit as "the" family; this can serve as a basis for programming and brainwashing the children. [1]

Desire to move or leave a geographical area - this can serve as a basis for programming and brainwashing, more so for women than for men. [1]

Dictator - another term for brainwasher. [1]

Discovery - The process of gathering information to present at a hearing or trial. [3]

Disdain - a technique of expressing direct hostility to something in a other parent's life. [1]

Dispute - The conflict that the court is being asked to resolve. [3]

Distortion - taking a set of facts or circumstances and re-working their meaning so that they fit a particular programme. [1]

Divorce - A legal decision that ends a marriage. [3]

Divorce Agreement – A legal agreement between a divorcing husband and wife regarding keeping the peach, division of property, spousal support, and responsibility to children. [2]

Divorce Ceremony – An informal way for the parents, children, family, friends, and others to acknowledge the ending of a marriage and the beginning of the parting couple's separate lives. Also called divorce ritual. [2]

Dysfunctional families - families that do not contribute positively to the physical, social, psychological, spiritual, educational, and medical potential of a child. [1]

- E -

Elaboration - a technique of providing infinite detail concerning a situation/person. The detail points out the "badness" of the other parent. This is often pair with character assassination. [1]

Emancipation - When a minor child demonstrates freedom from parental control, and the parents have no more obligations to the child. [3]

> The legal status of independence for children of divorcing parents. States recognize any age range from 17-23. Most states recognize 18 years of age as the point where parents have no further legal or financial obligations for a child's support. [2]

Embittered-chaotic - a term employed by Wallerstein and Kelly for parents who have intense anger and do not shield the child from (any of) the divorce bitterness and chaos. [1]

Emotional bases - the psychological bases for the programming/brainwashing which include revenge, rejection, survival, confusion, anxiety, control, hostility, fear of loneliness, and guilt. [1]

Empowerment of the child - an impact factor whereby a programming/brainwashing parent overtly or covertly assists a child in gaining inappropriate power for his or her age and status. [1]

Enmeshed - the degree to which parents become intensely involved in the life of their child and vice versa. [1]

Entrenched - when children become stuck in particular behavioral and attitudinal patterns from which they find it difficult to extricate themselves. [1]

Equitable parent - A parent who is not the biological or adoptive parent, but who nevertheless may be granted custody or visitation. [3]

Equitable distribution of property – Method of dividing marital property based on a number of considerations such as length of marriage, differences in age, wealth, earning potential, and health of partners involved that attempts to result in a fair distribution, not necessarily an equal one. [2]

Escalation - the seventh stage of programming/brainwashing; it involves a broadening of the programmes and the brainwashing techniques to encompass more areas of life. [1]

Evidence - Proof presented to the court that supports allegations. [3]

Exaggeration - a technique of overstating a comment, fact, circumstance, belief, behavior, and/or value. [1]

Ex-parte - A procedure that allows only one side in a dispute to address the court. [3]

Exhibit - Physical evidence used to prove a point. [3]

Expert - A person who is a recognized authority. An expert witness is allowed to give his or her opinion in court. [3]

Expert Witness – In court proceedings, professional whose testimony helps a judge reach divorce decisions. These experts may work in many areas including mental health, education, and finance (appraisers of home, business, tangible property.)

Exposure process - the process of exposing the child to the "truth" or the stages of revealing "information" to the child. Any fact, thought, belief, or value shared with children to control them or damage their image of the other parent is part of the exposure process. [1]

Extracurricular Activities - Any activity that a child participates in, including sports, theatre, music, chorus, peer group activities, church activities, after school activities or other child enrichment activities.

- F -

Fabrication - the making up of facts that have no reality basis. [1]

Family and women are synonymous - a belief to which many women adhere that family life is more connected to them than to a man. [1]

Family law - The body of law involving marriage, separation, custody, support, and so on. [3]

Family Support - A taxable form of support combining child support and spousal support into one payment.[3] Family support may be tax deductible to the paying parent, child support may not (CA).

Fear - a social-emotional basis for programming/brainwashing that usually revolves around concern for the loss of a child by a parent or the loss of the parent by the child. [1]

Fear of contact with the other parent - a detection factor that involves a child's expressing fear in being with a parent; the fear is usually related to overt and covert messages sent by the programmer/brainwasher. [1]

Federal Parent Locator Service - (FPLS) - A service run by the Office of Child Service Support Enforcement (OCSE) to help locate parents who owe child support. [3]

Feigned disinterest - a technique used by programming/brainwashing parents to let children know that they have no interest in what transpires at the other parent's home. It is used to diminish the value of the other parent. [1]

Female identity and parenting - the belief that many women hold that their social-psychological identity is more bound up with children than that of men. [1]

Financial-support-needs - the economic issues that surround the relationship between separating /divorcing parents and their children. Women's needs (because of decreased access to the marketplace) are often more critical; this can serve as a basis for programming and brainwashing. [1]

Financial Statement - A court paper containing a parent's income and expense information. [3]

Forensic - the relationship(s) between mental-health/family issues and the legal processes/ system. [1]

Full faith and credit - The legal principle requiring a judge in one state to enforce a decision made by a judge in another state. [3]

- G -

Game Plan - an overall (parental) strategy developed to obtain custody, interfere with the custodial arrangements of the other parent, and/or control information revealed in the legal and/or mental health arena. [1]

Good parent versus bad parent - a distinction used in the detection of brainwashing/ programming whereby the assaultive parent attaches labels to the other parent. The programming and brainwashing parent is always the good parent, the other parent is the bad parent. [1]

Goodwill – The value of a business beyond its sales revenue, inventory, and other tangible assets; includes prestige, name recognition, and customer loyalty. [2]

Guardian - A person appointed by the court to be responsible for a child.[3] An individual, usually an attorney, appointed by the court to advocate the rights and interests of the children in a divorce – most often when the parents are unable to arrange a custody agreement. [2]

Guardian ad litem - A person appointed by the court to represent a child in a legal matter. [3]

- H -

Hearsay - An out-of-court statement offered to prove something. [3]

"Ho-hum" approach - a brainwashing technique whereby a parent refuses to respond to the excitement and joy children may have about their relationship with the other parent. [1]

Hold harmless – One party assumes responsibility for an existing or potential debt and promises to protect the other party from any related loss or expense. [2]

Hostage- a term that refers to captivating the child for some past grievance, present hostility, or need that the programming brainwashing parent possesses. The term is used to imply that the child is in a middle-ground position in order for the programming and brainwashing parent to obtain his or her goal(s). [1]

Hostile witness - A witness who is antagonistic to the party who called him. [3]

- I -

"I don't know what's wrong with him" syndrome - a cluster of techniques whereby programming/brainwashing parents create or exaggerate differences between themselves and the other parent (in front of the child.) [1]

"I'm the only one who really loves you" syndrome - this is a cluster of techniques employed by programming/brainwashing parents in order to convince the child that the other parent or those associated with the other parent are not sincere in their loving and caring for the child. [1]

Inadmissible - Evidence that is not allowed to be introduced. [3]

Inappropriate and unnecessary information - a technique employed by parents whereby they inculcate information into the child concerning areas such as support or past life-style, sexual interests, and orientations of the other parent. [1]

Indirect statements - attacks of the target parent that the programmer/brainwasher inserts covertly into the dialogue with the child. These are often subtle messages and are difficult to detect. [1]

Inferior status - a technique of making children feel like "second class citizens" so that the programmer/brainwasher can better control them. [1]

Injunction - An order requiring someone to do something, or preventing someone from doing something. ^ A permanent restraining order. [2]

Insight - The degree of knowledge and/or awareness that one has into the damaging effects of the programming/brainwashing process. [1]

Instigator- another term for brainwasher. [1]

Intentional process - when programming/brainwashing parents are consciously aware of their motives, goals, objectives, and/or techniques. [1]

Interlocutory - Temporary orders. [3]

Interrogatories - Written questions one side asks the other. [3]

Issue - The items being disputed.

- J -

Jealousy - a social-emotional basis for programming/brainwashing involving envy of some aspect of the other parent's life. [1]

Joint Custody - An arrangement allowing for mutual sharing of the children. Joint legal custody involves shared decision making, and joint physical custody allows for equal time with the children. [3]

Judge - The official who presides over a courtroom. [3]

Judgment - The official decision of the court. [3]

Jurisdiction - A court's authority to hear a case. [3]

- L -

Latchkey children – Children who finish their school day while their parent (s) are still at work. These children may spend part of their day at home alone. [2]

Lawsuit - A legal proceeding that settles a private dispute between two people. [3]

Leading Question - A question that suggests how a witness should answer. [3]

Legal custody - The right to make major decisions for the child. [3] The authority, after divorce, to make legal decisions for a minor child regarding health, education, and general welfare. Can be held solely by one parent or jointly by both parents. [2]

Legal Separation Decree – Court ruling on division of property, spousal support, and responsibility to children when a couple wishes to separate but not to divorce. A legal separation is most often desired for religious or medical reasons. [2]

Loss of Identity - a social-psychological basis for programming/brainwashing whereby parents may come to think or feel that some or all of their identity may be lost if they lose full control of the child. [1]

Loyalty conflicts - dilemmas created for the child that tear them between their feelings of commitment to, love for, and desire for affiliation with both parents; resolution is often only possible by choosing one (according to the programmer/brainwasher.) [1]

Loyalty Measures - a stage of programming and brainwashing whereby the programmer/ brainwasher seeks to determine how loyal the child is to the brainwasher's values, views, opinions, suggestions, and attitudes. [1]

- M -

Maintaining the marital/adult relationship through conflict - a basis for programming/ brainwashing whereby a conflict-oriented parent employs various techniques in order to stay connected to the other parent. This allows for the continuation of the relationship, albeit on a non-healthy basis, with the child often in a middle-ground position. [1]

Manipulator - another term for brainwasher. [1]

Marital property – All property in which either party has an interest, however and whenever acquired (equitable distribution viewpoint) or all property acquired during a marriage, except for property purchased with only the proceeds of separate property or excluded by valid agreement (community property viewpoint). Each states has a slightly different way of determining whether assets that are inherited, received as a gift, or acquired before marriage will be considered marital property. See community property, Common-law division of property, and Equitable distribution of property. [2]

Materialistic demands - an impact factor whereby children come to increase their demands for consumer items; at times, the children create a situation of "competitive bidding" between the two parents. [1]

Mediation - A form of alternative dispute resolution where the two sides meet with a third person who tries to help them resolve the dispute.[3] The mediator has no power to make or enforce decisions. [2]

Mental Health Professional - A psychiatrist, psychologist, marriage counselor, or licensed social worker. [3]

Merits - The essential issues in a case. [3]

Middleman syndrome - a cluster of techniques that involve communication with the child in regard to inappropriate subjects. These techniques place the child in middle-ground position. [1]

Mirror image of programmer - a detection factor that is identified if the child has a one-to-one correspondence of attitudes, feelings, values, opinions, ideas, and behaviors with the programming/brainwashing parent. [1]

Modification - When a court revises an existing order. [3]

Motion - A formal request to a court for an order or ruling. [3]

- N -

Negative imaging - When a parent (or other important individual) programs the child negatively toward another person. These individuals have influence in the child's life, and are able to create a negative 'image' of the target individual. This brainwashing technique is particularly effective when the target parent has minimal physical contact with the child.

Negative modeling - when children imitate behavior that is destructive to themselves and/or other healthy relationships. [1]

Negative opinions of men's capacity to parent - a view many women adhere to that can serve as basis for programming/brainwashing. [1]

Neglect - Ignoring a child's needs. [3]

Negotiation - The attempt to resolve a dispute through discussion. [3]

Non-custodial parent - A parent who is not responsible for raising the children.[3] The parent who does not have physical custody of his/her children after a divorce and therefore generally is obligated to pay child support to the custodial parent with whom the child resides. [2]

Nonverbal messages - a detection tool revealed by body language and tonal qualities of speech that may contradict and/or reinforce the spoken word. Programming and brainwashing parents often use these messages in conjunction with or separate from the spoken word. They are powerful but sometimes hidden factors in developing attitudes and behaviors in children. [1]

- O -

Opportunity - a factor that results because women often have more time with the children, therefore, can programme and brainwash more then men. [1]

Order - Instructions from the court. [3]

- P -

Paramour factor - the real or perceived presence of another man or woman in the life of the other parent. It serves as one of the most powerful motivators for programming and brainwashing by women (and men). [1]

Parenting Coordinator - A designated, professional individual who oversees the family structure, helps negotiate parenting agreements and monitors compliance of the written agreement.

Parallel Parenting - A parenting model that promotes a parallel structure in each household, and also promotes non-interference and autonomy in each home. The primary needs of the child are supported by the parallel structure (agreement on health, education and welfare) yet each household is managed independently of the other.

Passive participant - a child who is not aware of the desired ends of the programming/ brainwashing process. [1]

Pavlonian technique - a brainwashing technique whereby a particular reward or punishment often follows a stimulus presented by the parent. [1]

Peer-group expectations - a social pressure perceived more by women that serves as a basis for programming and brainwashing; friends, siblings, parents, and others are seen as a pressure to maintain control of the child(ren). [1]

Perjury - A false statement made under oath. [3]

Performer - anther term for brainwasher. [1]

Perpetrator - another term for brainwasher. [1]

Personal history - beliefs about how life should be interpreted/lived according to how the past is presented. [1]

Physical custody - The right to have the children live with you.[3] Refers to the actual residence of a child following divorce. Physical custody may be solely with one parent, jointly with both parents (when the child spends alternating periods of time with each parent), or split between the parents (each parent has physical custody of one or more of their children.) [2]

Plaintiff - The person who files a lawsuit. Also, petitioner.[3] The spouse who initiates the legal divorce process by filing a complaint stating that the marriage is over and listing the grounds and claims against the other spouse. [2]

Pleading - A court document that outlines the issues in a dispute. [3]

Point of no return - the ninth factor in the deprogramming process; it refers to children who are "beyond repair" and cannot reestablish a healthy relationship with the other parent (and/or others). [1]

Polarized - a result of the alliance process. A child is forced by the programming/brainwashing parent to move toward an acceptance and belief in one parent or the other. There is little or no room for the other parent in the life of the child. [1]

Power - the ability to influence the acts and decisions of others (even if they resist for a time.)[1]

Power, influence, control and domination - bases for programming and brainwashing in order that one parent may maintain complete direction over a child's life. One of the primary goals here is to (in) directly control the life of the other parent. [1]

Precedent - The decision in a case that influences future cases that are similar. [3]

Prejudice - When a judgment is made with prejudice, the issues cannot be re-litigated. When a judgment is made without prejudice, the issues may be retried. [3]

Prejudicial error - A mistake made in a decision by a court that justifies a reversal by an appellate court. [3]

Prenuptial agreement – A contract signed by a couple before marriage that lists the assets and liabilities each partner is bringing into the marriage and provides a framework for financial limits to rights of support, property, and inheritance after the marriage and in the event of a divorce or death. Also called ante nuptial agreement. [2]

Primary caretaker - The parent who provides most of the daily care for the child. [3]

Programme - the content material employs as a basis in assaulting the other (target) parent, usually based on ideologies ("Mothers are superior parents," "Fathers must have an equal part"). It includes a set of directions on how to interpret reality ("If your mother cared, she would be home"). [1]

Programming - the formulation of a set or sets of directions based on a specific or general belief system directed toward another (target) in order to obtain some desired end or goal. [1]

Propria persona - Pro per and pro se are Latin terms that describe individuals who represent themselves. [3]

Proprietary perspective - a social-emotional basis for programming/brainwashing based on the idea that one parent has a greater right to possession and ownership of the child. [1]

Psychosomatic illness - the developing of physical ailments in children (headaches, stomach pain) as a way of coping with the programming and brainwashing; it is a form of acting in. [1]

Pseudo-adult - an unchildlike role that children sometimes adopt as a result of being overly involved with one or both parents; one characteristic of this role is becoming the problem solver for the parents' dilemmas. [1]

- Q -

Quash - A decision to void or cancel a court order or judgment. [3]

- R -

Rationalize belief - a belief based on an inaccurate, distorted, or partial view of the circumstance. [1]

Re-affiliate - the process whereby a child renews his or her bonds with a target parent (and/or others). [1]

Rebuttal - Arguments or evidence used to disprove. [3]

Reinterpreting an experience - a technique whereby a parent modifies the perception of a child from the positive to the negative regarding the other parent by supplying another way of looking at the set of facts and/or circumstances. [1]

Relevant - Evidence which directly addresses an issue. [3]

Renunciation - getting the child to turn against his or her own view of the past and to speak against the other parent. [1]

Repeating the cycle - an impact factor whereby children who are programmed and brainwashed may themselves become participants in the process - either with their siblings or with their own children if they become separated or divorced. [1]

Repetition - a technique employed to reinforce a message whereby an idea, word, or action is performed over and over again. It creates a mind-set or habitual pattern of acceptable thinking. [1]

Respondent - The person being sued.

Restriction of permission to love or be loved - a technique employed by programmers and brainwashers that may be physical and/or socio-psychological; it facilitates a divorce between the child and the other parent. It has some of the most serious social-psychological consequences of all techniques employed, as the child is disallowed from physically or mentally reaching out to the other parent . The ultimate fear is the withdrawal of love from the programming and brainwashing parent. [1]

Revenge - a social-emotional basis for programming and brainwashing whereby the goal is to get even with the other parent for perceived hurts of the past. These retaliatory needs usually blind the assaultive parent to the needs of the child. [1]

Rewriting history - a brainwashing technique involving getting children to distort their views and opinions of the past; the process whereby the programming/brainwashing parent changes certain facts and/or interpretations in order to restructure the beliefs and opinions of the child. [1]

Rewriting-reality syndrome - a cluster of techniques employed by programming and brainwashing parents in order to convince a child to doubt his or her own abilities to perceive reality. [1]

- S -

Sanction - A penalty for violating a court order. [3]

School related problems - a result of programming and brainwashing; acting out, social withdrawal, grade fluctuations, insubordination, and truancy may result. [1]

Scripted views - detection tool; revealed by children who doubt their own perceptions because of scripts that have been inculcated by the programming and brainwashing parent. [1]

Secret keeping - an expectation of a programming/brainwashing parent in regard to whatever he or she has defined as "special information"; the child is expected to communicate this special information only to the programming and brainwashing parent. Judges, lawyers, therapists, the target parent, and other are all defined as "off-base" or not legitimate sources with whom they can communicate openly. [1]

Secret wishes - an impact factor whereby children begin to develop ideas (which they may not relate freely) to see, love, and know the target parent. One of the most common wishes the children have is that their parents will stop fighting. [1]

Seeing the light - the child interprets the world as the programmer/brainwasher wishes. [1]

Self-centered - a vulnerability characteristic that predisposes children to greater negative impact from the programming/brainwashing process; the greater the self-centeredness, the greater the vulnerability. [1]

Self-doubt - a result of the programming/brainwashing process whereby children come to be unsure of their own beliefs, ideals, values, and opinions. [1]

Self-protective - a social-emotional motive for programming/brainwashing based on the parent's need to hide or keep secret certain deviant or problematic aspects of his or her life-style from the target parent and other members of society. [1]

Self-righteousness - a social-emotional motive for programming/brainwashing that may stem from a genuine belief of being the better parent. [1]

Sense of past history - a social-emotional motive for programming/brainwashing whereby one parent believes her or she is the most competent because of the past involvement with the child. [1]

Separate Property – Generally considered any property owned before marriage (earned or acquired by gift or inheritance), acquired during marriage by one partner using only that partner's separate property, or earned after a formalized separation. [2]

Separation Agreement – The legal document listing provisions for peace between the divorcing couple, division of property, spousal support, and responsibility for children of the marriage. The couple's agreement or court-ordered terms are part of the divorce decree. [2]

Settlement - When two sides come to an agreement without a trial. [3]

Settlement agreement - A written agreement between the two sides. [3]

Shuttle Mediation - A mediation model designed to provide separate meetings between the parties for more efficient, non-productive communication. Shuttle mediation, also known as shuttle diplomacy specifically reduces the opportunity for conflict when parents may fight during face-to-face negotiations.

Sibling conflict - an impact factor whereby children intensify or create sibling conflict as a result of programming and brainwashing. [1]

Significant change of circumstance - The minimum requirement for changing an existing court order. [3]

Social isolation - a technique of keeping the child separate from experiences contradictory to the desired programme. [1]

Socially/emotionally kidnapped - children who are not necessarily physically removed from contact with the target parent, but are denied the right to love, think about, core for, desire, and otherwise have positive thoughts and feelings about the parent. [1]

Sole Custody - An arrangement where the children are raised by only one of their parents. [3]

Special Events - Events that may only occur once, such as graduations, championship games, recitals and religious ceremonies.

Split Custody - An arrangement where the time with the children is divided between the two parents. [3]

Spousal support – Money paid by one partner to the other for the recipient's support following a divorce. Support may be a lump sum or mandated for a specific period of time (long-term or short-term) and is based on the needs of the recipient, ability to pay, and economic differences between the partners. Also called alimony or maintenance. [2]

Spy - a child who is covertly or overtly instigated by the programming and brainwashing parent to retrieve information about the other parent that will eventually be used against that parent. Children who have been used as spies often elicit high levels of anxiety and guilt. [1]

Standard of living - The relative comfort the children were accustomed to before the parents separated. [3]

Stipulation - An agreement between the two sides in a lawsuit. [3]

Stripping process - a technique of taking away old bases of social identity: forced changes in appearance, clothing, ("You look like your mother, and it's cheap"), speech (Don't call him Daddy"), access ("You can't see her on Wednesdays anymore"). [1]

Subpoena – A court order requiring a person's appearance in court as a witness or to present documents or other evidence for a case. [2]

Symbiotic - the intertwined relationship between the programming/brainwashing parent and the child; it results in both of them having similar behaviors and attitudes toward the target parent. The child who is in a symbiotic relationship with a programmer/brainwasher becomes incapable of developing a separate social-psychological identity. It may lead to a fusion of identities between the programming/brainwashing parent and the child. [1]

- T -

Tainted - a process whereby a parent, stepparent, grandparent, school, neighborhood, or any other feature associated with the target parent is given a negative slant. [1]

Target parent - the parent who is defined as the enemy, evil one, and outsider. There may also be target lawyers, judges, siblings, grandparents, therapists, and others who are perceived and defined as the "enemy." [1]

Temporary restraining order (TRO) - An order that prohibits someone from doing something until a hearing can be heard. ^ A court order intended to prevent one person from harming another (domestic violence cases), taking children (in custody battles), or removing property/ squandering assets while a divorce is in process. The court will hold a second hearing to decide if the TRO should be made a permanent order. A permanent restraining order is called an injunction. [2]

Testimony - A statement made under oath. [3]

Testing of effectiveness - the fifth stage of programming and brainwashing whereby the programmer/brainwasher seeks to have a "feedback assessment" in order to evaluate the success of the techniques. [1]

Thought control - the way the term brainwashing has been used in regard to political goals and activities. It is derived from the Chinese term hso nao (literally "to wash the brain"). This implies the ability to direct people's thoughts and beliefs against their will.[1]

Threat-of-withdrawal-of-love-syndrome - a cluster of techniques revolving around the fear of rejection or the fear of loss of love from a parent if a child expresses love or desire to be with the other parent. [1]

Transcript - A written record of court proceedings. [3]

- U -

Unchildlike statements - a detection tool that has as two of its primary characteristics consistency and over rigidity on the part of the child; child make statements that are not in line with their maturity level. [1]

Unconditional love - a love modeled or taught by a parent that is not based on expectations of performance or hostility to the other parent. The child is loved even if he or she loves the other parent. [1]

Unintentional process - when the parent (and/or child) is not aware of (their own) motives, goals, objectives, and/or techniques. [1]

Unpredictably - an impact factor whereby children come to feel that their world is unpredictable; this results from the chaotic nature of the assaults they experience. [1]

Unprotected and alone - two impact factors whereby children come to feel that no one is able to protect them. [1]

- V -

Venue - A place where a trial can be held. [3]

Victim - brainwashee; a term for the recipient of programming and brainwashing. [1]

Visitation - The time a non-custodial parent spends with the children.[3] When one parent has sole physical custody of the children, regular visits with the children are authorized for the non-custodial parent. This right is usually automatic unless there are extenuating circumstances. Parents may work out the visitation schedule or the court will order specific visitation terms. [2]

- W -

War within the home - an impact factor that is a specific type of sibling conflict. It often occurs between children who respond differently to the programming and brainwashing process. [1]

"Who me?" Syndrome - a cluster of techniques employed by the programming or brainwashing parent that involve indirect attached against the other parent, with the basic pattern being an attack against the other parent's character and life-style while feigning innocence. [1]

"Winner" - the feeling statement made by programmers/brainwashers when their strategies have been successful. [1]

Withdrawal of love - a technique whereby parents deny a child physical and/or emotional demonstrations of affection and/or other rewards if the child does not conform to their views. [1]

Witness - A person who testifies under oath. [3]

Writ - A court order requiring someone to do something. [3]

(Endnotes)
1. Clawar, S. S., & Rivlin, B. V. (1991). *Children Held Hostage: Dealing with Programmed and Brainwashed Children*, Chicago, Illinois: American Bar Association.
2. Engel, M. L. (1994). *Divorce Help Sourcebook*, Detroit, Michigan: Visible Ink, a division of Gale Research Inc..
3. Watnik, W. (1999). *Child Custody Made Simple: Understanding the Laws of Child Custody and Child Support*. Claremont, CA: Single Parent Press.

24.

Selected Readings and Bibliography

Abraham, Jed H., *From Courtship to Courtroom: What Divorce Law Is Doing to Marriage,* Bloch Publishing Company, Inc., New York, 1999.

Ahrons, Constance R., *The Good Divorce, Keeping Your Family Together When Your Marriage Comes Apart,* Harper Collins Publishers, Inc., New York, 1994.

Allen, Robin, *The Complete Guide to Parallel Parenting: Establishing Appropriate Boundaries for Families of Divorce,* Nipomo Publishing Company, California, 2004.

Blau, Melinda, *Families Apart: Ten Keys to Successful Co-Parenting,* G.P. Putnam's Sons, New York, 1993.

Brennan, Carleen, and Brennan, Michael, *Custody for Fathers, A Practical Guide Through the Combat Zone of a Brutal Custody Battle,* Fourth Revised edition, Costa Mesa, CA, 1994.

Campbell, Terence W., Ph.D., *Smoke and Mirrors: The Devastating Effect of False Sexual Abuse Claims,* Insight Books, Plenum Press, New York, 1998.

Clawar, Stanley S., and Rivlin, Brynne V., *Children Held Hostage: Dealing with Programmed and Brainwashed Children,* American Bar Association, 1991.

Engel, Margorie L., *Divorce Help Sourcebook*, Visible Ink Press, Detroit, MI, 1994.

Folberg, Jay, *Joint Custody and Shared Parenting, Second Edition*, The Guilford Press, New York, 1991.

Forman, Deborah L, *Every Parent's Guide To The Law: Everything You Need to Know About Legal Issues Affecting Parents and Children From Pre-Birth Through the Child-Rearing Years*, Harcourt Brace & Company, 1998.

Gardner, Richard, *The Parental Alienation Syndrome, A Guide for Mental Health and Legal Professionals*, Second Edition, Creative Therapeutics, Inc., 1992 (First edition), 1998 (Second Edition).

Garrity, Carla B. and Baris, Mitchell A., *Caught in the Middle: Protecting the Children of High Conflict Divorce*, First edition, Lexington Books, Macmillan, Inc., 1994.

Greif, Geoffrey L., *The Daddy Track and the Single Father, Successfully Coping with Kids, Housework, a Job, an Ex-Wife, a Social Life, and the Courts*, Lexington Books, 1990.

Gross, Linden, *Surviving a Stalker: Everything You Need to Know to Keep yourself Safe*, Marlow and Company, New York, 1994.

Hawkins, Alan J. and Dollahite, David C., *Generative Fathering, Beyond Deficit Perspectives*, Sage Publications, Inc., Thousand Oaks, CA 1997.

Herman, Stephen P., M.D., *Parent vs. Parent: How You and Your Child Can Survive the Custody Battle*, Pantheon Books, 1990.

Johnston, Janet R.. and Campbell, Linda E.G. *Impasses of Divorce: The Dynamics and Resolution of Family Conflict*, Free Press, A Division of Macmillan, Inc., New York, 1988.

Johnston, Janet R., and Roseby, Vivienne, *In the Name of the Child: A Developmental Approach to Understanding and Helping Children of Conflicted and Violent Divorce*, The Free Press, New York, 1997.

Kimball, Gayle, Ph.D., *50/50 Parenting: Sharing Family Rewards and Responsibilities*, Lexington Books, Massachusetts, 1988.

Lawson, Christine Ann, Ph.D., *Understanding the Borderline Mother, Helping Her Children Transcend the Intense, Unpredictable, and Volatile Relationship*, Jason Aronson, Inc., Northvale, New Jersey & London, 2000.

Leving, Jeffrey M., and Dachman, Kenneth A., *Father's Rights: Hard Hitting and Fair Advice for every Father Involved in a Custody Dispute*, Basic Books, New York, 1997.

Levy, David, L., *The Best Parent is Both Parents, A Guide to Shared parenting in the 21st Century,*, 1993.

Major, Jayne A. *Creating a Successful Parenting Plan: A Step-by-Step Guide For the Care of Children of Divided Families,* Living Media 2000 Int'l, Inc., 1998.

Marston, Stephanie, *The Divorced Parent: Success Strategies for Raising Your Children After Separation,* William Morrow and Company, Inc., New York, 1994.

Mason, Mary Ann, Ph.D., J.D, *The Custody Wars: Why Children Are Losing the battle and What We Can Do About It,* Basic Books, New York, 2000.

Mason, Paul T. and Kreger, Randi, *Stop Walking on Eggshells: Taking Your Life Back When Someone You Care About Has Borderline Personality Disorder,* New Harbinger Publications, Inc., Oakland, CA, 1998.

Meloy, J Reid, *The Psychology of Stalking, Clinical and Forensic Perspectives,* Academic Press, Harcourt, Brace & Company, Publishers, 1998.

Neuman, Gary M., LM.H.C., with Romanowski, Patricia, *Helping Your Kids Cope With Divorce the Sandcastles Way,* Times Books, a Division of Random House, Inc. 1998.

Parnell, Teresa F. and Day, Deborah O., *Munchausen by Proxy Syndrome: Misunderstood Child Abuse,* Sage Publications, Thousand Oaks, 1997.

Ricci, Isolina, Ph.D., *Mom's House, Dad's House, Making Shared Custody Work, How Parents Can Make two Homes for Their Children After Divorce,* First Edition, Macmillan Publishing Company, New York, 1980.

Ricci, Isolina, Ph.D., *Mom's House, Dad's House, Making Two Homes for Your Child: A Complete Guide for Parents Who Are Separated, Divorced, or Remarried,* Fireside, New York, Second Edition, 1997.

Seidenberg, Robert, *The Father's Emergency Guide to Divorce-Custody Battle*, JES Books,, Inc, 1997.

Simons, Ronald L. & Associates, *Understanding the Difference Between Divorced and Intact Families, Stress, Interaction and Child Outcome,* Sage Publications, Inc., Thousand Oaks, CA, 1996.

Turkat, Ira Daniel, Divorce Related Malicious Parent Syndrome, *Journal of Family Violence,* Vol. 14, No. 1, p. 95-97. (1999).

Warshak, Richard A., *Divorce Poison,* Regan Books, An imprint of HarperCollins Publishers, New York, New York, 2001.

Watnik, Webster, *Child Custody Made Simple: Understanding the Laws of Child Custody and Child Support,* Single Parent Press, Claremeont, CA, 1999.

Appendix A

Parallel Parenting Order
(Sample)

IN THE COURT OF QUEEN'S BENCH OF ALBERTA
JUDICIAL DISTRICT OF EDMONTON

BETWEEN:

[APPLICANT'S NAME]

-and-

[RESPONDENT'S NAME]

BEFORE THE HONOURABLE MR./MADAM) On _____, the _____ day

JUSTICE _____) of _____, 20_____.

PARALLEL PARENTING ORDER

UPON NOTING THAT the Applicant and Respondent are jointly referred to in this Order as the "Parents" of the children named in this Order.

AND UPON NOTING THAT this Order is founded upon principles of mutual respect of one Parent for the other and both Parents accepting responsibility to parent their children while focusing on the needs of the children;

AND UPON NOTING the names and birth dates of the children of the marriage or relationship:

> [CHILD 1 NAME], born [CHILD 1 BIRTH DATE]
> [CHILD 2 NAME], born [CHILD 2 BIRTH DATE]
> [CHILD 3 NAME], born [CHILD 3 BIRTH DATE]

IT IS HEREBY ORDERED THAT:

(1) [APPLICANT'S NAME] and [RESPONDENT'S NAME] will have joint custody of the children with the following Parenting Times:

    (a) [APPLICANT'S NAME: SPECIFY PARENTING TIMES]
         [RESPONDENT'S NAME: SPECIFY PARENTING TIMES]

    [OPTIONAL:]

    (b) Holidays and birthdays

         [APPLICANT'S NAME]   SPECIFY OCCASION(S) AND DATE(S)]
         [RESPONDENT'S NAME]   SPECIFY OCCASION(S) AND DATE(S)]

    [OPTIONAL:]

    (c) Vacations

         [APPLICANT'S NAME]   SPECIFY DATE(S)]
         [RESPONDENT'S NAME]   SPECIFY DATE(S)]

(2) The child(ren) shall not be prohibited from placing telephone calls to the Parent in the other household. Telephone calls will be placed by the child(ren) at the following times:

[SPECIFY DATES AND TIMES OF TELEPHONE CALLS]

(3) Each parent will make all decisions concerning the child(ren) during their respective Parenting Times and each Parent will be solely responsible for all decisions concerning community activities for the child(ren) during their respective Parenting Times, without interference from the other Parent. Neither Parent will plan or schedule activities for the child(ren) during the other Parent's Parenting Time.

(4) Neither Parent will contact the other Parent, except by way of:

    (a) e-mail

    (b) a third party [OPTION: SPECIFY NAME OF THIRD PARTY] other than the child(ren);

    (c) a parenting notebook to be exchanged between the parties via a third party other than the child(ren);

    (d) [OPTION: SPECIFY OTHER MEANS OF COMMUNICATION]

(5) A parent may only contact the other Parent in accordance with the terms of this order with the only exception being a case of an absolute emergency requiring the immediate attention of the other Parent.

(6) Neither Parent will use the child(ren) to relay messages, notes or any other communications.

(7) Each Parent will provide the other Parent with information on schedules, school events and other activities which will only be communicated in accordance with the terms of this Order.

(8) Any agreements and discussions of matters concerning the child(ren) which are not addressed in this order will be made in writing and communicated with the other Parent in accordance with the terms of this Order.

(9) Each Parent will provide the other Parent any change in contact information such as address, home and work phone numbers and place of employment.

(10) This order will be followed by both Parents without variation. [Optional: If either Parent wishes to change any term of this court order, such change will only be valid by further order of this Honourable Court OR such change will only be valid by written agreement.]

(11) The parents will attend post-separation/divorce counseling with [name of counselor/ psychologist or program] [OPTIONAL: and a brief written report will be submitted to the Court].

(12) The above named counselor may contact the Court directly if the said counselor has concerns about the counseling, the behavior of the parties or the best interests of the children.

OPTIONAL CLAUSES

(i) Appointment of Counsel for Children

The Parents will make an application for appointment of legal counsel by the Legal Aid Society of Alberta to act on behalf of the children.

(ii) Child Care

The Parents will chose child care provider(s) for the child(ren) who will provide all care outside of each Parent's residence, except when an emergency arises and the child care provider is unavailable. [OPTIONAL: Child care will be provided by [SPECIFY CHILD CARE PROVIDER].

(iii)   Exchange of Children and Transportation

Exchange of the children at the beginning of each Parenting time will take place at [SPECIFY LOCATION OF EXCHANGE OF THE CHILDREN]. [APPLICANT'S NAME] or [RESPONDENT'S NAME] will provide transportation for the children as follows: [SPECIFY TRANSPORTATION ARRANGEMENTS]

(iv) Medical and School Decisions

The Parents will chose a medical practitioner for the child(ren) who will provide all medical care except when the medical practitioner makes a referral to a specialist or a medical emergency arises.

OPTIONS

Each Parent will be solely responsible for all medical and school decisions for the children during their respective PARENTING times.

or

[APPLICANT'S NAME] or [RESPONDENT'S NAME] will be solely responsible for all medical and school decisions.

(v) Religious Upbringing

[APPLICANT'S NAME or [RESPONDENT'S NAME] will be responsible for overseeing the children's religious education.

(vi) Child Support

[SPECIFY CHILD SUPPORT ARRANGEMENT(S) - SHARED CUSTODY CALCULATION V. PRIMARY RESIDENCE CALCULATION]

(vii)   Special or Extraordinary Expenses

[SPECIFY CHILD SUPPORT ARRANGEMENT(S) RE: S.7 EXPENSES SHARED CUSTODY CALCULATION V. PRIMARY RESIDENCE CALCULATION]

(viii) Clothing and Setting up Households

Each parent will be solely responsible for providing all clothing and household furnishings for the children during their Parenting Time.

(ix) Mediation

When any dispute arises between the Parents, both Parents will attend mediation in an attempt to settle all disputes prior to returning to Court.

(x) Geographical Moves

Neither Parent will relocate their residence or make a geographical move without first notifying the other Parent in writing of an intended change of residence at least [# OF DAYS] before the change and shall specify in the notice the date on which the change will be made and the new place of residence.

_____

JUSTICE OF THE COURT OF QUEEN'S
BENCH OF ALBERTA

ENTERED this _____ day of
_____, 20_____.

_____

Clerk of the Court
Court Generated Orders Project
Law Courts Building
#1A Sir Winston Churchill Square
Edmonton, Alberta T5J OR2
Tel (780) 415-0404

PARALLEL PARENTING ORDER
web site information:
www.albertacourts.ab.ca/familylaw

Appendix B

Extraterritorial Custody Agreement

Sample

EXTRATERRITORIAL CUSTODY AGREEMENT

THIS AGREEMENT is entered this _____ day of _____, 20____, by and between [Name of Petitioner], of [County and State] (the "Father") and [Name of Respondent] of [County and State] (the "Mother").

WHEREAS, Father and Mother are subject to the jurisdiction of the [County and State] Superior Court (the "Court") with respect to the dissolution of their marriage and the legal custody of their two minor children (the 'Children") [see In re Marriage of [Name], [File Number, Date]; and

WHEREAS, it is the paramount desire of both the Father and the Mother that the best interests of the Children be considered and that such best interests, in the opinion of both Father and Mother, are being and will be served as determined currently and on an ongoing basis by this Court; and

WHEREAS, both Mother and Father are currently residents of [County and State]; and

WHEREAS, Father is an American Citizen and has remarried to an American citizen, Mother is a [nationality] citizen and remains, as of this date, unmarried, and Children are both American citizens; and

WHEREAS, Mother's parents are residents of [County, State, Country], and Mother has expressed an interest in visiting her parents, together with the Children; and

WHEREAS, [Name of Country] [is or is not] a treaty signatory nation to the Hague Convention on the Civil Aspects of international Child Abduction (the "Hague Convention") and , as a matter of fact and law, recognizes no extraterritorial application of this Court's Orders; and

WHEREAS, the Father desires to accommodate the reasonable requests of the Mother with respect to the opportunity for the Children to travel to [Name of Country] for the limited purpose of visiting [Relationship of Relatives or Reason for Travel]; and

WHEREAS, the parties acknowledge that under the current state of the law in [name of Country], the issue of custody of the Children would be considered without binding reference to the existing jurisdiction and findings of this Court; and

WHEREAS, it is the reasonable desire of the parties that for the limited purpose of establishing without question the superior custody rights of the Children in the Father in the event of a custody hearing in [Name of Other Country], pursuant to which Finding in favor of the Father's custody rights the Children would be directed to be returned to the jurisdiction of this Court.

WITNESSETH

NOW THEREFORE, in consideration of the premises and as hereinafter stated, the Mother and Father agree as follows:

FIRST: The jurisdiction of and custody Order issued by the [County, State], Superior Court on [date of divorce] in the matter of [Name of Divorce], op. cit., are agreed and accepted by both parties and will be observed an obeyed wherever the parties may be located, resident, domiciled, traveling or temporarily visiting, regardless of the enforceability of such jurisdiction, Order or agreements under the local laws of such ex-[Name of State] situs.

SECOND: The parties hereto agree that in the event either party seeks to establish custody rights over the Children in contravention of or in addition to the Court's directions herein, in any situs wherever situate in the World, whether or not a Hague Convention signatory country, country disposed to giving extraterritorial application to this Court's Orders, or a country by its laws and practices either indisposed or forbidden to accord such United States' courts full faith and credit or comity, the party seeking such de novo custody rights shall incorporate as a material disclosure in its pleadings for such custody rights not only the Order of this Court regarding these rights but also this Agreement which specifically commits the parties to the observance of such Order as such Order is in the best interests of the Children.

THIRD: For the purposes of confirming the Father's rights to custody in the event the Mother seeks to have such custody rights as have already been established by this Court considered by a [Name of other Country] court, the Mother hereby agrees without reservation to the following statements:

(a) That Father is a fit and proper person to have the care, custody and control of the Children, that Father and his present wife provide the Children with a loving and nurturing home in [Name of County, State, Country] and that it is in the best interest of the Children that they continue to enjoy the benefits of such close and continuous association with the Father and his family.

(b) That the Children also currently enjoy all of the material benefits of a superior standard of living in their current living arrangement in Father's home in [Name of County, State, Country] including the benefits of a superior education and extracurricular activities of an athletic and musical nature.

(c) That both the Children have resided in [Name of County, State, Country] since birth, and have extended family in, and in the proximity of [Name of County] as well as close friendships with many of their school classmates and neighborhood playmates.

(d) That under no foreseeable circumstances would it be in the best interests of the Children to be removed from the regular custody of the Father and his family home in [Name of County, State, Country.]

(e) That for the purpose of returning the Children to {Name of County, State, Country], Father's rights with respect to the Children are superior to those of the Mother, and for this purpose, Father shall be deemed to have sole custody of both of the Children.

Further, the Mother shall not dispute or seek to contradict the foregoing in any application in [Name of other Country] for custody of the Children, and as identified in Exhibit A hereto, shall appoint a member in good standing of the Bar of [Name of City, State, Country] as her agent for service of process in the event Father is compelled by Mother's acts or omissions to seek to have his custody rights established for the return of the Children to this Court's jurisdiction. Also as identified in exhibit A hereto, [Name and address of Petitioner's Attorney and Firm in Other Country], shall at all times during Mother's visit to [Name of Country] with the Children be advised of the Children's physical whereabouts in [Name of Country], to facilitate communication with and delivery of service upon the Mother in the event same becomes necessary because of her breach of the agreement by which the Children are permitted to travel with the Mother to [Name of Country], or to receive Notice from her due to Force Majeure, as defined hereinbelow.

FOURTH: The parties hereto agree that such declarations of superior custody rights as are stated in paragraph THIRD herein are made for the purpose of confirming the Father's rights to have the Children returned to the jurisdiction of this Court; when within said Court's jurisdiction, such declarations are not to be considered as admissions but are considered to be without prejudice to the rights of the Mother to challenge or to dispute any matters properly within this Court's jurisdiction.

FIFTH: It is specifically acknowledged and agreed that although the primary purpose of this Agreement is to minimize to the extent possible the permanent removal to [Name of Other Country] of the Children from the jurisdiction of this Court in connection with a planned visit to [Name of Other Country] by Mother and the Children during [Dates of Travel], in the spirit of equity Father and Mother shall each be prepared to execute this Agreement on a case-by-case basis in substantially the same form for each proposed removal of the Children to a non-Hague Convention country by either parent, with the Agreement modified to assert the custodial rights and virtues of the non-traveling party and the non-contestability of same by the traveling party.

SIXTH: All costs and fees, including attorneys' fees, associated with the enforcement of this Agreement shall be borne by the traveling party, except as otherwise set forth in Paragraph SEVENTH herein, provided, however, that such enforcement is necessitated by the unauthorized act or omission of the traveling party in seeking to deny the non-traveling party its Court-mandated custody rights in a country where such rights are not accorded full faith and credit pursuant to the Hague Convention or through extraterritorial application of this Court's Orders.

SEVENTH: The parties agree that the non-traveling party, the Father, may seek to have his superior rights to the custody of the Children established by the appropriate forum in [Name of Other Country] on an emergent basis, should the traveling party, the Mother, unreasonably fail to return the Children to the jurisdiction of this Court on a timely basis; for this purpose, the parties shall agree in advance of the trip to [Name of Other Country] by the Children as to the commencement and return dates for such visit, and the failure of the Mother to meet the return date, as agree, shall be deemed a representation of her intent to change domicile to [Name of Other Country] and to prevent the Children from returning to the jurisdiction of this Court. The parties shall designate their respective agents for service of process and for notice of a force majeure occurrence, as required herein per Exhibit A of this Agreement. For the purposes of this Agreement, "Force Majeure" shall include, but not be limited to, acts of God, riot or insurrection, acts of the [Name of Other Country] Federal or provincial governments prohibiting departure from the country, illness of either Child which is certified by a duly licensed physician as barring that Child's travel, which shall be subject to corroboration by a second physician of the Father's, or his [Name of Other Country] agent's choice in [Name of City in Other Country] or similar events or occurrences which as a factual matter make it impossible for the Children to return to the jurisdiction of this Court on or before the agreed return date.

"Notice" shall mean telephone notification to the [Name of Other Country] agent and to the [Name of County, State] attorney of record, or if the latter is not available for any reason, also to the Father, AND both fax and telegraphic written notice as soon as possible but in any event within not more than forty-eight (48) hours of the occurrence of or reasonable knowledge of the probability of such Force Majeure.

In the event of such extraordinary, unforeseen circumstance as would constitute Force Majeure and a corresponding delay in the return of the Child to [Name of Home County, State] on the agreed return date, the traveling party shall provide Notice, as stated herein, of such Force Majeure and of the earliest date by which the Children shall be returned. The failure of the traveling party to provide Notice within forty-eight (48) hours of the agreed return date shall be the basis upon which the non-traveling party may seek to establish his rights hereunder. TIME IS OF THE ESSENCE.

If the non-traveling party moves to establish his superior custody rights, notwithstanding the traveling party's fulfillment of the Notice requirement herein, a rebuttable presumption shall arise against the non-traveling party that such motion shall be without merit. If the presumption remains unrebutted, the non-traveling party shall bear all costs and fees of both parties arising from such motion. However, in the event the traveling party's Notice is subsequently determined to be fraudulent or otherwise without merit, the traveling party shall bear all costs and fees of both parties associated with the enforcement of this Agreement.

EIGHT: The terms of this Agreement shall be subject to approval by and incorporation as appropriate by this Court.

NINTH: The parties acknowledge and agree that they have, and each of them has, entered this Agreement freely, willingly, and with the advice of Counsel, and without duress or undue pressure having been placed upon either party, with the firm belief that this will serve the best interests of the Children.

TENTH: This Agreement shall be subject to and interpreted in accordance with the laws of the [Name of State and Country].
IN WITNESS WHEREOF, the parties hereto have executed this Agreement as of the day and year first above written.

Signatures:

_____   _____
Attorney for Father   Name of Father
                                                     Signature of Father

_____   _____
Attorney for Mother: Name of Mother
                                                     Signature of Mother

EXHIBIT A TO
EXTRATERRITORIAL CUSTODY AGREEMENT

SUPERIOR COURT OF [NAME OF STATE, COUNTRY]

[NAME OF COUNTY]

In re Marriage of   )   Case No: _____
)
Petitioner :   [Name of Petitioner])   DECLARATION OF
)   [Name of Traveling Parent]
                                    (TRAVELING PARENT)

and   )

Respondent   [Name of Respondent])

By agreement of the parties, I shall travel to [Name of Country] with our [#] of minor children. Our dates of travel are as follows:

SCHEDULED DEPARTURE DATE: _____

SCHEDULED RETURN DATE: On or before: _____

My agent for Service of Process is: _____ whose address in [Name of Other Country] and telephone and fax numbers are:

    Address: _____
    Telephone: _____
    Fax: _____

I understand that the Non-Traveling Parent's Agent for Notice in [Name of Other Country] is _____, whose address in [Name of Other Country] is:

    Address: _____
    Telephone: _____
    Fax: _____

I agree to be bound by all of the terms of the Extraterritorial Custody Agreement dated
_____, 20____, which is attached hereto, incorporated by
reference herein and made a part hereof as Exhibit A.

DATED: _____   _____

                                             [Signature of Traveling Parent]

                                             _____

                                             [Printed Name of Traveling Parent]

NON-TRAVELING PARENT'S CONSENT

        I consent to the travel described above and to the terms of the Extraterritorial
Custody Agreement, Exhibit A.

DATED: _____   _____

                                             [Signature of Non-Traveling Parent]

                                             _____

                                             [Printed Name of Non-Traveling
                                             Parent]

How To Order

Fax orders - (415) 435-1887   **Telephone Orders - (866) 897-9200**

Name/Title _____

Organization _____

Address _____

City _____ State _____ Zip _____

Daytime Phone (____) _____

E-mail _____

Payment Method

[ ] Visa   [ ] Mastercard   [ ] Discover   [ ] AmEx

Card Number _____

Exp. Date _____

Name on Card _____

Signature _____

Qty	Title	Price (U.S.)
_____	When Divorce Consumes the Maternal Instinct	29.95
_____	The Complete Guide to Parallel Parenting	34.95

Shipping & Handling Charges:
(Based on USPS Priority & Global
Priority Shipping Costs by weight,
plus Handling)

Currency rates based on date of order.

Total Cost of Books   _____
Sales Tax (CA only)   _____

Shipping & Handling   _____

Total Order   _____

Nipomo Publishing Company
P.O. Box 407
Belvedere, CA 94920

(415) 435-1887 (fax)   (866)- 897-9200 (toll free)

nipomopublishing.com